Victorian Architecture
& Dynasticism

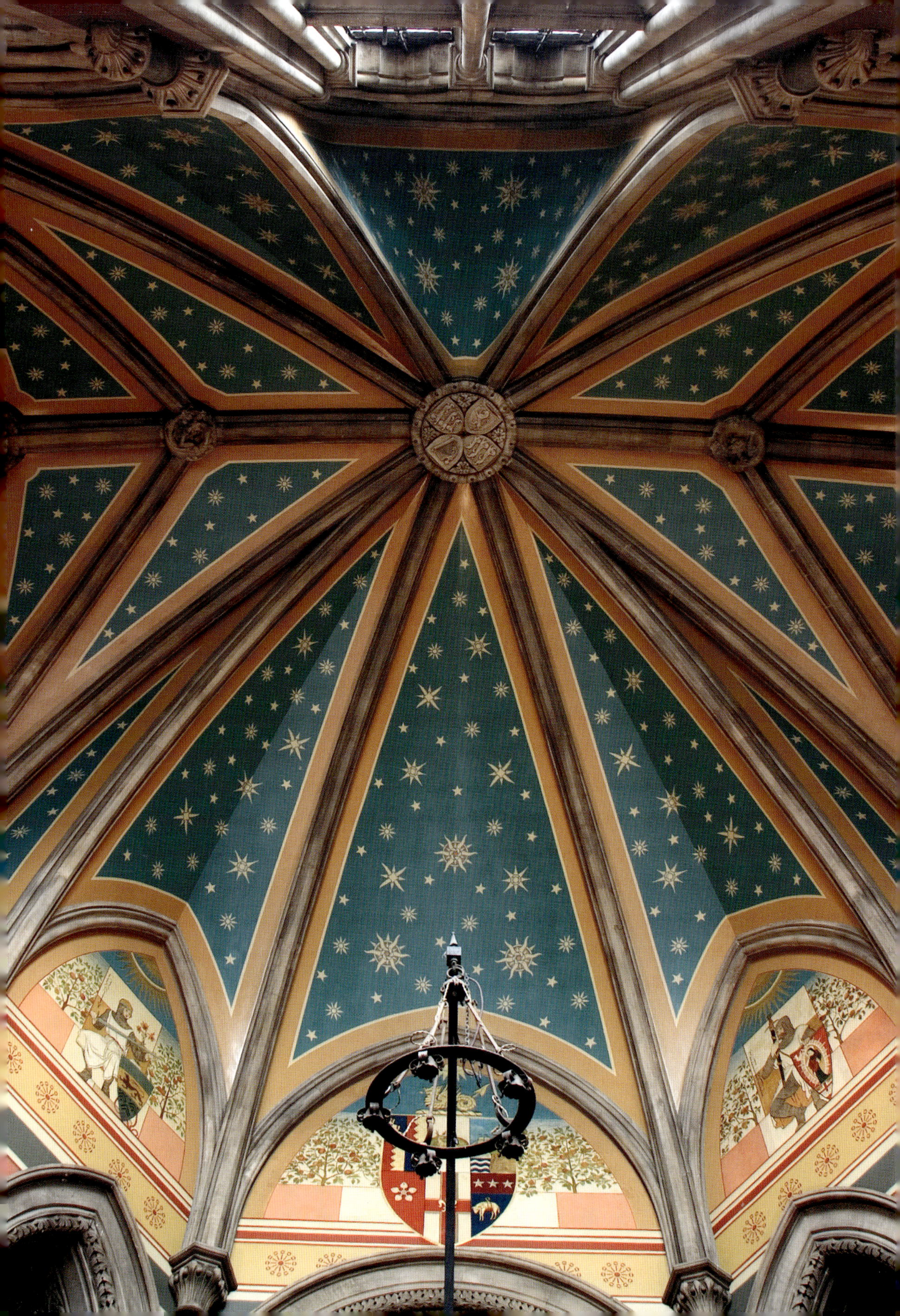

The Victorian Society
Studies in Victorian Architecture and Design
Volume Nine

Victorian Architecture & Dynasticism

Edited by Joshua Mardell

London · 2025

The editor wishes to thank Simon Bradley, James Hughes, Hilary Laurence, Jonathan Makepeace, Ben Mehigan, Sanders of Oxford, John Seaton, the Royal College of Art (for providing a grant to cover image costs), and especially Andrew Saint.

The Victorian Society is the champion for Victorian and Edwardian architecture and related arts in England and Wales.

Lectures, walks and tours are organised for members, who also receive this journal and *The Victorian*, our thrice-yearly magazine. For information contact: The Victorian Society, 1 Priory Gardens, London W4 1TT

www.victoriansociety.org.uk

ISBN 978-0-901657-58-9
ISSN 1756-6460

Design/Typography: Dale Tomlinson (after Dalrymple); Typeset in Ravenscar (text) and Miller.

Printed and bound by GPS Colour Graphics Ltd.

Front cover: Watercolour sketch of various architectural projects by John Buckler. Left to right from back left: the Lady Chapel and central tower of York Minster, Durham Cathedral, Salisbury Cathedral and the spire of Chichester Cathedral. In the centre; Winchester Cathedral and Canterbury Cathedral. In the foreground from the left; Peterborough Cathedral, Tewkesbury Cathedral and Iffley Church. Within the frames in the courtyard are illustrations of King's College Chapel, St. George's Chapel at Windsor, and the tower at Magdalen College, Oxford. *c.*1823–44. Courtesy Sanders of Oxford.

Back cover: One of the bench ends at Sheepstor, Devon, designed and carved by Violet Pinwill, 1914–17. Helen Wilson.

Frontispiece: Interior of the former Midland Grand Hotel, St. Pancras (George Gilbert Scott, 1868–76). Neil Setchfield/Alamy.

Victorian Architecture & Dynasticism

STUDIES IN VICTORIAN ARCHITECTURE & DESIGN · VOLUME 9

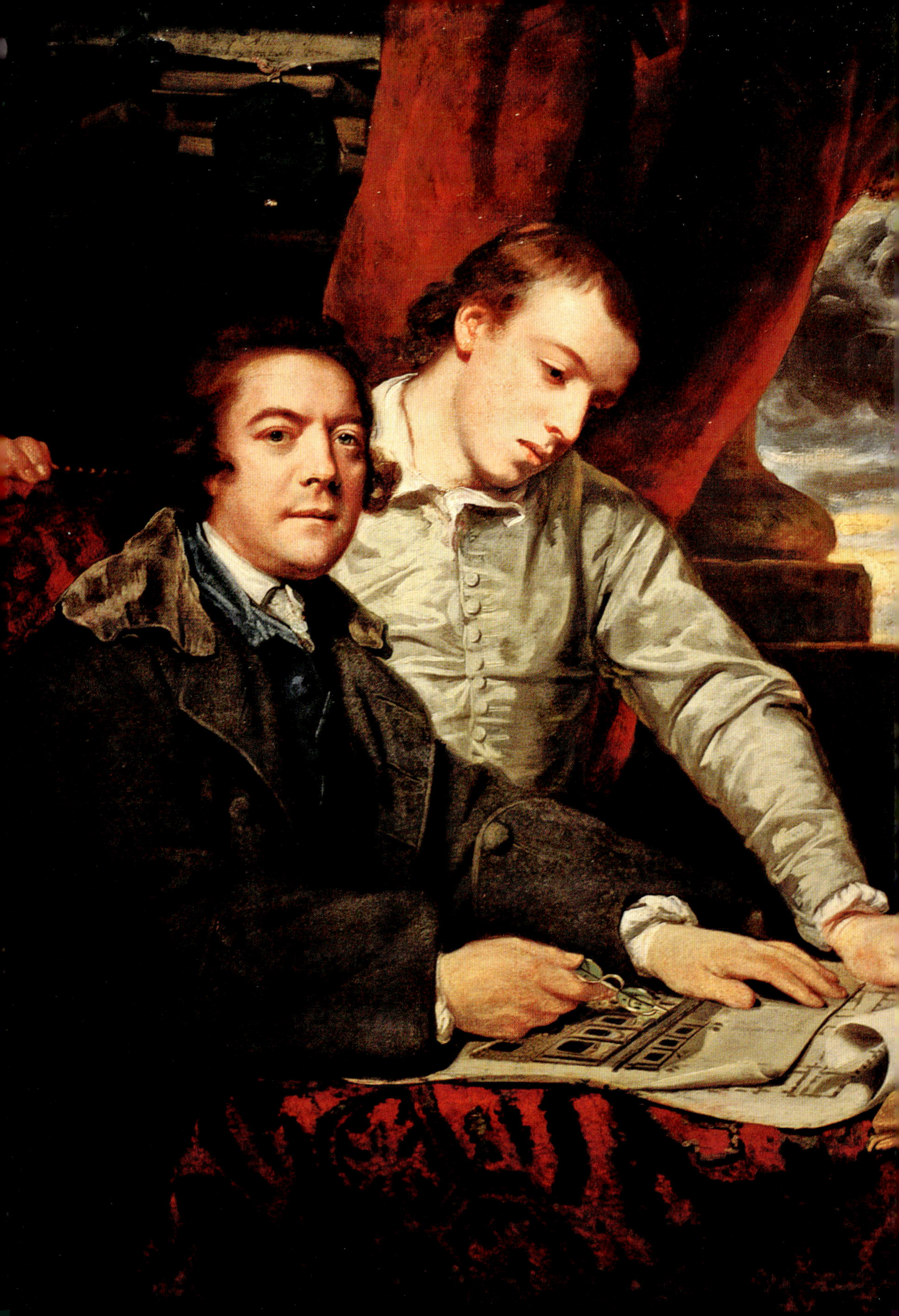

1 · Introduction

JOSHUA MARDELL

A dynasty is not just a family. A dynasty is a cultural construction: a family aggrandised with a historical agency.[1] A dynasty becomes one when it has something to pass on. Thus, the 'ism' in the title of this special issue, Victorian Architecture & Dynasticism, is used decidedly. Dynasticism refers to the ways that dynasties operated within architectural culture. By exploring them as a continuum of individuals in the longue durée of architectural history, this special issue hopes to offer new hereditary perspectives on Victorian architecture. While this volume centres on the Victorian era, the lens of dynasticism necessitates situating it in a broader chronology.

Revealingly caricatured in Alan Brownjohn's poem, in which the titular 'Dynasty' 'passes the bomb from hand to hand', dynasticism is also captured in portraiture (Fig. 1.1).[2] In Sir Joshua Reynolds' painting of the architects James Paine Senior and James Paine Junior (1764), the younger Paine, aged 20, leans over his father, who nurtures his son's examination of the design of the Palladian villa, Worksop Manor. It is suggestive of the patrimonial relaying of skills including knowledge and draughtsmanship, patronage, and the nurturing of a commitment to a style or tradition.[3] Furthermore, the self-mythologising of Reynolds' dynastic subjects – their great sense of self-importance – is powerfully depicted. Their stance is echoed in John Lucas' portrait of the engineers George and Robert Stephenson (Fig. 1.2).

The end of the eighteenth century (the roots of many of the protagonists of this special issue) is an essential turning point for locating dynastic aspirations because of the combined political and economic upheavals of democracy and industrialisation across Europe. Throughout this period, a new or growing bourgeois and capitalist social order threatened to displace the power of the aristocracy (or land-based inherited wealth) and the established church. The old institutions had to be re-strengthened, and the self-constructed stability of a dynastic house (whether hereditary or architectural) could be seen as one response.

Fig. 1.1 | Joshua Reynolds, 'James Paine, Architect and his Son, James.' Ashmolean Museum. 1764. Alamy.

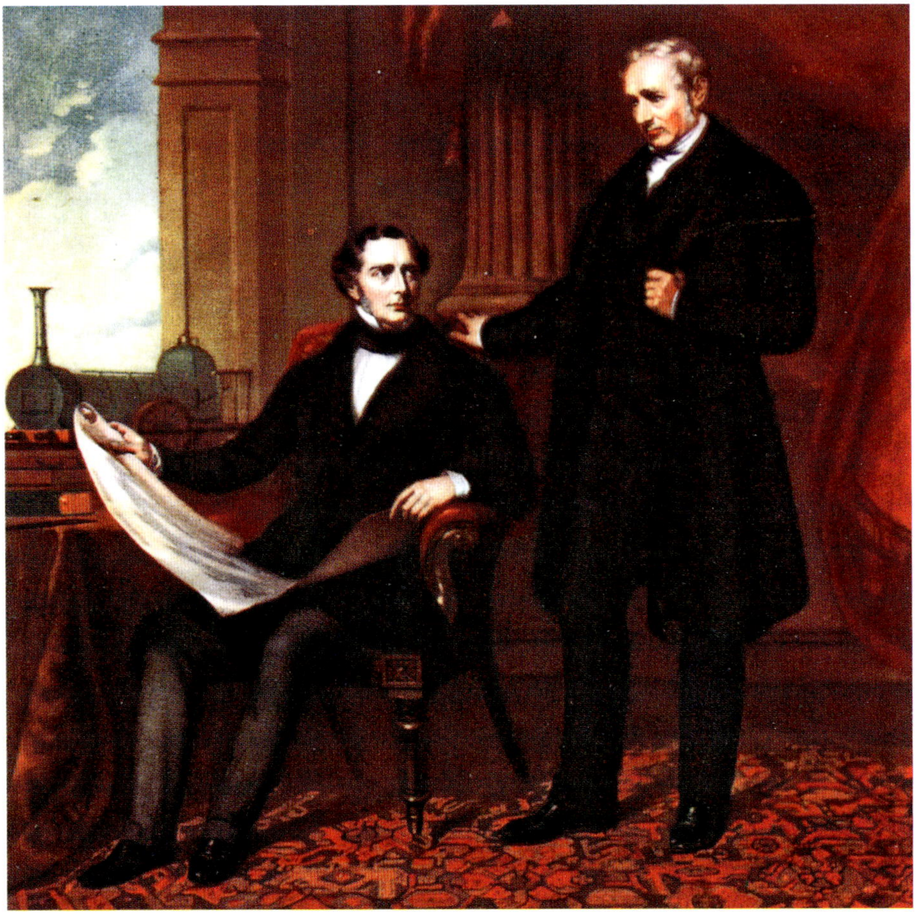

Fig. 1.2 | John Lucas, 'George Stephenson and Robert Stephenson.' 1851. Alamy.

If weakened by the modern turn, dynasties are remarkable for the paradox of their persistence in the face of modernity. A cursory glance at the indexes of the county-by-county *Buildings of England* series will immediately reveal how prevalent they were in both pre- and post-medieval British architecture. Absolutely defining features of the profession, a roll call of famous architects in Britain, such as the Mylnes, Adams, Pugins and Wyatts, would necessarily include them. We can see dynastic behaviours in the sixty-year history of the Wren office, too, or in the form of master-pupil relationships (albeit, outside of the focus of this issue).[4]

Dynasticism extended beyond famous names. The Newcastle-based Oswalds – Septimus (1823–1894), Joseph (1852–1930), Harold (1874–1938) and Gilbert (1896–1952) – ran a practice that shaped the architecture of the North-East of England. Atkinson Brierley in York, however, is likely the UK's longest-serving architectural dynasty. Still operating today, it descends from John Carr of York, via Peter Atkinson (1735–1805) and Walter Brierley (1862–1926). Yet, it has never been approached as a total entity. Many of the family's architectural drawings survive at the Borthwick Institute for Archives, a record of professional continuity that evidences key moments of transition in architecture, revealing (local) changes in office organisation and (broader) changes in the profession, such as how it became more specialised and codified, with increased professionalisation and bureaucratisation. The Atkinson Brierley example also reveals cases in which the trained became trainers, and how the archive was used intergenerationally to self-construct and preserve the dynasty itself, suggesting an almost mythic linearity.

Both Georgian and Victorian architecture aimed to historicise the present. Indeed, some architects seemingly desired to possess a *super*individual quality. Léon Vaudoyer (1803–1872), second in line in a dynasty of French architects who spanned the lifetime of architecture at the Ecole des Beaux-Arts, for instance, 'inherently sensed his place in a structure – both familial and institutional – larger than himself.'[5] While the Ecole could be said to have enabled dynasties through the lineage of its atelier structure, inter-dynastic training through family businesses may have perpetuated an inherited bias towards a particular style or method, even lengthening a stylistic, religious or intellectual project. The later members of the Pugin dynasty – Peter Paul (1851–1904), Cuthbert Welby (1840–1928) and Sebastian Pugin Powell (1866–1949) – are a case in point. Acutely conscious of their inheritance, they historicised the present through the very creation of 'dynastic' buildings. This might explain the remarkable atavism of St Robert Bellarmine, Glasgow (1955–1959, by H. C. Purcell of Pugin & Pugin).

Several sons of well-known Victorian architects succeeded in developing distinctive practices, including Robert Lutyens (1901–1972) and Sebastian Comper (1891–1979), although their reputations have been obscured by those of their famous fathers, and by the division of architectural history into periods that often sever the relationships between generations.[6] George Frederick Bodley (1827–1907), though, had frustrated dynastic ambitions. His son Hamilton had no feeling for architecture, so Bodley offered his parental affections to his pupils, establishing a surrogate dynasty. The Georgian, Sir John Soane (1753–1837), can be seen in parallel. While his own children did not take up the dynastic mantle either, so obsessively focused upon his own dynastic future, Soane crystallised his own dwelling, thanks to an official act of parliament, into a permanent museum to his own biography.[7] Soane created a 'dynasty of influence' on the Victorian architectural profession.

Thus, one can also think queerly about issues of inheritance. In his work on the National Trust, for example, Michael Hall has argued that, while the Trust presents an 'overwhelmingly heteronormative face' in focussing on the preservation of family legacies, the very act of taking homes away from them – and thereby dissolving the ties of inheritance – is 'challengingly queer'.[8] Elsewhere, Matthew Reeve has explored the 'queer genealogies' (biological and architectural) of Horace

Walpole and his homoerotic circle of friends in eighteenth-century England.[9] They created a family of Gothic buildings, challenging the then-dominant Palladian idiom. Walpole's most famous creation, Strawberry Hill, inspired Thomas Barrett's Lee Priory. As Reeve put it, 'From Walpole's perspective, his own 'queer family' of Barrett and others had created offspring in the built environment, and Strawberry Hill in particular – Walpole's architectural 'spouse' – had created progeny.'[10]

Beyond alternative forms of dynasticism, a family's lack of renewal – in the face of a strengthening notion of progress, a reforming labour market, increasing state patronage, the obsolescence of traditional skills, increasingly codified training, and a new ethically-driven professionalism in the nineteenth and twentieth centuries – could also have a devastating impact on the survival of architectural dynasties. An emphasis on an individual's self-establishment (as opposed to hereditary privilege) viz. Samuel Smiles' popular ideas on self-help, put further pressure on them.[11] Yet, they persevered. The UK Terrys are a case in point (Fig. 1.3),

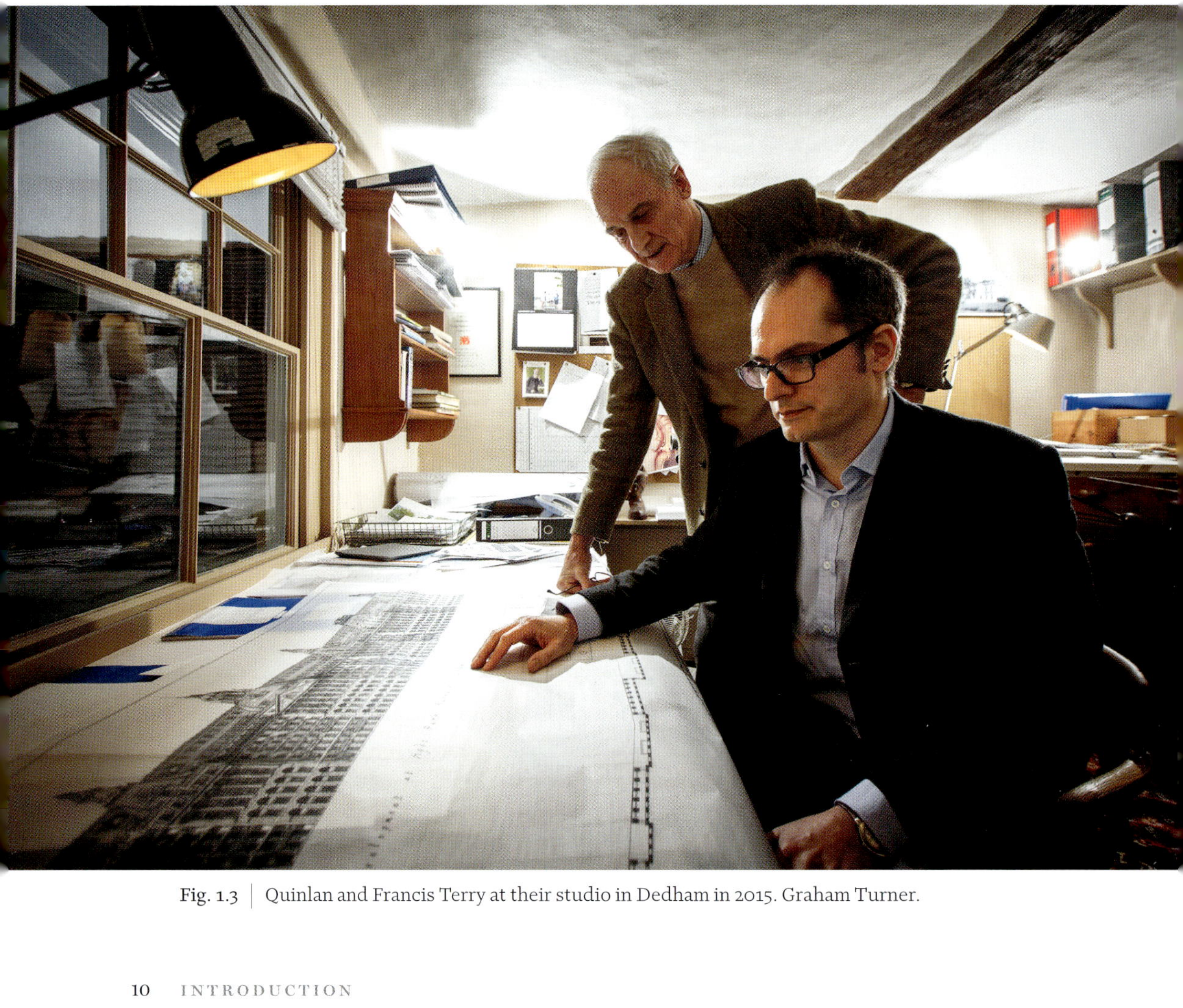

Fig. 1.3 | Quinlan and Francis Terry at their studio in Dedham in 2015. Graham Turner.

as are the century long Böhm dynasty, Germany's most famous architectural family, 'a phenomenon of its own kind', with a 'specially dynastically structured office'.[12] Echoes of dynasticism are present, too, in the constructed 'families' of the architectural avant-garde.[13]

Nepotism never really went away. A 1998 study of architecture's elitism in the USA argued that architects' 'success owes at least as much to their social background ... [as] ... native talent'.[14] In 2003, the social commentator Adam Bellow discovered no less than a 'boom in generational succession' in Western professions as a whole.[15] In 2024, Igea Troiani stressed the ongoing 'reputational capital' of dynasticism in the field.[16] Thus, the phenomenon can also help to historicise conditions still recognisable in architectural practice today, such as perpetuating the idea of architecture, not as salaried labour but as a vocation, 'a calling', opening up practitioners to potential exploitation.[17]

With modern architectural history in Britain usually constructed around individual lives, architectural dynasties have barely entered scholarly awareness.[18] Several studies have adopted dynastic groupings to frame their studies, however.[19] In *The Wyatt Dynasty* (1979), John Martin Robinson argued that the Wyatts' significance 'is due to their cumulative effect as a dynasty. Though they produced individually great architects it is their total contribution to England's architecture, sculpture and the decorative arts over a long period which makes them so interesting'.[20]

What it actually *means* to be an architectural dynasty is less resolved in the scholarship. Beyond architecture, this shortcoming was addressed at the conference, 'The Modern Invention of Dynasty: A Global Intellectual History, 1500–2000', at the University of Birmingham (2017). As Liesbeth Geevers and Mirella Marini, summarised, 'the concept of 'dynasty' remains underdeveloped. Authors generally use the term without being aware of what exactly they mean by it.'[21] Dynasties warrant attention beyond a self-evident biological grouping, as some studies have examined. Heinz Jürgen Sauermost has researched the cumulative trans-generational character of the German late Baroque Asam brothers of architects and sculptors.[22] Angus Taylor has examined the long-term reliance on marble and slate (and the inter-reliance of the family's own marble and quarrying business) of the Websters of Kendal in the North-West of England.[23] Barry Bergdoll has analysed continuities in the drawings of the Vaudoyers.[24] Scholars working on the eighteenth-century Adam dynasty, furthermore, have shown how, as a dynastic group, they had an advantage over individual practitioners in influencing the development of taste, ultimately enabling them to supplant a dominant Burlingtonian dynasty with a neo-classical, even Adamite, one.[25] After all, they famously adopted the motifs of their relatives with the self-referential 'Adam window'. The degree to which inherited advantage was a major factor of the Adams' success remains under-developed, though; the usual focus has been on the architect 'genius'.[26]

This special issue offers a more nuanced understanding of several aspects of architectural culture including patronage; education; style and historicism; the development and dissemination of knowledge; and the self-understanding of one's professional status. Moreover, it examines how a dynastic identity offered a distinctive means for dynasts to pass on their patrimony by constructing an idea of themselves through lineages. The above, however, does not only include architects. Dynasticism permeated all aspects of the profession in the Victorian period, including – as covered in this volume – in topographical draughtsmanship, publishing, model making and woodcarving.

Dynasticism is concretised in this volume through case studies of well-known, and lesser-known, families. Julian Pooley analyses the influence of the Nichols dynasty of antiquarian printers whose publications brought inspiration to many architects and craftspeople. Exploring their practice over three generations sheds new light on the genealogies of the Gothic Revival as it evolved across the period, enabled in no small part by the dynasty's own attempts to record their achievements for posterity. Matthew Wells examines the Day dynasty of model makers, a participatory medium that architects employed to help 'articulate the different material qualities of a design'. Wells also explores the notion of a 'transdisciplinary' dynasticism through the example of the Vulliamy family, through whose lineage he traces an example of an 'emerging technical or operative culture within the economy of production'.

The maleness (and whiteness) of the three illustrations in this editorial have not escaped my notice. It is as though dynasties helped perpetuate a caste hierarchy in architecture. Helen Wilson's article serves as a vital reminder of the distinctive agency that women exerted over the Victorian built environment.[27] Wilson discusses the influence of the ecclesiastical woodcarving company, Rashleigh, Pinwill & Co., established in Devon in 1890 by the Pinwill sisters, whose work was prevalent across the South-West of England. Their business was self-determinedly seen 'as a viable alternative to the inevitability of marriage and children or dependent spinsterhood', and thus an alternative form of dynasticism. The Pinwills benefited from an inter-dynastic patronage, with much of their work deriving from the Sedding dynasty.

Architectural dynasticism, lest we forget, was a pan-European phenomenon. Mikołaj Getka-Kenig focusses on the Polonized-Italian Marconi family, whose dynastic grouping helped reproduce its members' social statuses while helping them find favour with wide-ranging aristocratic and entrepreneurial patrons in Congress Poland. The classicism in which they specialised and helped develop offered clients 'an architectural instrument of social legitimacy'. The Marconis' enterprises over two centuries provide a lens to monitor diversifying architectural agency, industrialisation, and the development of Polish architecture. The Buckler dynasty in the UK also offered a form of legitimacy through its command, not of classicism, but of medievalism. In my essay, I show how the construction of a dynastic identity was seen by many of the Bucklers' clients as a means of establishing a sense of continuity of a family over the ages. Their traditional patronage came under threat, however, in the face of new open competition systems. John Chessell Buckler came second to Barry (and Pugin) in the Palace of Westminster competition. Beyond his Gothic erudition, it may it have helped that he employed 'the too-obvious rebus of an R inside a buckle' on his (ostensibly anonymous) entry; Charles Hanbury-Tracy, Chairman of the Commission, had previously invited Buckler to design his estate, Toddington Manor, Gloucestershire.[28] Reflecting on the extent to which Catholic architecture was a product of a dynastic organisational social structure, Peter Howell offers portraits of two entwined dynasties: the Bonomis and the Goldies and their deep-rooted Catholic lineages. These span from the appointment of Bonomi the Elder as architect to St. Peter's, Rome in 1804, through the work of his grandson, George Goldie (designer of the York Oratory, 1862–4), to his great-great grandson Joseph Goldie's 'large and powerful' church of the Assumption, Englefield Green, Surrey as late as the 1930s.

This special issue concludes with a conversation with the architect Nick Gilbert Scott. Echoing Harold Bloom's 'anxiety of influence', he reflects on his own – at times ambivalent – sense of filial duty to the Scott dynasty from which he descends.[29] Seeking to find 'Scottness' in his own practice, Nick shares particular artistic kinship with George Gilbert Scott Junior (1839–97), who 'expressed feeling, spirit and soul in his work'. Fittingly, Scott Junior died in the dynastic setting of his father's most famous creation, the magnificent Midland Grand Hotel.

NOTES

1. My own definition takes inspiration from Wolfgang Weber, "Dynastiesicherung und Staatsbildung: Die Entfaltung des frühmodernen Fürstenstaates," in: *Der Fürst: Ideen und Wirklichkeiten in der europäischen Geschichte*, ed. W. Weber (Köln, Weimer, Wien: Buchbeschreibung Böhlau, 1998), 91–136. A further source of influence in conceptualising dynasticism is Daniel Schönpflug, "Dynastic Networks," in *European History Online (EGO)* (Mainz: Institute of European History, 2010).
2. Alan Brownjohn, "Dynasty," *Times Literary Supplement*, September 17, 2004, 7.
3. Both James Paine Jnr. and James Paine Snr. supplemented their training by attendance at the St. Martin's Lane Academy.
4. Christopher Wren junior assembled the family history, *Parentalia: or Memoirs of the Family of the Wrens* (London: T. Osborn, in Gray's Inn, and R. Dodsley, 1750). On master-pupil relationships, see, for instance, the genealogical tree in Andor Gomme and David Walker, *Architecture of Glasgow* (London: Lund Humprhies, 1968), 282.
5. Barry Bergdoll, *Léon Vaudoyer: Historicism in the Age of Industry* (New York: MIT Press, 1994), 5.
6. Officially, Jean-Baptiste Sebastian Comper. Robert Lutyens did not have formal training as an architect. He worked as an interior designer working largely in partnership with Robert Wemyss Symonds.

7. John Soane, *Description of the House and Museum on the North Side of Lincolns-Inn-Fields, the Residence of John Soane* (London: James Moyes, 1830). "Dynasticism" can be explored through several biographies of leading architects of the period, written or compiled by their sons, including: Arthur Edmund Street, *Memoir of George Edmund Street, R. A., 1824–1881* (London: J Murray, 1888); Alfred Barry, *The Life and Works of Sir Charles Barry, R.A., F.R.S.* (London: John Murray, 1867); George Gilbert Scott, *Personal and Professional Recollections* (London: S. Low, Marston, Searle, & Rivington, 1879).
8. Michael Hall, "Queering the National Trust," Society of Architectural Historians of Great Britain blog, 17 June 2020, https://www.sahgb.org.uk/features/queering-the-national-trust.
9. Matthew Reeve, *Gothic Architecture and Sexuality in the Circle of Horace Walpole* (Pennsylvania: Penn State University Press, 2021).
10. Matthew Reeve, "Lee Priory," in *Queer Spaces: an Atlas of LGBTQIA+ Places & Stories,* ed. A. N. Furman and Joshua Mardell (London: RIBA, 2022), 46.
11. Samuel Smiles, *Self-help: with Illustrations of Character and Conduct* (London: John Murray, 1859).
12. Francis Terry has described how "sketching with my father is the corner stone of my architectural education," https://www.qftarchitects.com/essays/essay-sketching (accessed 27 June 2023). Deutsches Architeketurmuseum, "Raum ist Sehnsucht: Der Kirchenbauer Dominikus Böhm 1880–1955," exhibition (April–June 2005), http://dam-online.de/portal/de/Ausstellungen/RaumistSehnsucht/1777/0/57401/mod1487-details1/1594.aspx (accessed 5 February 2024)
13. Igea Troiani, "Edited by Alison Smithson: a censored history of the 'Team 10 family'" in *The Politics of Making*, ed. Mark Swenarton, Igea Troiani and Helena Webster (London: Routledge), 148–158.
14. Gary Stevens, *The Favored Circle: The Social Foundations of Architectural Distinction* (Cambridge, MA: MIT Press, 1998), 1.
15. Adam Bellow, *In Praise of Nepotism: A Natural History* (New York: Bantam, 2003), 9.
16. Igea Troiani, *Work-Life Balance in Architecture Playing the Game* (London: Routledge, 2024), 90.
17. Peggy Deamer, ed., *The Architect as Worker: Immaterial Labor, the Creative Class, and the Politics of Design* (London and New York: Bloomsbury, 2015).
18. See Malcom Airs and William Whyte, eds., *Architectural History After Colvin* (Stamford: Paul Watkins, 2013). Albeit, while not extending specifically to architecture, Reaktion have established a new series on dynasties with similar goals to that of this volume: https://reaktionbooks.co.uk/series/dynasties
19. Including: Geoff Brandwood and Martin Cherry, *Men of Property: the Goddards and Six Generations of Architecture* (Leicester: Leicestershire Museums, Arts and Records Service, 1990); Hermoine Hobhouse, "Philip and Philip Charles Hardwick: an Architectural Dynasty," in *Seven Victorian Architects*, ed. Jane Fawcett (London: Thames and Hudson, 1978), 32–49. Gavin Stamp catalogued the Scotts as a dynastic group, resulting in Joanna Heseltine, ed., *Catalogue of the Drawings Collection of the Royal Institute of British Architects: the Scott Family* (Amersham: Gregg International, 1981).
20. John Martin Robinson, *The Wyatts: an Architectural Dynasty* (Oxford: Oxford University Press, 1979), 230.
21. Liesbeth Geevers and Mirella Marini, eds., *Dynastic Identity in Early Modern Europe: Rulers, Aristocrats and the Formation of Identities* (Farnham: Ashgate, 2015), 15. They were referring to their interest in the House of Nassau.
22. Heinz Jürgen Sauermost, *Die Asams als Architekten* (Munich and Zurich: Schnell & Steiner, 1986).
23. Angus Taylor, *The Websters of Kendal: A North-Western Architectural Dynasty* (Kendal: Cumberland & Westmorland Antiquarian and Archaeological Society, 2004), 55.
24. Barry Bergdoll, *Les Vaudoyer: Une dynastie d'architectes* (Paris: Éditions de la Réunion des musées nationaux, 1991).
25. E.g. Deborah Howard, *William Adam* [Architectural Heritage, vol. 1] (Edinburgh: Edinburgh University Press, 1990), 92.

26. Eileen Harris, *The Genius of Robert Adam: His Interiors* (New Haven: Yale University Press, 2001); Julius Bryant, *Robert Adam, 1728–92: Architect of Genius* (London: English Heritage, 1992).
27. As explored in the Victorian Society's 2025 lecture series "Victorian and Edwardian Women in Architecture," which will thereafter form a special issue of this journal.
28. M. H. Port, ed., *The Houses of Parliament* (New Haven and London: Yale University Press, 1976), 43.
29. Harold Bloom, *The Anxiety of Influence* (New York: Oxford University Press, 1973).

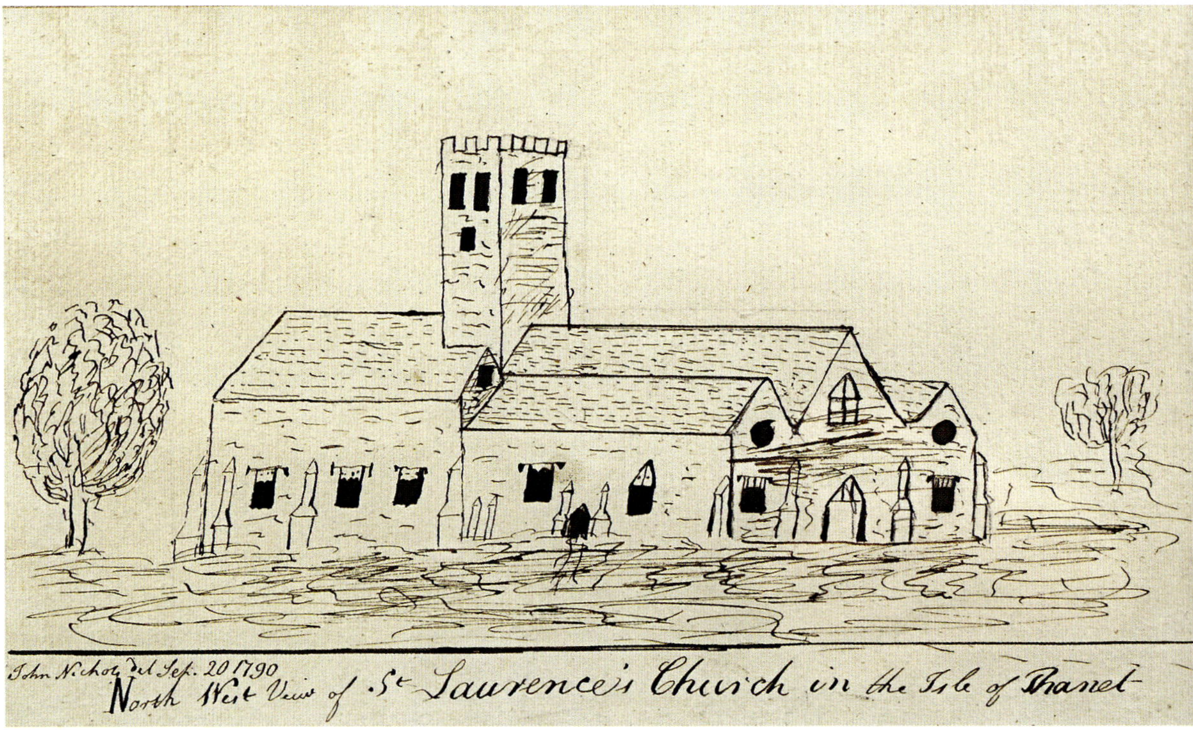

Fig. 2.1 | North West View of St. Lawrence's Church in the Isle of Thanet. Signed John Nichols 20 September 1790 but in fact drawn by his son, John Bowyer Nichols, aged eleven. Private Collection.

2 · Printers and Patronage: the Nichols Dynasty of Antiquaries and Printer-Publishers

JULIAN POOLEY

Framed above my desk there is a naïve ink drawing of St. Lawrence's church in the Isle of Thanet (Fig. 2.1). Although signed 'John Nichols' and dated 20 September 1790, this is unlikely. John Nichols (1745–1826) was a printer, antiquary and patron of topographical draughtsmen and, although no other drawings by him are known, at forty-five he might have done better than this. In fact, the handwriting is that of his son, John Bowyer Nichols (1779–1863), then aged eleven. It is hardly an auspicious start for a lad who succeeded his father as printer and editor of the *Gentleman's Magazine* and producer of most of the great late-Georgian county histories, but it encapsulates the family's immersion in the antiquarian endeavour of the late eighteenth century and points towards Bowyer Nichols's later role as a patron of architectural artists and contribution to conservation campaigns in the next century. His son, John Gough Nichols (1806–1873), was third in line of this dynasty of antiquarian printers.[1] His interest in sepulchral monuments and medieval tiles would inspire the designs of architects and craftsmen throughout the Victorian period. For three generations the Nichols family was synonymous with the research, writing and publication of local history, and their large archive allows us to follow the developing links between antiquarianism and architecture through one family over more than a century. This essay will show how their interests, channelled through their printing business, patronage and intellectual network, helped to lay foundations for the steady professionalisation of topographical research and publication between the mid-Georgian period and the reign of Victoria.

The Nichols archive is now scattered globally between over a hundred libraries and several private collections. My interest in the family was ignited when I bought a small volume of pocket diaries in The Flask Bookshop in Hampstead in 1982. I found that the writer was Mary Anne Nichols (1813–1870), granddaughter of John Nichols, daughter of Bowyer Nichols and sister of Gough Nichols. Her diaries cover 1823 to 1834, taking us into her domestic world, centred around her family's printing business in Parliament Street and a succession of homes in the quieter villages of Clapham and Hammersmith.[2] She records visits to London attractions and historic buildings and also family dinner parties for like-minded antiquarian friends.[3] My research led me to discover four volumes of travel journals kept by Mary Anne between 1844 and 1866 that survived in private hands. They provide a personal record of what she called her 'architectural pilgrimages' through Britain with her father and the architectural writer, John Britton, visiting churches and ancient monuments (Fig. 2.2).

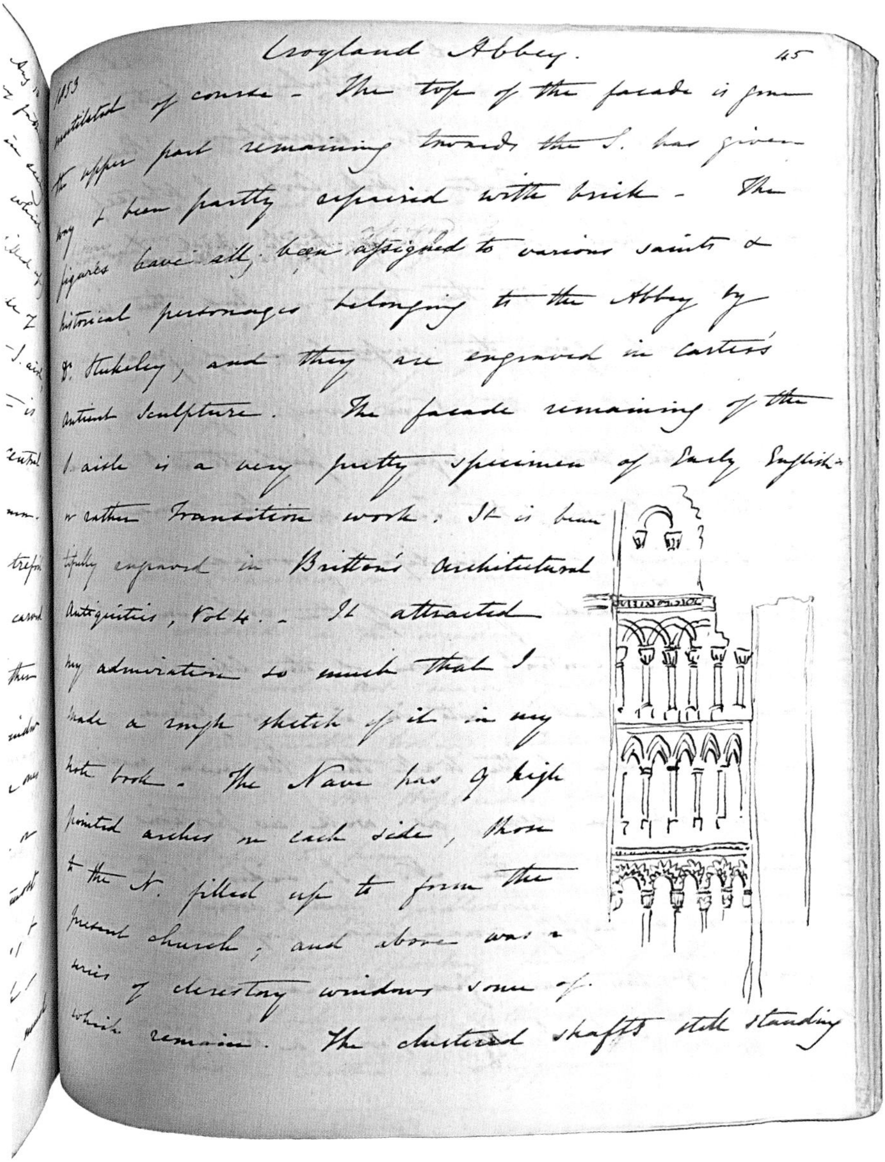
Croyland Abbey. 45
1853 mutilated of course – The top of the facade is gone
the upper part remaining towards the S. has given
way & been partly repaired with brick – The
figures have all been assigned to various saints &
historical personages belonging to the Abbey by
Dr. Stukeley, and they are engraved in Carter's
Antient Sculpture. The facade remaining of the
S aisle is a very pretty specimen of Early English –
or rather Transition work. It is beau-
tifully engraved in Britton's Architectural
Antiquities, Vol 4. – It attracted
my admiration so much that I
made a rough sketch of it in my
note book. The Nave has 9 high
pointed arches on each side, those
to the N. filled up to form the
present church; and above was a
series of clerestory windows some of
which remain. The clustered shafts still standing

Fig. 2.2 | Travel journal of Mary Anne Nichols recording her visit to Croyland abbey, Northamptonshire, on 18 August 1853. Alongside her sketch of the façade of the south aisle, her description testifies to her familiarity with the work of William Stukeley, John Carter, and John Britton. Private Collection.

Further study showed that significant collections of Nichols business and personal papers were held by the British Library, Bodleian Library, Folger Shakespeare Library, Yale University and Columbia University in New York. These could be traced to a series of Sotheby's sales of the Nichols libraries and collections between 1843 and 1951, but I also tracked down thousands of letters remaining in private hands.[4] Detailed calendars of these letters, in both private and public collections, are now managed and searchable via the Nichols Archive Database.[5] They allow us to map the networks of friendship and influence of this remarkable dynasty of antiquaries and printers, and assess their contribution to the recording, preservation and shifting understanding of ancient buildings and sculpture in the late Georgian and early Victorian age.

JOHN NICHOLS

James Boswell described John Nichols as being 'joyous to a pitch of baccanalian vivacity,' whose hearty dinner parties piled 'more solid victuals upon the table' than he had ever seen at a private house.[6] Nichols successfully mixed his conviviality with what he termed 'an irresistible impulse to proceed' both in his business as a leading London printer and his diverse research interests and publications (Fig. 2.3).[7] His *Literary Anecdotes of the Eighteenth Century* (9 vols., 1812–1815) and *Illustrations of the Literary History of the Eighteenth Century* (8 vols., 1817–1858) are fundamental for the study of the Georgian book trade and its customers.[8] His *History and Antiquities of the County of Leicester* (4 vols., 1795–1815) is still valued by local historians, and Renaissance scholars esteem his *Progresses of Queen Elizabeth* (4 vols., 1788–1823) for preserving in print an extraordinary range of sources for the life and culture of the Elizabethan court.[9] He was one of the earliest biographers of Hogarth, an editor of Swift and printer and research assistant for Samuel Johnson's *Lives of the Poets*.[10] Many people also knew him as 'Sylvanus Urban', pseudonymous editor and printer of the *Gentleman's Magazine*.[11]

Son of an Islington baker, in 1757 Nichols was apprenticed to the London printer, William Bowyer.[12] Personally involved in editing and correcting the works of Greek, Latin and Biblical scholarship, literary biography, science and antiquities that passed through his press, he inspired his apprentice with a love of research that would shape his career.[13] Bowyer printed for learned societies, particularly the Society of Antiquaries whose Director, Richard Gough, was the most influential antiquary of his day. As Bowyer's partner and successor, Nichols printed the Society's transactions, *Archaeologia*, but his friendship with Gough was forged during their completion of John Hutchins's county history of Dorset following Hutchins's death in 1773.[14] Nichols later admitted that his work with Gough steered his research interests away from literature into the 'dry, thorny and barbarous paths of National and Local Antiquities.'[15]

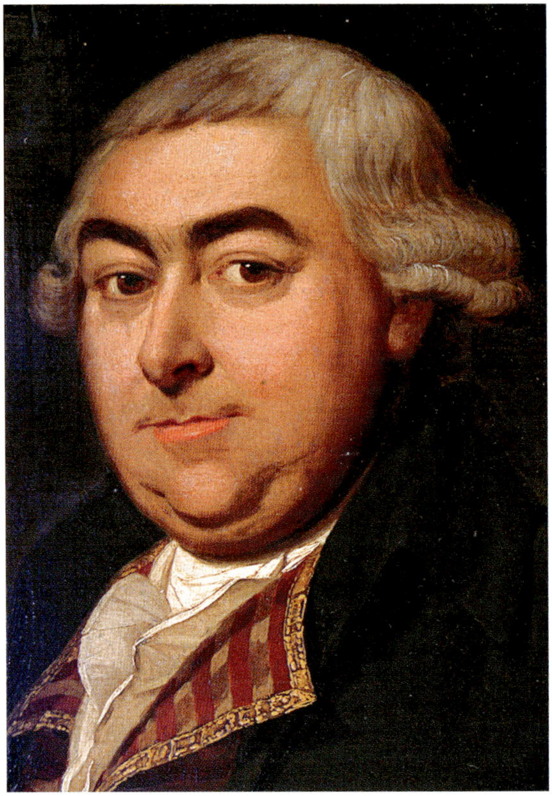

Fig. 2.3 | John Nichols. Portrait by Gerard van der Puyl, 1787. Oil on canvas. Private Collection.

These paths led in several directions. Immediately after Bowyer's death, Nichols began a memoir of him that grew into a biography of his press. By listing the titles of the hundreds of works he had printed, providing biographies of their authors, and printing their correspondence the work grew into the *Literary Anecdotes* and *Literary Illustrations* providing an encyclopaedia of literary and antiquarian culture across the long eighteenth century. Bowyer had been a Fellow of the Antiquaries and his press had printed many topographical works, so these volumes underpin any study of the work of the Society and its Fellows throughout the Georgian period. Nichols remained the Society's printer after inheriting Bowyer's business in 1777, but his relationship with the Society was not always easy. Though Gough proposed him for election in November 1777, this came to nothing. Bowyer Nichols later remarked that this was because the Society could not 'entertain the idea that their printer should be a Fellow' but it may also have been because Nichols's own publications at that time focussed on literary biography rather than on antiquities.[16] He was eventually elected on 17 May 1810.[17]

NICHOLS AND THE *GENTLEMAN'S MAGAZINE*

Another pathway was through the *Gentleman's Magazine*, established in 1731 by Edward Cave which by the 1770s had a monthly print run of some 10,000 copies reaching an estimated audience of over 40,000 people.[18] It boasted a huge readership of individuals, families, book-clubs, debating societies, and circulating libraries across Britain and beyond. Nichols bought a share in it 1778 and by 1782 was printer and editor. It remained at the heart of the Nichols family's business and personal life until 1856 when they sold it to John Henry and James Parker, booksellers and architectural writers of Oxford. Under Nichols the magazine became the main conduit of antiquarian research to a national audience as he and Gough (reviews editor from 1786) regularly reviewed the latest county histories, and promoted the study of the material remains of Britain's past. In 1783 Nichols doubled the size of each issue, allowing more space for topographical and antiquarian topics. This placed the magazine and its reader-contributors at the centre of debates surrounding the study and classification of medieval architectural styles and the growing tensions concerning their conservation.

The magazine propagated larger projects. In 1780 Gough and Nichols established the *Biblotheca Topographica Britannica* to raise public awareness of the nation's antiquities and improve standards of topographical research.[19] These short, specialist publications made Nichols a far more successful communicator of antiquarian research than the Society of Antiquaries. When his own history of Hinckley in Leicestershire appeared in the *Bibliotheca* in 1782 the magazine's reviewer noted that 'This printer to the Society of Antiquaries moves faster than his constituents. And the reason is obvious. All communications are welcome to him, and this is encouragement enough to communicate to him.'[20] It was clear that though Nichols was the Society's printer, he was more energetic than its Council in publishing antiquarian research. The magazine's review of *Archaeologia* in 1783 noted that as three years had passed since the previous volume, there was a risk that half the monuments of antiquity would decay or be destroyed before the next appeared. In 1784 an unidentified contributor observed that by giving more space to antiquities, the magazine was becoming 'A REPOSITORY… in which may be collected, for public reference and use, all the scattered accounts of facts respecting the History and Antiquities of our country'.[21]

As editors of the *Gentleman's Magazine* Nichols and his successors placed it at the heart of arguments surrounding the nation's appreciation of its architectural legacy in the late Georgian period. The essays, letters and architectural studies featuring in each number made it a powerful agent of debate in an age that witnessed a series of vociferous campaigns about the conservation of historic buildings. No other printing firm was so strongly involved with the architectural arguments that resonated across the country in the late Georgian and early Victorian age.

By giving a voice to key players in these debates through their press, their research and private correspondence they allow us to navigate the turbulent history of the Gothic Revival. Throughout the 1780s and 1790s Nichols focussed the magazine's attention on the controversies surrounding James Wyatt's heavy-handed campaign of 'Improvement' at the cathedrals of Salisbury, Hereford, Lichfield and Durham, allowing Gough, the architectural draughtsman Jacob Schnebbelie, the architect John Carter as well as John Milner to criticise Wyatt's proposals and work in a series of excoriating letters. When Wyatt was elected a Fellow of the Antiquaries in 1797 Gough resigned as Director and continued to lead an epistolary war against Wyatt and his supporters in the magazine. Working with Gough and Carter in this way, Nichols enhanced public appreciation of the distinctive qualities of Gothic architecture.[22] Their contributions encouraged a new generation of antiquaries who valued ancient buildings as monuments to be preserved rather than adapted to contemporary taste. Nichols encouraged his readership to see churches and cathedrals as historical documents, reflecting the manners and customs, art and culture of earlier centuries. It may not be a coincidence that Nichols lost his

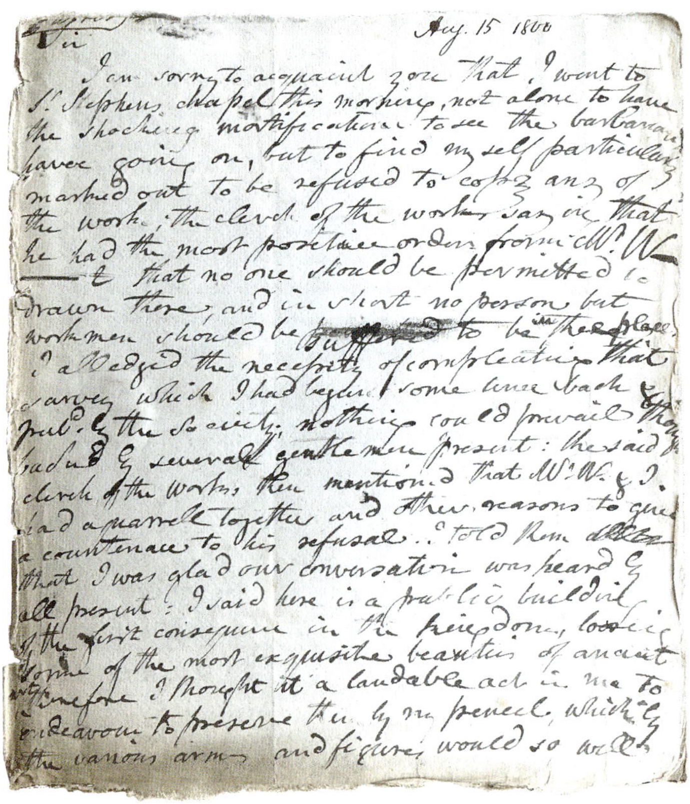

Aug. 15 1800

Sir

I am sorry to acquaint you that I went to St. Stephens Chapel this morning, not alone to have the shocking mortification to see the barbarous havoc going on, but to find myself particularly marked out to be refused to copy any of the work; the clerk of the works saying that he had the most positive orders from Mr. W— that no one should be permitted to draw there, and in short no person but workmen should be suffered to be in the place. I alledged the necessity of compleating that survey which I had begun some time back for the Society, nothing could prevail tho backed by several gentlemen present: the said clerk of the works then mentioned that Mr. W. & I had a quarrell together and their reasons to give a countenance to his refusal.. I told them that I was glad our conversation was heard by all present: I said here is a public building of the first consequence in the kingdom, boasting some of the most exquisite beauties of ancient therefore I thought it a laudable act in me to endeavour to preserve them by my pencil, which by the various arms and figures would so well

Fig. 2.4 | John Carter to Richard Gough, 15 August, 1800 reporting his 'shocking mortification of seeing the barbarous havoc going on' under Wyatt's direction at St. Stephen's, Westminster. Private Collection.

contract as the Society's printer the following year. Although the Council explained that it was due to his high costs and their preference for the new fashion of 'fine printing', they must have been irritated whenever the magazine criticized Wyatt's work or compared Nichols's energetic antiquarian press to their own inertia.

Undeterred, Nichols consolidated the magazine's role as a public voice in support of national antiquities, by printing a series of over two hundred campaigning essays by John Carter called 'The Pursuits of Architectural Innovation' between 1798 and 1817. Rosemary Sweet likens these to a war correspondent's report from the front of architectural damage and destruction.[23] They covered the whole country, chronicling the destruction of buildings by insensitive repair or unchecked decay but focussed on Wyatt's proposed work at Westminster, where St Stephen's chapel and its newly uncovered painted chamber had been earmarked for alterations. Carter's letter to Gough in August 1800 reporting his 'shocking mortification of seeing the barbarous havoc going on' under Wyatt's direction at St. Stephen's is preserved in the Nichols archive (Fig. 2.4).[24] His journalism established in the public's mind the importance of Westminster abbey as the embodiment of national history and glory. The concept of national heritage was nurtured by Carter, supported by Nichols, through the pages of the *Gentleman's Magazine*.[25]

RECORDING A DYNASTY

At the same time, John Nichols's son and daughters began their work to preserve their own heritage on both a business and personal level. Bowyer Nichols was apprenticed to his father on 6 August 1793 while still at St. Paul's school. On completing his apprenticeship on 5 August 1800, he was made a Freeman of the Stationers' Company and became a partner in the family business (Fig. 2.5). Eight years later he oversaw the firm's reconstruction following the fire that destroyed its printing office and warehouse in Red Lion Passage, Fleet Street, on 8 February 1808. Though William Bowyer's printing ledgers and John Nichols's own collection of early newspapers survived because they were stored in a garret of the adjacent home that escaped the flames, the Nichols's own business records and the large archive of the *Gentleman's Magazine* were lost.[26] Bowyer Nichols's work to gather and preserve what remained was boosted in 1809 when Richard Gough bequeathed his working set of

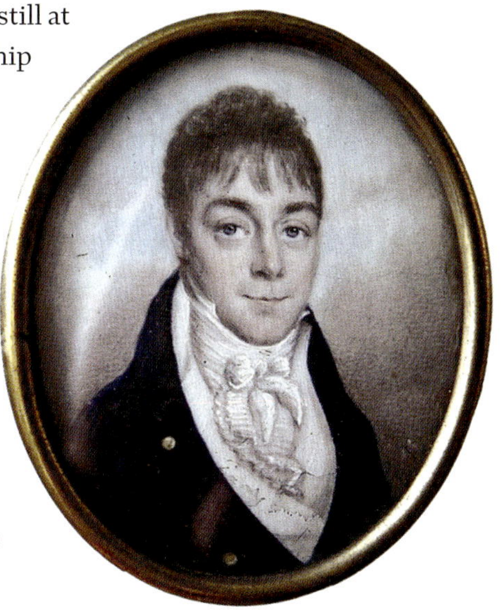

Fig. 2.5 John Bowyer Nichols, Cameo portrait miniature, *c.*1815. Artist unknown. Private Collection.

the magazine to John Nichols. These volumes, filled with letters and annotations identifying thousands of anonymous and pseudonymous contributors were continued by Bowyer Nichols and his family for the next fifty years.[27] Helped by his sisters, Isabella and Anne and his son, Gough Nichols, he created an archive that mapped their editorship of the magazine and links to its network of correspondents. Simultaneously, they collected letters, illustrations, printed ephemera, and other papers into a series of albums called 'Family Records' that chronicle their dynasty through key events and friendships in their business and personal lives between *c*.1765 and *c*.1854. These, alongside many other volumes of correspondence were plundered by Mary Anne Nichols when forming her extensive collection of autograph letters in the 1830s and 1850s.[28] These different parts of the Nichols family and business archive link the three generations between John Nichols and the death of Gough Nichols in 1873 (Fig. 2.6).

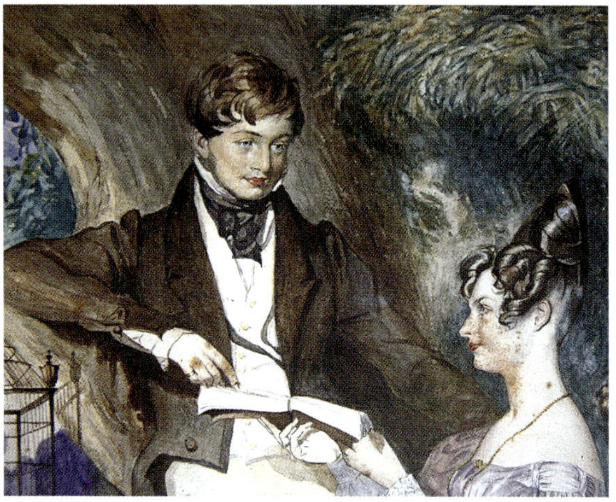

Fig. 2.6 | John Gough Nichols and his sister, Mary Anne Nichols. Detail of 'The Children of John Bowyer Nichols' by Daniel Maclise, 1831. Watercolour copy. Private Collection.

THE NICHOLSES AND THEIR ILLUSTRATORS

It is this archive that records the conservation interests of the Nichols dynasty and their enduring relationships with leading topographical draughtsmen and engravers of their day. Richard Goddard has shown how four generations of the Basire dynasty were employed by successive members of the Nichols family to illustrate the *Gentleman's Magazine* and other works that they printed. Thirty plates by James Basire were included in the *Bibliotheca Topographica Britannica* for example, over a hundred in Nichols's history of Leicestershire, and a hundred more by successive members of the family featured in the magazine. The patronage provided by the Nicholses and their friends, notably Gough, Carter and Sir Richard Colt Hoare ensured the longevity of this leading family of engravers and can be traced throughout their archive.[29] We are indebted to the skill of the Basires and other draughtsmen patronised by the Nicholses for what we know about buildings and sculpture now either destroyed or drastically repaired by later generations. These included: Jacob Schnebbelie, Barak Longmate, Thomas Prattent, James Peller Malcolm, George Hollis and his son Thomas. All too often they remain shadowy figures, leaving little behind besides their name as artist or engraver in the plate-mark of a published print, but John Nichols preserved his correspondence with them because it recorded his financial relationship with them and because many of them shared his antiquarian interests. Many of these men struggled financially, relying on the Nicholses for support. Jacob Schnebbelie regularly accompanied Nichols into Leicestershire to sketch churches for his county history (Fig. 2.7). When he died tragically young in 1792 Nichols and Gough raised a subscription for his widow and completed the publication of his *Antiquaries Museum* in tribute to him and to benefit his family.[30] In 1795 Schnebbelie's widow Caroline, whose poverty was relieved by engraving plates for the magazine, sent her son Robert to Bowyer Nichols with a volume of his own sketches hoping that he would employ him as well.[31] He used his work in the magazine and engaged him as drawing master for his children.[32]

Jacob Schnebbelie's place as John Nichols's preferred draughtsman was filled by James Peller Malcolm. Though a regular contributor of plates to the magazine, and author of several antiquarian works including *Londinium Redivivum,* Malcolm's financial situation was never secure.[33] The Nichols papers show that John Nichols frequently rescued him from financial disaster by advancing money in return for drawings to illustrate in his own publications. Nichols saw these cash injections to cover rent, butchers' bills and fines for infringing the Hair Powder Act as debts

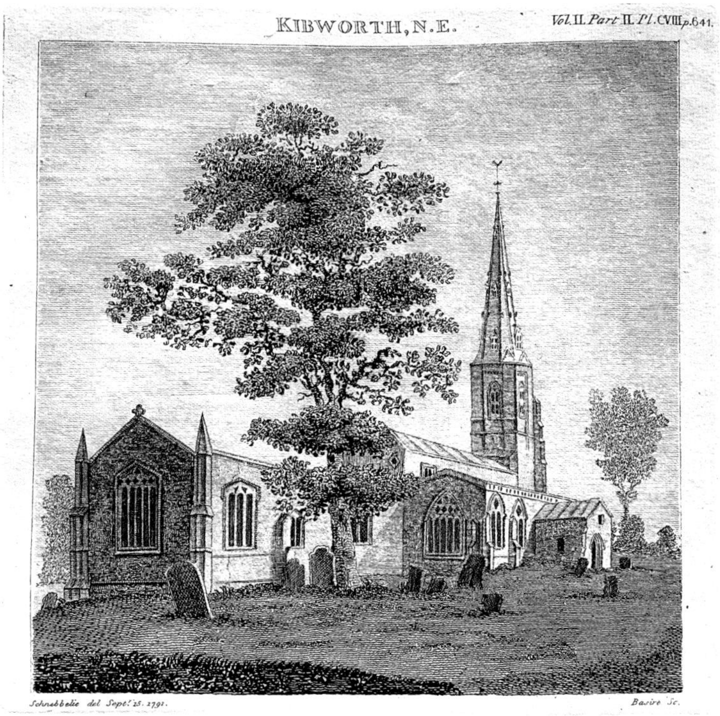

Fig. 2.7 | Kibworth church, Leicestershire. Drawn by Jacob Schnebbelie 15 Sep 1791 and engraved by James Basire. J. Nichols, *History and Antiquities of the Town and County of Leicester*, vol. 2, part 2, plate 108, 641.

of gratitude that tied Malcolm closer to his press and his own research.[34] Without Nichols's help Malcolm would have been bankrupt; without Malcolm's dependence upon him Nichols's works might not have been so abundantly illustrated (Fig. 2.8). When Malcolm followed Schnebbelie to an early grave in 1815, Nichols and his son raised a subscription for his family.[35]

Thomas Prattent was also employed by Nichols to engrave plates for the magazine and history of Leicestershire following Schnebbelie's death in 1792 (Fig. 2.9). When in 1802 'a nervous fever and inflammation of his eyes' prevented him from working and he was confined in Southwark's grim Marshalsea prison for debt, Nichols described him as 'our ingenious but unfortunate correspondent' when he printed Prattent's first-hand description and drawings of the Marshalsea's shabby interior in the magazine. Although Nichols paid him, Prattent was still in the Marshalsea in 1804, when he sent more pictures seeking further financial support.[36]

Although the patronage by John Nichols and his son of talented yet impoverished topographical artists helped to nurture their work and ensure it reached a wide audience, it was not without its risks. George Hollis engraved plates for the magazine from 1816, and in 1839 they joined with him and his son Thomas in a project to continue Charles Alfred Stothard's *Monument Effigies of Great Britain*.[37] Part one appeared on 1 June 1840 and, perhaps encouraged by the names of Nichols and Hollis appearing as joint publishers on the title page, Thomas wrote to Gough

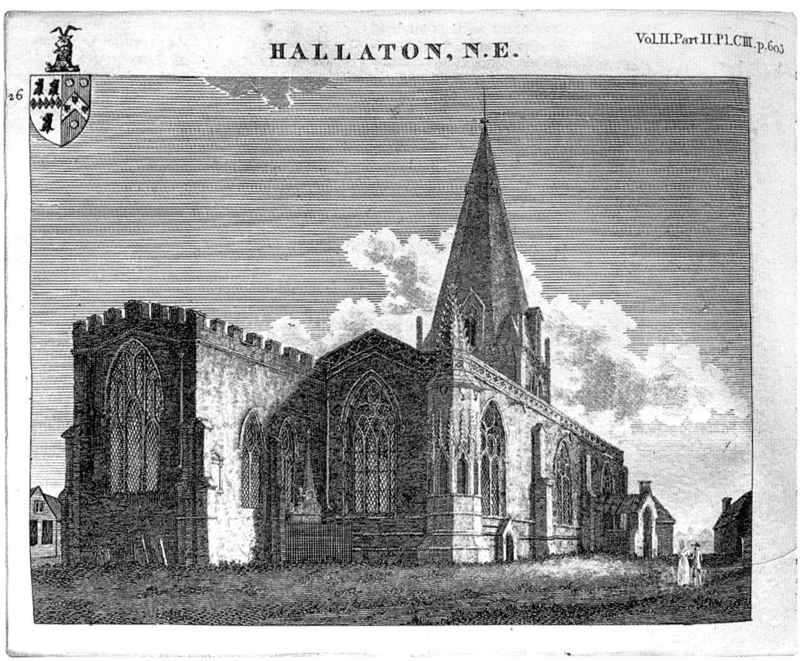

Fig. 2.8 | Hallaton church, Leicestershire. Drawn and engraved by James Peller Malcolm. J. Nichols, *History and Antiquities of the Town and County of Leicester*, vol. 2, part 2, plate 103, 603.

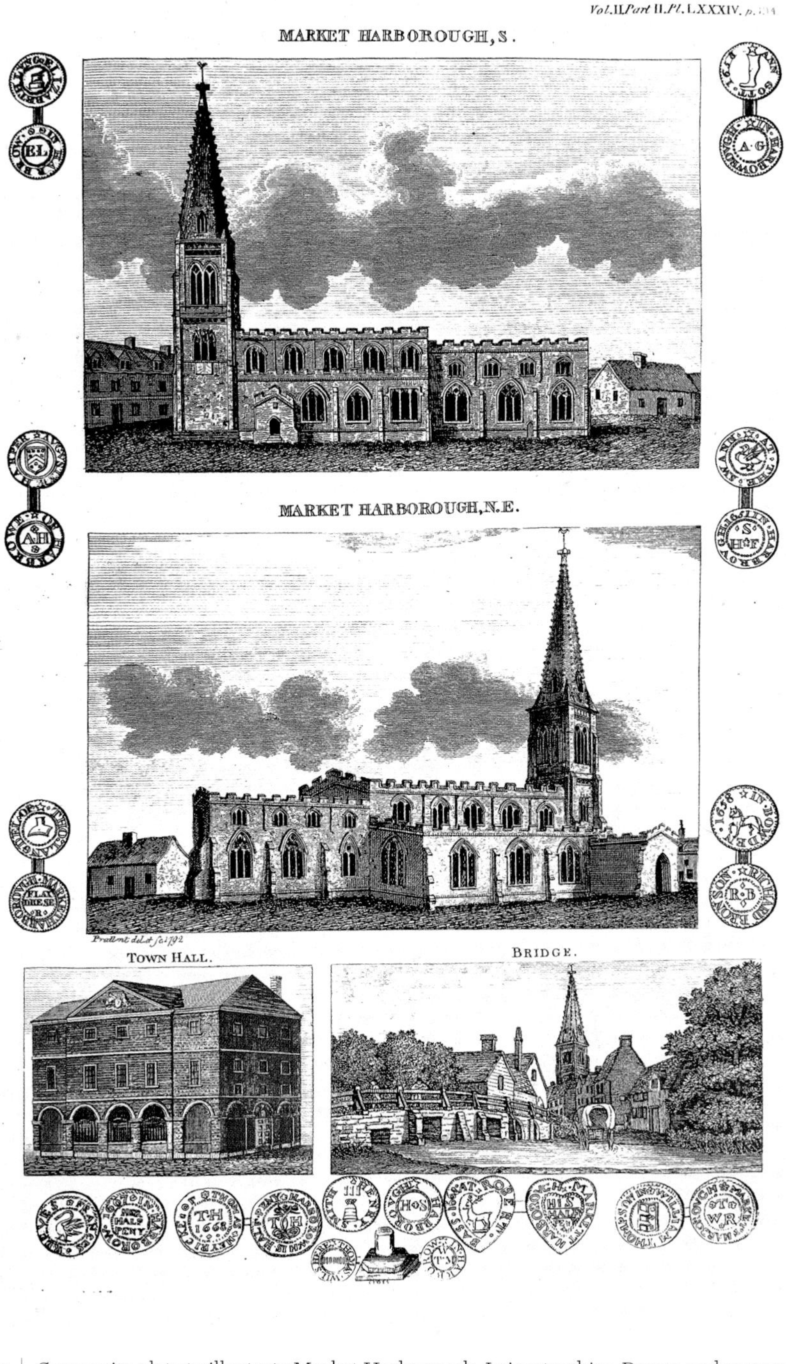

Fig. 2.9 | Composite plate to illustrate Market Harborough, Leicestershire. Drawn and engraved by Thomas Prattent. J. Nichols, *History and Antiquities of the Town and County of Leicester*, vol. 2, part 2, plate 84, 494.

Nichols three weeks later to express 'the deepest regard for one of [his] good and virtuous Sisters'.[38] He hoped that as he advanced in his profession, he might find favour in her sight and obtain her consent and her parents' approval. Gough Nichols replied promptly and negatively, stating that a young man in Hollis' position should defer all thoughts of marriage until he was established in his profession and able to provide for a family. No man had the right to expect to depend on his wife's property, and Hollis was end his visits to the family home with immediate effect.[39] Clearly, patronage would not intrude on the dynasty. Five further numbers of the *Monumental Effigies* appeared before George Hollis died in January 1842. In the magazine's obituary, Bowyer Nichols paid tribute to his skills, noting that his 'talented son' planned to complete the work. Sadly, the task broke Thomas's health, and he died aged just 25 on 14 October 1844.[40]

THE *MAGAZINE* AS A FORUM FOR DISCUSSION

As editors of the magazine the Nicholses enabled readers across the country to promote interest in ancient buildings and their preservation. Most issues include views and descriptions of churches and sculpture alongside letters from readers eager to participate in discussions surrounding the development and description of architectural styles. J. Stone's letter in 1798 describing medieval effigies inside Aldworth church, Berkshire, is typical and one of the first to include a view of the interior showing its gallery, box pews and sepulchral monuments (Fig. 2.10).[41] Other letters called attention to neglect and ruin, such as George Lipscombe's descriptions of the Buckinghamshire churches of Quarrendon and Pitchcot which

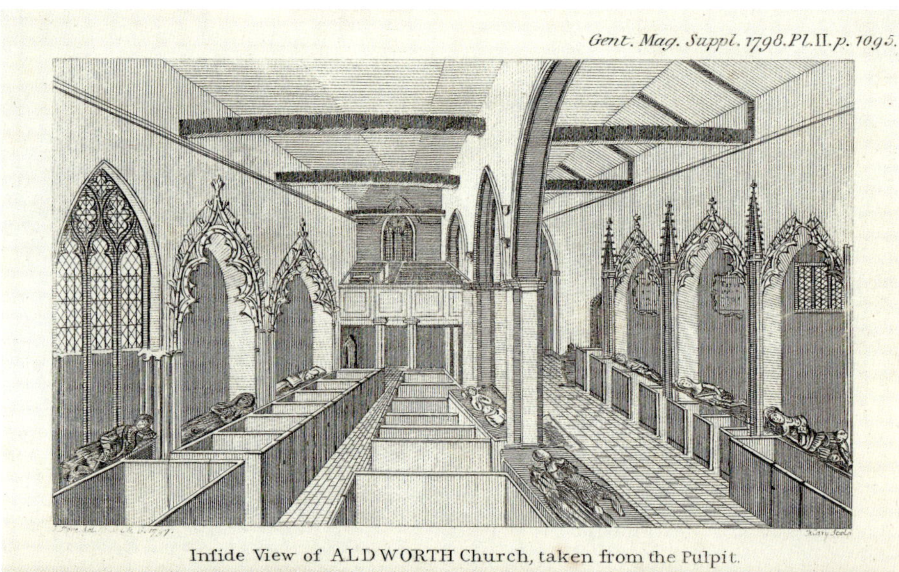

Fig. 2.10 | Aldworth church, Berkshire. *Gentleman's Magazine*, 1798 part 2, 1094.

Nichols printed in 1817.[42] Readers also used the magazine to promote local campaigns. In 1818 'Well aware of the zealous and effective support which you have given to civil and ecclesiastical establishments, and knowing of your regard even to ecclesiastical architecture', George Henry Law (1761–1845), bishop of Chester, asked Nichols to insert a circular seeking subscriptions for repairs to the cathedral fabric.[43]

JOHN BOWYER NICHOLS

As a boy, Bowyer Nichols accompanied his father, Richard Gough and Jacob Schnebbelie on topographical tours around Britain. His first identified contribution to the *Gentleman's Magazine* in July 1800 under the initials 'B.I.N.', was an account of West Twyford church, Middlesex, in which he provided epitaphs omitted by Lysons in his *Environs of London* and hoped 'Mr Malcolm, or other ingenious correspondent' might be encouraged to draw it.[44] Even before he assumed greater editorial responsibility after 1817 he was contributing church notes on a monthly basis and using the magazine to champion the recording and preservation of ancient monuments. In 1818 he was elected a Fellow of the Antiquaries and frequently spoke at their meetings. In 1819, during a brief appointment as printer to the Corporation of London, he published *A Brief Account of the Guildhall of the City of London* assisted by the 'pen and pencil of that ingenious young Draughtsman, Mr. J. C. Buckler' who had himself been contributing architectural sketches and essays to the magazine since 1812.[45] Its brief account of the Guildhall was based on printed authorities but it focused on the contemporary state of the hall, chapel and courts following their recent restoration by the Corporation, paying tribute to the 'skill and good taste of the Nineteenth Century' evidenced in their 'judicious arrangement of the monuments and regularity and display of the ancient and modern designs and enrichments'.[46] It demonstrates his knowledge of architectural style, the value he placed upon sensitive repairs and his enthusiasm to work with an emerging generation of skilled architectural draughtsmen like Buckler.[47] The work is in marked contrast to his revised edition of Andrew Coltée Ducarel's *Account of the Royal Hospital and Collegiate Church of St Katharine, near the Tower of London* (London, 1824). Ducarel's work had first appeared in the *Bibliotheca Topographica Britannia* in 1782 but was now scarce, following the warehouse fire in 1808. In his Preface Bowyer Nichols explained that he had been prompted to reprint it by Parliament's plans to redevelop the area for new docks. 'Though every Lover of his Country' he wrote, 'must rejoice at the Commercial prosperity which requires this additional accommodation for the Port of London – the Antiquary, alive to the venerable remains of distant years, cannot but regret the anticipated destruction of the Collegiate Church of St. Katharine.'[48] The work was announced in the magazine in April 1824 and reviewed (probably by Bowyer Nichols himself) in June.[49] Like his father, Bowyer Nichols understood the magazine's potential for raising public awareness and appreciation of the nation's architectural heritage, especially when it was at risk. When the last service was held in St. Katherine's on 30 October 1825, the magazine carried two letters that were highly critical of the building's destruction. The first, by 'N.P.' described the solemnity of the Rev. Bailey's last sermon which alluded to the 'unfeeling and encroaching hand of Commerce'.[50] The second, by Edward John Carlos writing under his usual initials of 'E.I.C.' raged against the 'sacrilegious destruction' and expressed 'just feelings of indignation against the ruthless destroyers of the ill-fated building'.[51]

CAMPAIGNING THROUGH PRINT

Though highly regarded for his honourable dealings, mild manner and genial company, Bowyer Nichols did not hesitate to unleash the full force of his printing press in the fierce campaign to preserve St. Saviour's church in Southwark. Concern was first voiced by Buckler in the magazine in 1826.[52] Praising the magazine as 'foremost among the advocates for our national architecture', he hoped the editor would give his 'powerful aid to the protection of St. Saviour's church'. Plans to halt recent repairs by George Gwilt and re-build the nave with 'cumbrous galleries' for the expanding congregation, would consign the choir to a mere mausoleum and destroy the unity of the entire fabric. Throughout the coming years of struggle, Bowyer Nichols opened the pages of the magazine to Buckler, Carlos and Alfred John Kempe who campaigned to raise local and national appreciation of the architectural importance of St. Saviour's and the potential loss to the nation's heritage. In December 1828 Carlos expressed astonishment that 'so fine a Church should remain in a state of neglect and decay, in an age when the preservation of our national antiquities is so much encouraged'.[53] The vestry's plans to close off the nave with temporary walls and benches would reduce the interior to the state of a dissenting meeting house, 'little better than a barn'. He petitioned for space in the magazine to call public attention to the subject and entreat readers with influence to make the repair of St. Saviour's a national concern.

In February 1830 'Suthriensis' told readers that St. Saviour's was about to be destroyed as part of plans to redevelop roads serving the new London Bridge, and called on Parliament and the Society of Antiquaries to ensure that it was repaired and could form a central feature of the view from the bridge.[54] In April Carlos told readers that St Saviour's was the 'finest specimen of pointed architecture in existence' and an ornament to the Metropolis.[55] On 25 March 1831 Kempe called for public support towards the repairs but just five days later Carlos reported that there were now plans to demolish the Lady Chapel, as it obstructed plans for wider highways leading from London bridge into Surrey.[56] In August Bowyer Nichols printed another letter from Carlos, reporting that the vestry had resolved to remove the roof from the nave of the church in order to ruin the fabric. He urged the

Diocesan to intervene and a public subscription to be established for the repair of the entire building.[57]

By early 1832, the magazine's campaign was gaining traction, and large parts of the January issue were devoted to it. Carlos told readers that 'The friends of this ancient building are gaining strength; a sensation is excited in its favour, which is mainly to be attributed to the notice bestowed by the public press.'[58] His praise for the magazine was seconded by Kempe in a letter thanking the Bishop for refusing his assent to the destruction of the Lady Chapel but voicing indignation that Parliament was planning to overrule his decision.[59] Bowyer Nichols followed these letters with details of a parish meeting on 5 January in which the future of the Lady Chapel had been warmly debated, and printed a powerful report by the architects James Savage and Lewis Nockalls Cottingham giving their esteemed opinions on why the chapel should be restored.[60] He concluded with news that a meeting 'of architects, antiquaries and men of taste' had been held at the Freemason's Tavern on 28 January, where it was resolved to restore the Lady Chapel through public subscription. His editorial the following month supported this subscription. Although signed by 'Sylvanus Urban', it concluded by saying that 'When the Report had been read, J.B. NICHOLS, Esq. moved that it should be received by the meeting. Having witnessed the exertions of the Committee, he felt it his duty to come forward and declare his high sense of their conduct' (Fig. 2.11).

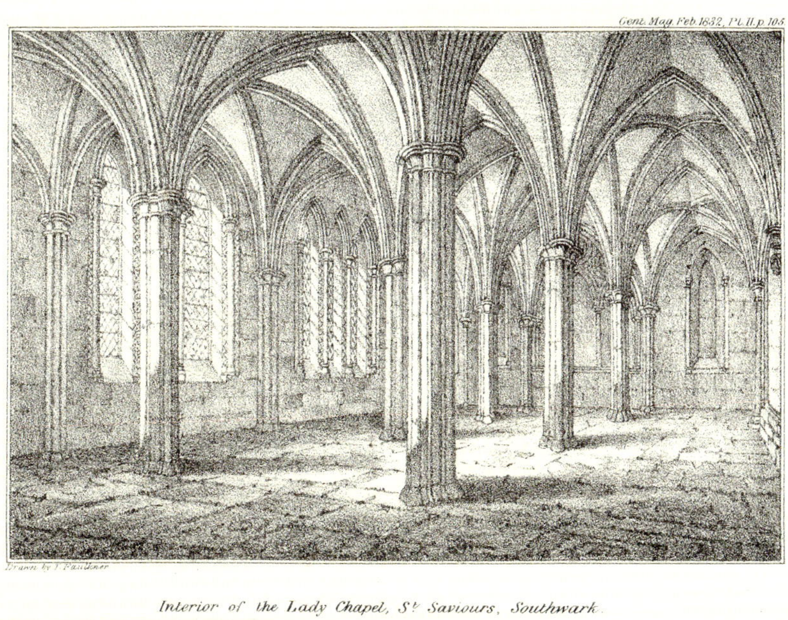

Fig. 2.11 | Lady Chapel at St. Saviour's church, Southwark. Lithograph by Thomas Faulkner *Gentleman's Magazine* 1832, part 1, 105.

Bowyer Nichols had shown himself to be a worthy successor to his father in using the magazine and its vociferous correspondents to raise public awareness of the threat to ancient buildings and oppose destructive redevelopment. As 'Sylvanus Urban', John Nichols had worked with Carter to oppose Wyatt in the 1790s and criticise the brutal 'restoration' of Henry VII's chapel in Westminster Abbey by Dean William Vincent after 1807; but Bowyer Nichols went further, stepping forward from pseudonymity in 1831 to give his name, in capital letters, to publicly endorse the campaign for the Lady Chapel (Fig. 2.12). His family joined in the endeavour. On 5 July 1832 Mary Anne Nichols recorded in her diary that she and her mother and sisters had been 'to Mr. Kempe's New Kent Road where we had luncheon. We then proceeded with 2 of the Miss Kempes to the Fancy Fair at the Surrey Zoological Gardens for the Ladye Chapel, Southwark. It was very pretty Papa and John met us there'. On 10 August she also recorded a visit with her family 'to the Fancy Fair at Vauxhall Gardens for the Ladye Chapel'.[61]

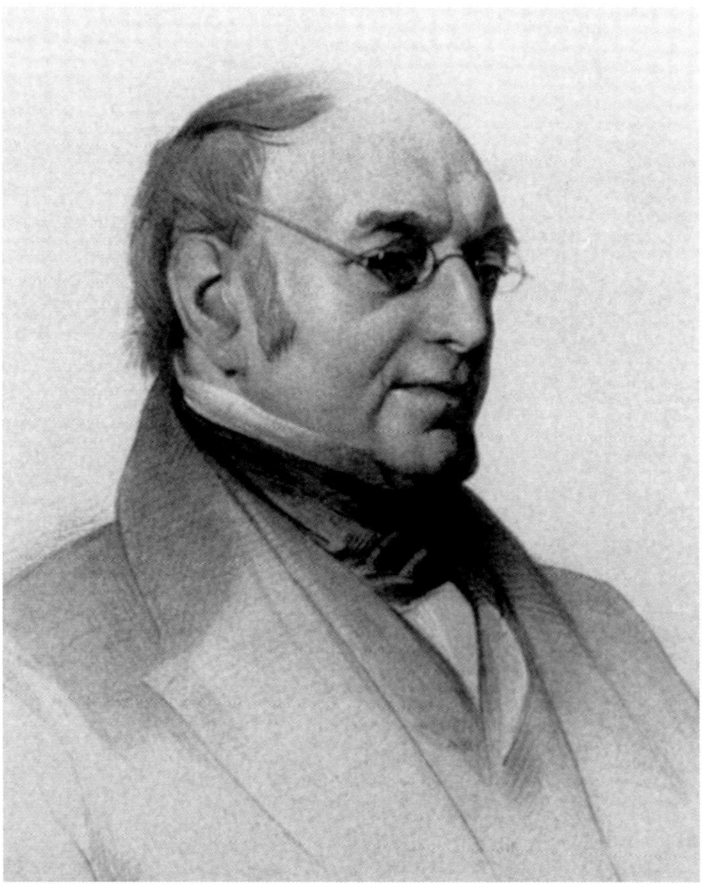

Fig. 2.12 | John Bowyer Nichols drawn by Samuel Laurence in chalk, lithographed by J. H. Lynch, 1850. Private Collection.

ARBITERS OF TASTE

As editors of the *Gentleman's Magazine* the Nichols dynasty was part of a national discussion regarding style and taste. Alongside their preservation campaigns, they also printed critical reviews of modern ecclesiastical buildings. The Church Building Acts of 1818 and 1824 made money available to build churches and chapels in populous areas. Designs for these new churches were decided by competition, and architects submitted plans in a range of Classical styles as well as a 'late Georgian Gothic' reimagining of medieval architecture. Many of the new churches were appraised in the magazine by Buckler, Carlos, or local correspondents, such as Thomas Faulkner in Chelsea. Between 1824 and 1832 Carlos contributed thirty-three articles on 'New Churches' to the magazine. Though stridently critical of architects who failed to live up to the ideal style that 'prevailed in the reign of the Third Edward', he was happy to praise when merit was due, applauding D. Laing for designing 'a correct specimen of our ancient architecture' at St. Dunstan in the East and admiring the new church at Doncaster as 'a beautiful specimen of modern architecture, which, although not free from defects, possesses architectural merit in a very high degree.[62]

Bowyer Nichols also collected topographical books, prints and maps. His house, 'Chancellors', by the Thames at Hammersmith housed an important collection of artefacts ranging from Norman Romanesque sculpture to a Renaissance chimney-piece from Theobalds, Hertfordshire, once owned by Gough.[63] Like his father, he commissioned artists to draw antiquities for him. In 1819 he sent Buckler to inspect the painted chamber in the Palace of Westminster on his behalf and in the 1820s he paid Carlos to draw churches for him in Kent, Middlesex and Surrey.[64] These 'working tools' were used by his friends, including John Britton, John Adey Repton and Maria Hackett, the formidable campaigner who saved Crosby Hall.[65] Though some of his collections were sold by Sotheby's in 1843 and in a posthumous sale in 1864, significant parts were inherited by Gough Nichols, and can be traced in Sotheby's catalogues of his library following his death in 1873.[66] They showcase the scope and importance of these dynastic collections. The 1864 sale included Thomas Fisher's *Collections, Historical, Genealogical and Topographical for Bedfordshire*, illustrated by 114 copper plates, 67 additional plates and a set of Fisher's lithographs of monumental brasses.[67] There were also 69 drawings of monastic ruins by Francis Nicholson,[68] over 500 drawings of Suffolk churches by Maurice Johnson of Woodbridge[69] and 23 county portfolios of drawings.[70]

JOHN GOUGH NICHOLS

Gough Nichols maintained his family's close association with the magazine, helping to edit it from 1826 and continuing to have ultimate managerial control after responsibility was shared with the writer, John Mitford and antiquaries, James Temple

Mansel, Sir Frederic Madden and John Bruce between 1834 and 1850 (Fig. 2.13). Though sole editor from 1850 until its sale in 1856, his contribution to antiquarian scholarship stretched far beyond the magazine. He was a particularly active Fellow of the Antiquaries, attending meetings with his father from the age of twelve before his election in 1835. Throughout the 1830s and 1840s he and Kempe reported on the Society's meetings in the magazine in a monthly column called 'Antiquarian Researches'. Many of his contributions about churches, sculpture and genealogy were under the pseudonym of 'Nepos'. Just as his grandfather had used the *Bibliotheca Topographica Britannica* to raise the standards of antiquarian scholarship, so in 1834 Gough Nichols founded the *Collectanea Topographica et Genealogica* for topographical articles that were increasingly squeezed out of the magazine as it sought to 'embrace a larger circle of Literature'.[71]

The world of topographical printing was already changing when Gough Nichols joined the firm in 1826. The subscription county histories familiar to his father and grandfather were being replaced by specialised printing societies

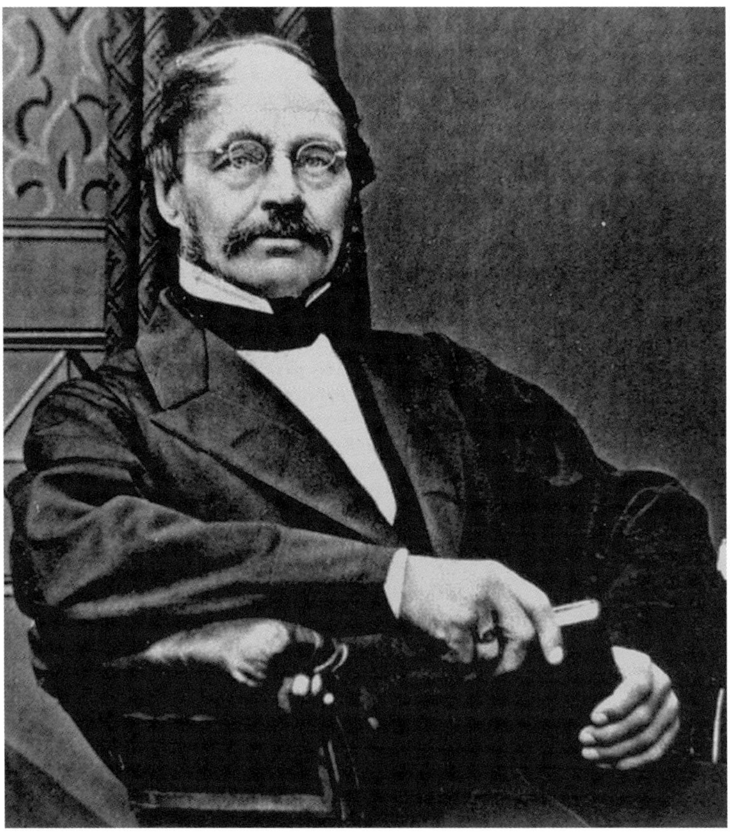

Fig. 2.13 | John Gough Nichols photographed by Hennah and Kent, Brighton, 1864 and printed by his brother, Robert Cradock Nichols in his *Memoir of the Late John Gough Nichols* (1874).

whose members received academic editions of historic documents in return for annual subscriptions. The first of these was the Surtees Society, of which Gough Nichols was a founder member in 1834. Inspired by its success in 1838 he, Thomas Wright and John Bruce formed the Camden Society to publish manuscripts and new editions of rare books. Gough Nichols edited eighteen texts for the Camden Society. His interests in medieval ornament were clear from 1838, when he published a *Description of the Church of St Mary, Warwick and of the Beauchamp Chapel* and *Ancient Paintings in Fresco discovered in 1804 on the Walls of the Chapel of the Trinity at Stratford upon Avon from Drawings by Thomas Fisher*. In 1837 he visited both towns to compare Fisher's drawings with the monuments. Writing from Leamington on 15 October, he told his father that everything was just as Fisher had drawn. 'He was very accurate. It will make a *Gentleman's Magazine* article of great interest to the architectural antiquarian'.[72]

Gough Nichols's immersion in the study and conservation of church monuments resounds through his correspondence. Throughout the 1840s he worked with the Suffolk antiquary, David Elisha Davy to repair the brasses and sculptures at Cobham, Kent.[73] Carlos had sent him 'some of the most curious' brasses to select for engraving in 1838, and by August 1840 he was working with Davy to fund their repair. The table monument to George, Lord Cobham (d. 1558) in the chancel was in a lamentable state, with the niche figures of children broken and strewn on the top of the tomb. Gough Nichols considered the monuments to be some of the finest of the Elizabethan age and was concerned that they were at risk from 'neglect in the absence of anyone to care much about them, to the wear and tear of a village school and the occasional pilfering of ignorant and dishonest admirers.'[74] He noted that the architect George Hammerton knew a modeller who was restoring sculptured ornaments at Rochester who might help with repairs.[75] After visiting Rochester and Cobham, he obtained quotes for repairs amounting to £26.00, using 'mastic which in a few minutes becomes harder than stone. It will permanently fix the brasses, prevent further violent injury and the slabs will appear as new.'[76] By February the the slabs were covered in mastic, the broken brasses restored, and the canopy figures would soon be preserved by 'a sort of permanent paint, which sinks into the mastic' which would 'represent perfect slabs of Purbeck marble.'[77] He arranged for iron railings to be erected, to 'prevent people from clambering upon the tomb'[78] and wrote a report on the project for the magazine.[79]

Gough Nichols's pioneering study, *Examples of Decorative Tiles, Sometimes Termed Encaustic* inspired contemporary taste and design.[80] In August 1833 he reported in the magazine how tiles found near an ancient kiln near Malvern proved that ornamental tiles found in medieval churches were of English, not Continental manufacture because they corresponded with those in Malvern's priory churches. In October he showed that many tiles in English churches were ornamented with heraldic shields appropriate to local families. In 1837 he published a letter from B.C. Taylor of Malmesbury reporting the discovery of an encaustic pavement during repairs at the abbey church, and endorsed a call by William Leverton Donaldson for the reintroduction of armorial and pictorial tiles in modern church design.[81] In May 1841 Albert Way, whose work on the tiles at Great Malvern was published in John Henry Parker's *Oxford Glossary of Architecture*, told him that he remembered seeing 'original tiles of interesting character' at the Nichols's home at Hammersmith and suggested that 'A treatise on them would be a pleasing addition to middle-age archaeology'.[82] Gough Nichols was already preparing a systematic study of figurative medieval ceramic tiles, and the survival of his interleaved copy of that work in the Mercer Collection of Bucks County Historical Society, Pennsylvania, allows us to follow his research and appreciate the support that he received from antiquaries and clergy around the country.[83] In June his cousin, William Lake Baker, sent details of tiles at Bushmead Priory, Bedfordshire, and in November George A Biederman (1782–1859), rector of Dauntsey, Wiltshire, told him that he had used some tiles he had found in a local, farmyard as a border in the entrance porch to his rectory.[84] With text and plates printed in brick-red ink to reflect the simple beauty of the medieval designs, Gough Nichols's study of encaustic tiles explicitly drew the attention of antiquaries and architects to ancient examples that 'if revived in a correct spirit, will be found at once decidedly beautiful and decidedly economical' (Fig. 2.14).[85] Industrial manufacturers responded enthusiastically. Chamberlains of Worcester were soon making tiles for 'ornamental pavements for modern churches, mansions, dairies &c', based on medieval patterns, while Mintons of Stoke on Trent designed and made tiles for the Temple church in London and St Mary's, Stafford. Gough Nichols's footnotes even provided details of their London agents and the dimensions of the tiles available.[86] J. French, a linen draper of Bolton le Moors, Lancashire used designs for tiles he had seen in the magazine for oil cloth, telling Gough Nichols that he wished to improve other articles of church furniture and had successfully introduced emblematic patterns on Communion linen and altar cloths. Gough Nichols's plates had enabled him to reproduce tiles in their original colour and arrangement.[87] Mary Anne Nichols shared her brother's interest in medieval tiles, telling him of some she had found in Cotheridge church, Worcestershire.[88]

John Gough Nichols's achievements as a topographical printer and champion of medieval style united the medieval antiquarian interests of his predecessors with the ideals of the Gothic Revival. He played a pivotal role in working with local antiquaries, architects and contractors to identify significant monuments, promote public awareness and ensure their survival both physically and through the incorporation of their craftsmanship in contemporary design. His work was the legacy of a dynasty of printing antiquaries stretching from the time of John Nichols, in the

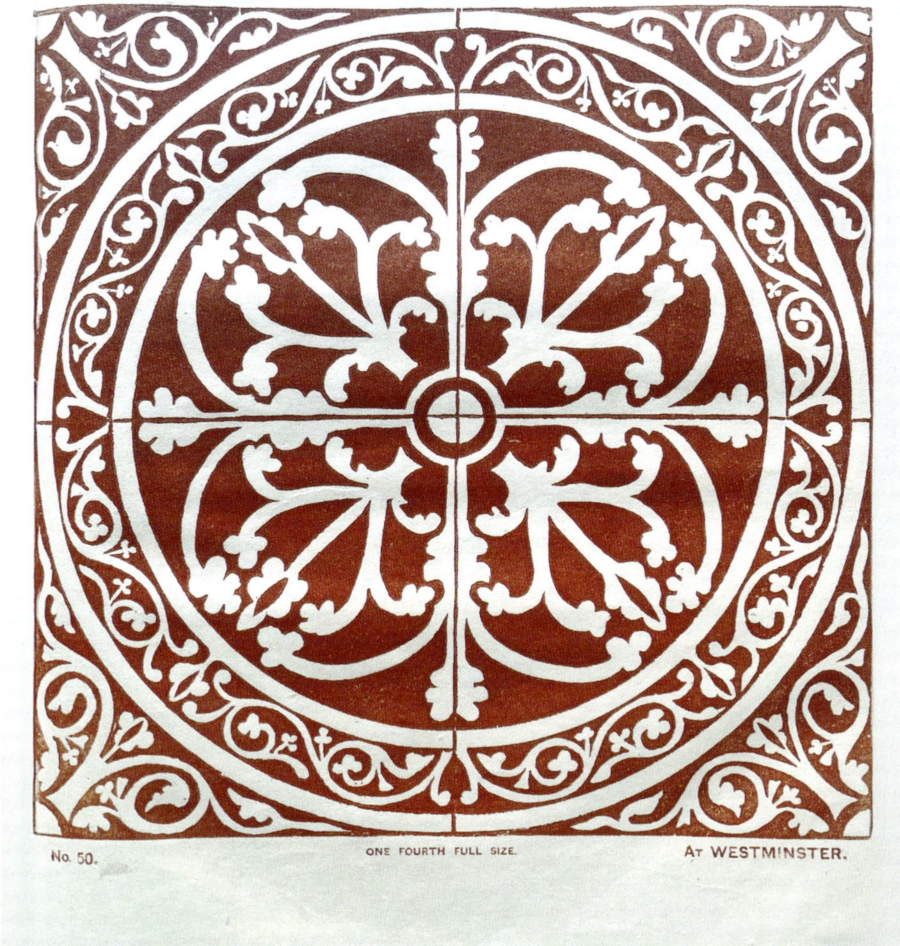

Fig. 2.14 | John Gough Nichols, *Examples of Decorative Tiles, Sometimes Termed Encaustic* (1845) plate 50, Westminster Abbey tiles. With permission from the Society of Antiquaries of London.

fractious years of James Wyatt's controversial works at English cathedrals in the 1790s to the immersion of Gothic forms in British ecclesiastical and domestic design in the mid-nineteenth century. While his father and grandfather had printed multi-volume county histories for gentlemen authors and patronised the work of talented draughtsmen, Gough Nichols worked on a larger scale, as a founder member of the Archaeological Institute (1844) and London and Middlesex Archaeological Society (1855) and contributor to the work of local archaeological societies. He became convinced that a national 'Topographical Society' with county branches would be the best means of promoting local historical research.[89]

Though he did not live to see the establishment of the *Victoria County History* in 1899, Gough Nichols's devotion to rigorous scholarly editing, assistance to the formation of national and county societies and promotion of medieval art in contemporary design ensured that the achievements of the dynasty established by John Nichols in the late eighteenth century, and the work of the draughtsmen and campaigners they supported, were embedded in the taste and culture of Victorian Britain. The large archive of the Nichols family provides a lens through which we can assess the immense contribution of this firm of printers and antiquaries to the development of architectural culture.

NOTES

1. Throughout this essay I will refer to these three generations as John Nichols, Bowyer Nichols and Gough Nichols respectively.
2. Baldwin Hamey, "London Street Views: Nichols and Son, printers," accessed, 21 Dec, 2022, https://londonstreetviews.wordpress.com/2018/09/26/nichols-son-printers
3. J. Pooley, "The Diary of Mary Anne Nichols, 1823–1834, a publisher's daughter in Hammersmith," *Transactions of the London and Middlesex Archaeological Society* 44 (1993) [1996]: 171–197.
4. J. Pooley, "'The Book That Changed My Life': Discovering the Archive behind the *Gentleman's Magazine*," *The Book Collector,* 70, no. 1 (Spring 2021): 11–24.
5. For details of the Nichols Archive Project, see https://le.ac.uk/english-local-history/about/collections/julian-pooley and http://www.bibsoc.org.uk/content/nichols-archive-project [accessed 20 August 2022]. I am grateful to the owners of private collections of Nichols papers for their continuing interest in and support for my work. Although the Nichols Database is not yet online, it may be consulted by appointment with me at Surrey History Centre, Woking.
6. Marshall Waingrow, *The Correspondence and Other Papers of James Boswell Relating to the making of the 'Life of Johnson'* (New Haven: Yale University Press, 2001), 388.
7. *Literary Anecdotes,* vol. 7 (1816), 491.
8. Referred to throughout this essay as the *Literary Anecdotes* and *Literary Illustrations.*
9. See Caroline Wessel, Julian Pooley and Robin Jenkins, *Nichols' History of Leicestershire. A Bicentenary Celebration 2015* (Leicester, Leicestershire Archaeological And Historical Society, 2015); Elizabeth Goldring, Faith Eales, Elizabeth Clarke and Jayne Elisabeth Archer, eds., *The Progresses and public processions of Queen Elizabeth: A New Edition of Early Modern Sources* (Oxford: OUP, 2014).
10. The first edition of John Nichols's *Anecdotes of Mr Hogarth,* 1780 grew with the assistance of Isaac Reed and George Steevens into *The Works of William Hogarth from the Original Plates restored by James Heath RA to which is prefixed a biographical essay on the genius and productions of Hogarth*, 1822. For Nichols's contribution to Swift studies, see Daniel Cook, "*Labor ipse voluptas:* John Nichols's Swiftiana," in *Authors and the Book Trade, ed.* Matthew Day (Delaware: Oak Knoll Press, 2012) 43-60. Nichols's relationship with Samuel Johnson is discussed by Roger Lonsdale in his edition of *The Lives of the Most Eminent Poets; with Critical Observations on Their Works* (Oxford: OUP, 2006). See also J. Pooley, "'Conciliating His Esteem': John Nichols's Contribution to Johnson's *Lives of the Poets*, to Biographies of Johnson and to later Johnsonian Scholarship," *The Age of Johnson* 21 (2011): 143–192.
11. For Nichols's work on Domesday, see *Domesday Book, seu liber censualis Willelmi Primi Regis Anglicæ,* 2 vols., (1782). For Nichols and the *Gentleman's Magazine,* see Edward Hart, "An Ingenious Editor: John Nichols and the *Gentleman's Magazine*," *Bucknell Review* (March, 1962): 232–242 and Gillian Williamson, *British Masculinity in the* Gentleman's Magazine, *1731–1815*, (Basingstoke, Palgrave Macmillian, 2016), 26–9.

12. Nichols entered Bowyer's office in 1757, aged twelve, but he was not enrolled in the Stationers' Apprentice registers until 6 February 1759, *Literary Anecdotes,* vol. 3 (1816) 286 and D. F. McKenzie, ed., *Stationers' Company Apprentices 1701–1800* (Oxford: Oxford Bibliographical Society, 1978), 44.
13. See Martin Maner, "'The Last of the Learned Printers': John Nichols and the Bowyer Nichols Press," *English Studies* 65, no. 1 (1984): 11–22.
14. John Hutchins, *The History and Antiquities of the County of Dorset* (London: W. Bowyer and J. Nichols, 1774). See also H. Smith, "John Nichols and Hutchins's History and Antiquities of Dorset", *The Library,* 5th series, 15, no. 2 (June 1960): 81–95.
15. Nichols's description was quoted by Sir Samuel Egerton Brydges in a letter to the magazine Dec 1823, 484–5.
16. Bowyer Nichols's comments are written on Gough's 'Testament' proposing Nichols for candidacy to the Antiquaries in 1777 now at Columbia University Library, New York, Spec MS Coll Nichols. No reference to his candidacy is given in the Society's minutes for November 1777, suggesting that it did not gather enough support to be voted on and so was not blackballed.
17. Society of Antiquaries of London, *Minute Book,* vol. 32 (1808–1811): 375. Nichols was described as 'a Gentleman deeply versed in the History and Antiquities of the United Kingdom, and Author of many valuable Topographical Publications' and his candidacy was supported by John Caley, William Bray, Francis Douce, Henry Ellis, Taylor Combe and Charles Combe.
18. Albert Pailler, *Edward Cave et le Gentleman's Magazine (1731–1754),* vol. 1 (1977), 459. See also J. Pooley, "The *Gentleman's Magazine:* A Panoramic View of Eighteenth-Century Life and Culture," *The Book Collector* (Autumn 2020): 407–21.
19. The *Bibliotheca Topographica Britannica* appeared in 52 numbers between 1780 and 1790, continuing as the *Miscellaneous Antiquities* in ten numbers 1791–1800. Significant issues which provided a template for further research included Andrew Coltée Ducarel's *History of the Royal Hospital and Collegiate Church of St. Katharine, near the Tower of London,* 1782, and Nichols's own *Collections towards the History and Antiquities of the Town and County of Leicester,* 1790.
20. *GM* 1783 pt. 1, 51.
21. *GM* 1784 pt. 2, 653.
22. Rosemary Hill, *Time's Witness: History in the Age of Romanticism* (London: Penguin, 2021), 63–64.
23. Rosemary Sweet, *Antiquaries: The Discovery of the Past in Eighteenth-Century Britain* (London: Hambledon and London, 2004), 291.
24. Private Collection, PC1/96/26 NAD8839, Carter to Gough, 15 August 1800. Items on the Nichols Archive Database have two references; a unique number generated by the database, prefixed NAD, and a reference number used by the public repository holding the original document or devised to preserve the order of the documents as found in the private collections.
25. Sweet, *Antiquaries,* 290–295.
26. Keith Maslen and John Lancaster, eds. *The Bowyer Ledgers,* (London: The Bibliographical Society, 1991); J. Pooley, "'A Copious Collection of Newspapers': John Nichols and his Collection of Newspapers, Pamphlets and News Sheets, 1760–1865," *Gale" A Cengage Company,* accessed, 24 December, 2022.
27. They are now at the Folger Shakespeare Library, see James M Kuist, The Nichols File of the 'Gentleman's Magazine', (Madison: University of Wisconsin Press, 1982).
28. See J. Pooley, "The Papers of the Nichols Family and Business: New Discoveries and the Work of the Nichols Archive Project," *The Library,* 7th Series, 2, no. 1 (March 2001): 10–52.
29. Richard Goddard, *Drawing on Copper: The Basire Family of Copper-plate Engravers and their Works* (Maastricht: Universitaire Pers Maastricht, 2016), 222–236 and 267.
30. Jacob Schnebbelie, *The Antiquaries' Museum: Illustrating the Antient Architecture, Painting, and Sculpture of Great Britain* (London: John Nichols, 1791–1800). Correspondence between Schnebbelie and his widow with Richard Gough and John Nichols, is Society of Antiquaries of London MS267.

31. Caroline Schnebbelie, letter to Bowyer Nichols, 5 October 1795, London, Society of Antiquaries of London, MS267 fo. 180 NAD10387. Caroline's letter shows that she had engraved a drawing of an ancient pavement found in Pancras Lane in June 1794. It was published in *GM* 1795 pt. 2, in the miscellaneous plate facing p. 985.
32. Diary of Mary Nichols, 11, 16, 19 and 30 June 1829, author's collection.
33. James Peller Malcolm, *Londinium Redivivum, or an Antient History and Modern Description of London*, 4 vols., (1802–7).
34. Rosemary Sweet, "John Nichols and his Circle," *Transactions of Leicestershire Archaeological and Historical Society* 74 (2000): 1–20. See also, Malcolm to John Nichols, 3 June 1795, Bodleian Library, MS. Eng. lett. c. 358 f. 165, NAD15225.
35. Subscriptions received by Messrs Longman for Mrs Malcolm between 3 May and 19 August 1815, Leicestershire Record Office, DE5463/15/2, NAD7938.
36. For Prattent's invoices to Nichols, see Leicestershire Record Office DE546/3/–NAD7881–8. Prattent's letters to Nichols from the Marshalsea are Bodleian MS. Eng. lett. c. 362 ff. 223, 225, 228 and 231. Nichols printed his contributions under the initials 'T.P.' in the GM 1803 pt. 2, 804 and 1804 pt. 1, 401. See also Jerry White, *Mansions of Misery. A Biography of the Marshalsea Debtors' Prison* (London: Bodley Head, 2016), 142–4.
37. See Phillip Lindley, "The Artistic Practice, protracted Publication and Posthumous Completion of Charles Alfred Stothard's 'Monumental Effigies of Great Britain'," *The Antiquaries Journal* 92 (2012): 385–426.
38. Thomas Hollis to John Gough Nichols, 21 June 1840, Yale University Library, OSB MSS 154 Box 8 NAD12568. The identity of the 'virtuous sister' remains unknown, as Mary Anne, Anna Octavia, Emma Onebye, Harriett Elizabeth and Isabella Georgina Nichols were all unmarried at this time. Mary Anne was the only sister to remain a spinster.
39. Gough Nichols to Thomas Hollis, June 1840, Yale University Library, OSB MSS 154 Box 8 NAD13657.
40. For George Hollis' obituary in the *Gentleman's Magazine* see 1842 pt. 1, 333–334. Thomas's obituary, by Edward John Carlos, was published in 1844 pt. 1, 101–202.
41. *GM* 1798 pt. 2, 1094.
42. *GM* 1817 pt. 1, 504 and pt. 2, 105–8 and 397–9
43. Law to John Nichols, 15 July 1818, Private Collection, PC1/5/47 NAD308.
44. *GM* 1800 pt.2, 732.
45. John Bowyer Nichols, A Brief Account of the Guildhall of the City of London (London: John Nichols and Son, 1819), i. John Chessell Buckler (1793–1894) became a regular contributor to the magazine.
46. *Ibid.*, 9–16.
47. Hill, *Time's Witness*, 69.
48. John Bowyer Nichols, *Account of the Royal Hospital and Collegiate Church of St Katharine, near the Tower of London* (London: John Nichols and Son, 1824), iii.
49. *GM* 1824 pt. 1, 353 and 543.
50. *GM* 1825 pt. 2, 391. 'N.P.' has yet to be identified.
51. *GM* 1825 pt. 2, 391–392.
52. *GM* 1826 pt. 1, 31–33.
53. *GM* 1828 pt. 2, 500–501.
54. *GM* 1830 pt. 1, 103.
55. *GM* 1830 pt. 1, 402–403.
56. *GM* 1831 pt. 1, 195–197 and 294–6.
57. *GM* 1831 pt. 2, 199.
58. *GM* 1832 pt. 1, 34–35.
59. *GM* 1832 pt. 1, 36–38.
60. *GM* 1832 pt. 1, 38–40.
61. Diary of Mary Nichols, 1823–1834, author's collection.

62. *GM* 1821 pt. 1, 35–38 and 1821 pt. 2, 17–20.
63. The chimneypiece was described by Gough Nichols in the *GM* 1836 N.S. vol. 5, 154.
64. J. C. Buckler to Bowyer Nichols, 1819, inserted in Edward Wedlake Brayley and John Britton, *The History of the Ancient Palace and the Houses of Parliament at Westminster*', 1836, University of California, Riverside, MS.303/1 NAD9209. I am grateful to Sara Stilley of San Jose University, California, for this information. Carlos's drawings are now British Library Add. MS. 25705–6.
65. John Britton described them as 'working tools, almost daily in demand,' in *The Autobiography of John Britton* (London, 1850), 300.
66. Parts of John Nichols's library were sold by Sotheby's on 16–19 April and 5 May 1828. The dates of the Sotheby sales of the libraries and collection of Bowyer Nichols and Gough Nichols were 10 February 1843, 11 July 1856, 26 May 1864, 4 December 1874, 5 April 1879, 18 November 1929, and 5 November 1951.
67. 26 May 1864 lot 201.
68. 26 May 1864 lot 1251.
69. 26 May 1864 lot 1459.
70. 26 May 1864 lots 1778–1801.
71. *GM* 1834 N.S Pt. 2, iii. See also Gough Nichols to Madden, 1 May 1832, British Library Eg. 2839 f.7 NAD1178; Sir Nicholas Harris Nicolas to Gough Nichols, 9 August 1832, Add. 369878 ff. 116–8 NAD9907; Gough Nichols to Joseph Hunter, 10 December 1832, Add. MS. 24872 ff. 201–2 NAD11938; Gough Nichols to David Elisha Davy, 3 October 1840, Add. MS. 19229 ff. 181–2 NAD11073.
72. Gough Nichols to Bowyer Nichols, 15 October 1837, Bodleian MS. Eng. Lett. c. 6165/4/ff. 435-6 NAD7126. For further information on Gough Nichols' involvement with this project, see Kate Giles, Anthony Masinton and Geoff Arnott, "Visualising the Guild Chapel, Stratford upon Avon: Digital Models as Research Tools in Building Archaeology," *Internet Archaeology,* vol. 32 (July 2012): 5.2.4
73. British Library Add MS. 19229 ff 173-9 and Add. MS. 19230 ff. 61–72. See also R.H. D'Elboux, 'The Brooke Tomb, Cobham', *Archaeologia Cantiana,* vol. 62 (1949), pp. 48–56.
74. Gough Nichols to Davy, 11 August 1840, British Library, Add. MS. 19229 ff. 173–5 NAD11081.
75. Gough Nichols to Davy, 3 September 1840, British Library Add. MS. 19229 ff. 176–7 NAD11174.
76. Gough Nichols to Davy, 30 October 1840, Add. MS. 19230 ff. 61–3 NAD11179.
77. Gough Nichols to Davy, 16 February 1841, British Library Add. MS. 19230 ff. 66-8 NAD11181.
78. Gough Nichols to Davy, 7 August 1841, British Library Add. MS. 19230 ff. 82–3, NAD11188.
79. *GM* 1841 N.S. 15, 306.
80. Initially issued in four parts between 1841 and 1845.
81. *GM* 1837 N.S. 8, 395 and 572.
82. Way to Gough Nichols, 25 May 1841, Bucks County Historical Society [hereafter BCHS], BM B.345 f. 380 NAD9567.
83. See Cleota Reed, "A Discovery in Pennsylvania – The 'Tiles' Guardbook of John Gough Nichols," *Journal of the Tiles and Architectural Ceramics Society* 6, (1996): 1–12.
84. Baker to Gough Nichols, 29 June 1841, BCHS, BM B.345 f. 265a NAD9564; Biederman to Gough Nichols, 25 November 1841, BM B.345 f. 383 NAD9570.
85. John Gough Nichols, *Examples of Decorative Tiles, Sometimes Termed Encaustic* (1845) [hereafter *Encaustic Tiles*] pt. 1, i.
86. *Encaustic Tiles* pt. 1, I note. See also Harvey Eginton to John Gough Nichols, 26 November 1841, BCHS, BM B.345 f. 385 NAD9572; Chamberlains to John Gough Nichols, 26 November 1841, BM B.345 f. 386 NAD9573.
87. French to Gough Nichols, 11 June 1842, BCHS, BM B.345 f. 412 NAD9602; French to Gough Nichols, 18 June 1842, BM B.345 f. 410 NAD9600.
88. Mary Anne Nichols to Gough Nichols, 31 March 1855, BCHS, BM B.345 f. 286 NAD948.
89. Gough Nichols to Davy, 8 July 1840, British Library Add. MS. 19229 f. 172.

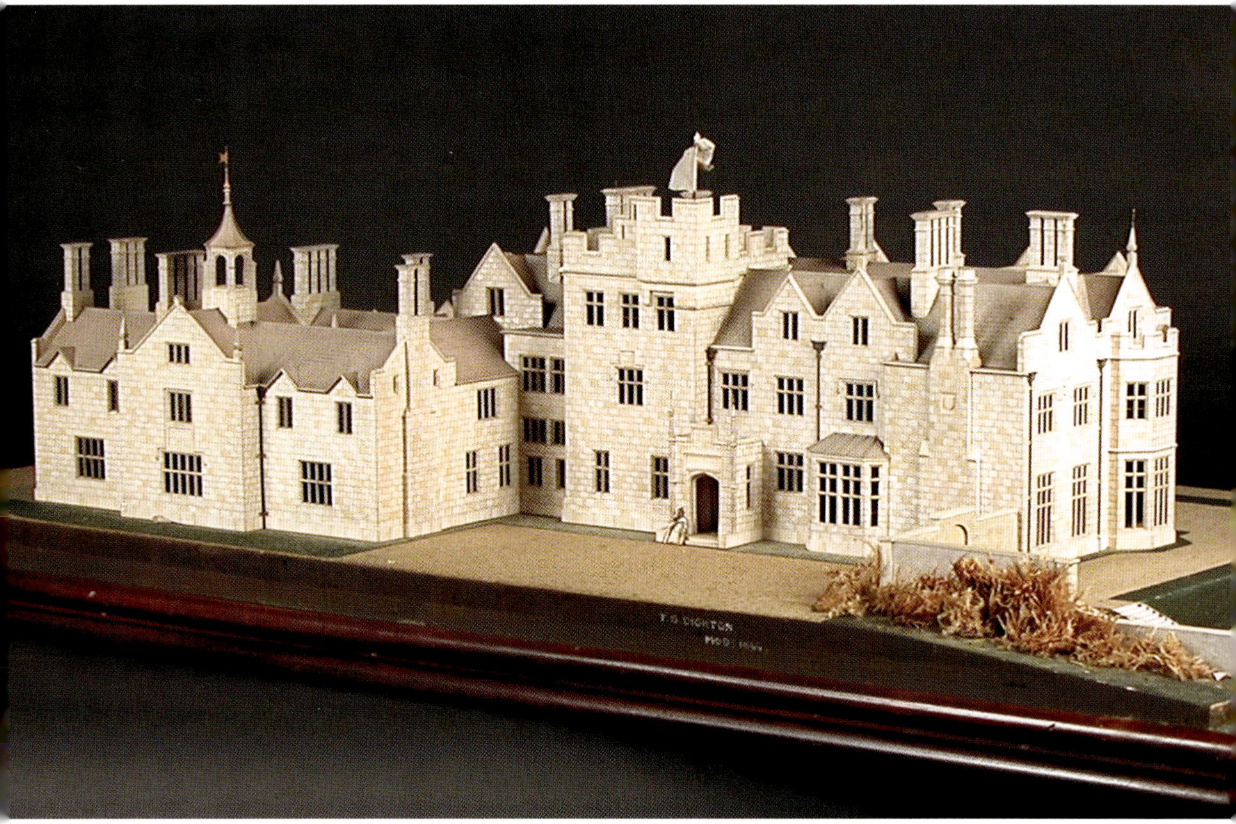

Fig. 3.1 | Anthony Salvin (architect), Thomas Dibdin Dighton (model-maker), Model of Scotney Castle, Kent. *c.*1836, National Trust 791941.

3 · Fire and Plaster: The Model-Makers Richard Day Senior and Junior

MATTHEW WELLS

Whether physical or digital, made to scale or replicating parts of a building at full size, architectural models have always played a critical role for architects, clients, and the wider public as easily understood representations of two-dimensional designs. Models have served as visualisations of individual elements, such as a staircase or a mantelpiece, or they might present a proposed building, a ruined monument, or a whole city in miniature. Models were an essential part of Victorian architectural practice with one exception: the medium appears to be entirely absent from construction documentation. Instead written contracts, specifications, and working drawings, more detailed documents than they eighteenth-century equivalents, took primacy when a design reached the construction site.[1]

The fabrication of models required the focused talent and artistry of model-makers. Nine individuals comprise the key architectural model-makers of the Victorian era in Britain: the central characters of this essay, Richard Day and Richard Day Jr, Thomas Dibdin Dighton, John Thorp, the Mabey family (James Mabey, his son Charles Henry Mabey, and grandson Charles Henry Mabey Jr), Stephen Salter, and Charles Newson Thwaite. Finding the information needed to comprehend the logistics, strategies, and processes of the model-maker is a challenging undertaking. These independent tradesmen lack specialised archives for their personal papers and company records, unlike nineteenth-century architects, builders, or cultural institutions. But, some residue of their work has survived, including trade directories, advertisements in the architectural press, and census and probate data. On occasion, especially related to the key protagonists for this essay, correspondence from a model-maker survive, filed away in the archives of architects or private clients. These traces provide a fresh perspective on Victorian architecture.

All these model-makers were based in the capital, although Thwaite began work from Manchester before moving to London in 1865, and Richard Day Jr left south London for Maidstone in Kent in the early-1860s. The location of their workshops varied across the city. Dighton remained in Westminster before moving to Devon at the end of his career. Following the relocation of his business from Manchester to the capital, Thwaite also operated from a workshop in south London before setting up close to the Strand from the mid-1860s. C. H. and J. Mabey were based out of a mews at Storey's Gate, Westminster, from around 1864 until 1889. The Mabey family produced scale models for architects of contemporary and antique buildings, harbours, bridges, exhibition pieces, and monuments in London and further afield.[2]

Unlike previous model-makers who had specialised in the replication of existing, often antique, buildings of Italy and Greece, which were displayed in the town and country houses of the Georgian upper classes, the work of this new generation centred on making models for new buildings in London.[3] Commissioned by architects and paid by private clients or institutional committees, the model-makers advertised their services in the architectural press, displayed their work independently at exhibitions, and supplemented their income with other activities when commissions were not forthcoming. In 1969 John Wilton-Ely argued that it wasn't until the end of the nineteenth century that model-making was a specialised activity.[4] Before that time, Wilton-Ely suggested, models were produced by architectural assistants or by the various craftsmen employed on the building.

Wilton-Ely's claim was accurate for the Mabeys at least as architectural model-making was a secondary source of income at best; their primary employment was the production of sculptural reliefs for buildings, from commissions for civic buildings, such as Todmorden Town Hall (completed in 1875) to producing an extensive stock and catalogue of plaster and cement readymade elements including 'ceiling flowers, cornice enrichment, capitals, trusses, enriched panels, chimneypieces, etc.' that architects and clients could view at their premises.[5] There were also occasions when the sculptor-model-maker produced both the architectural model of the building and carried out the work for the sculpture on the exterior of the building. One example of this was Charles Henry Mabey Junior who made a model for the County Hall, London, in 1911, and later completed the architectural carvings for the exterior to the designs of Ralph Knott between 1910 and 1922.[6]

One significant model-maker in early Victorian Britain was Thomas Dibdin Dighton (1799–1882), first based in Mayfair, before moving to Pimlico, and then operating from 2 Lower Grosvenor Place.[7] Dighton was active from *c.*1830 until the mid 1870s, working for a variety of architects and clients. Although Dighton's last recorded work appears to have been a model of Holborn Viaduct in 1872, the majority of his works were designs for new houses, including a model for the facade of Lacock Abbey for William Henry Fox Talbot in 1830.[8] Other country-house models were exhibited at the Royal Academy including a model of a house for the Duke of Athol, at Dunkeld in 1832, and a model Dighton made of a Somerleyton Hall, Suffolk, designed by John Thomas and exhibited in 1847.[9] Another client of Dighton's, Edward Hussey III, was a regular visitor to the Royal Academy Exhibition, and it was likely that he was aware of the model-maker's work. When Hussey commissioned Anthony Salvin to design Scotney Castle in Kent – a new house on the family estate to replace a fourteenth-century castle that had fallen into disrepair – Hussey himself also directly ordered a model from Dighton of Salvin's design.[10] From study of Hussey's diaries there was a close relationship between client and model-maker. Hussey went to see the model fifteen times at Dighton's workshop located in Pimlico, which was adapted and 'remodelled' several times between March 1836 and June 1837.[11] Iterations to the model was aided by its materiality. Dighton worked primarily in cardboard and coloured paper to articulate the different material qualities of a design. (Fig. 3.1)

Disciplinary background and training were paramount to the business and often determined the approach of the model-maker. Those with a sculptural background, such as the Mabey or Day dynasties, worked exclusively in plaster. Those coming from a graphic or architectural background worked in cardboard or paper applied to a timber structure. In addition to these less well-known model-makers were the eminent British sculptors Hamo Thornycroft and Frederick William Pomeroy. The latter made models in plaster for several London-based architects including John Belcher, Edward William Mountford, and Alfred Brumwell Thomas. Many of these models were exhibited at the Royal Academy, where Pomeroy's expertise was employed to render the formal massing and outline of a building in a spectacular manner. (Fig. 3.2)

Pomeroy was also involved in architectural education through lectures and classes at the Architectural Association (AA). From 1892 he gave an evening class titled 'Instruction in Modelling', which consisted of making relief copies from existing plaster casts in the AA studios. In a lecture in 1899 titled 'Curving and Modelling applied to Architecture', Pomeroy considered how 'Modelling might be used in architecture for a great variety of purposes', from details of ornament to scaled objects representing 'the whole of a building'.[12] What distinguished the lecture from others of this time was how he demonstrated this approach. On a series of pre-prepared clay surfaces, raised up on a blackboard for the audience to view, Pomeroy, aided by an assistant, gave 'a practical demonstration of both carving and modelling'. Through these different functions, Pomeroy believed 'a general idea of the general effect of light and shade' could be gained by architects before construction.

FROM DAY TO DAY

One significant example of this 'general idea' provided by architectural models can be found in the design for Dorchester House on Park Lane by Lewis Vulliamy (1791–1871). Built for the art and plant collector Robert Stayner Holford, the Italianate palazzo later described by Francis Sheppard as the 'most opulent of all

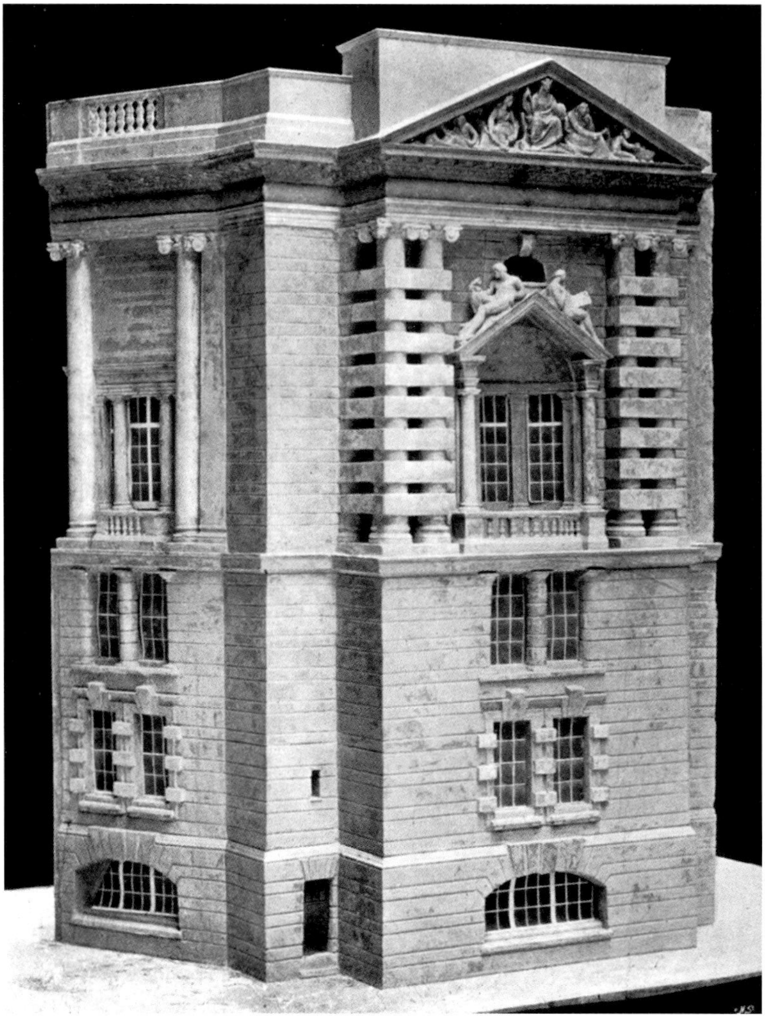

Fig. 3.2 | Edward William Mountford (architect), Frederick William Pomeroy (model-maker), Southwest Angle of New Museum and Technical School, Liverpool, 1898.

the Park Lane palaces', was to replace an existing house, one of a number of new mansions that were rising on the easterly edge of Hyde Park.[13] (Fig. 3.3) There have been several previous studies of Dorchester House written from the nineteenth century to the present day. These accounts focus on Holford's impressive collection of European paintings, the various artistic (primarily Italian Renaissance and neoclassical) influences on both the client and his architect, and the contribution of the sculptor Alfred Stevens to the interiors, especially the Carrera-marble chimneypieces for the Saloon and the Dining Room.[14] From the outset of the project the model-maker Richard Day (1786–1849) had been building a plaster model of Dorchester House for Vulliamy at his workshop in Southwark.

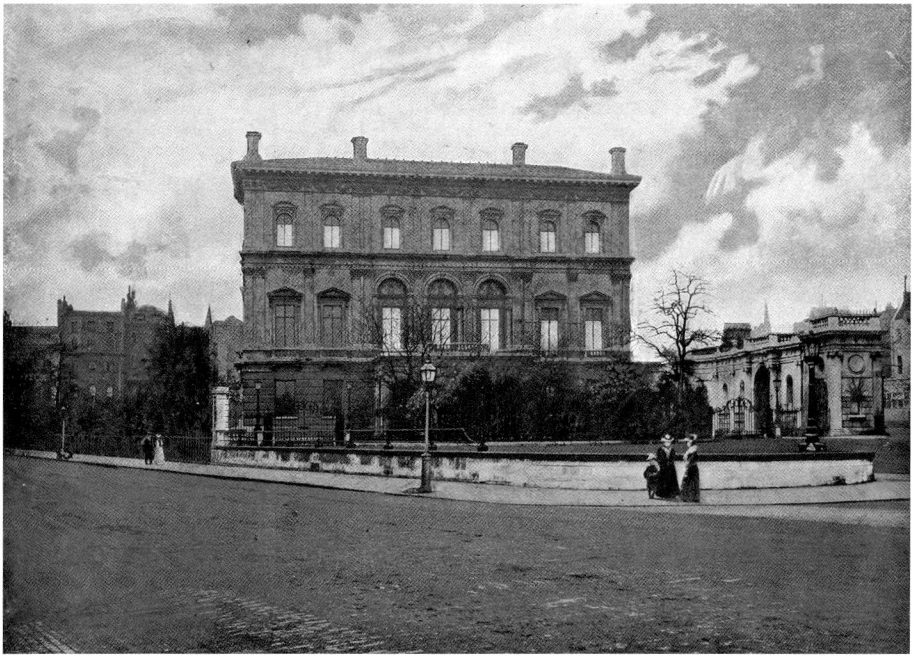

Fig. 3.3 | Dorchester House, view of south facade, Cassel and Co (photographer), in: *The Queen's London* (London: Cassell, 1896), 82.

The son of a mason, Day worked as a sculptor of funerary monuments before his involvement as a stone-carver on Buckingham Palace in 1827–28.[15] After exchanging architectural sculpture for model-making, his work was well known among Londoners as it was exhibited publicly for the display of new buildings across Britain. On the one hand, there was an increase in the number of public buildings, churches, and monuments commissioned, while on the other hand, following the 1832 Reform Act there emerged an urban 'public' with a desire for participation in the future of the built environment in Britain. Between 1831 and 1847, Day exhibited five times at the Royal Academy. Four of these were original compositions, while in 1837 Charles Fowler exhibited a design for the monument to Walter Scott in Edinburgh in the form of a model made by Day.[16] The model-maker was also well known amongst the emerging architectural profession, something he encouraged by showing 'numerous models' at a meeting of the Architectural Society in January 1834.[17] Around the same time Day produced a model for William Wilkins of the proposed National Gallery, which was exhibited in February and March 1834 to the public at the popular Gallery of Practical Science (or Adelaide Gallery), not far from the actual site at Trafalgar Square. The model was prepared in February 1833 and first shown to the client in August 1833 when Wilkins wrote to one of his supporters, the politician Thomas Spring Rice, to invite him to inspect the second model.[18] The exhibition included a selection of other scientific and mechanical models by Day in the gallery's Long Room before transferring to 13 King William Street in the City of London. (Fig. 3.4) Another model made by Day for William Tite's controversial design for the rebuilding of the Royal Exchange became part of public debate played out in the newspapers and committee rooms in the City of London during the summer of 1840.[19]

Despite his minor fame, the press reported that Day had been struggling for new orders ('he must either seek some other occupation or starve') and, praising the quality of his work, encouraged readers to commission him for new projects.[20] Similarly the *Builder* reported in July 1850 that 'there are several good architectural modellers, who have not more work than they can do'.[21] New techniques of imaging effected the role played by model-makers. An 1848 article on Thomas Dighton blamed the rise of cheap 'electrotyping, and other reproducing' technologies for the lack of model-making work.[22] A later essay in 1877 on the place of the architectural model in contemporary practice blamed the emergence of photography, 'by which any number of perspectives can be obtained'.[23] Despite this, there was still call for Day's expertise. George Bailey, first curator of the Sir John Soane's Museum, recorded in his diary that Day visited the museum in July and August 1847 to repair several 'models of temples' in the collection.[24]

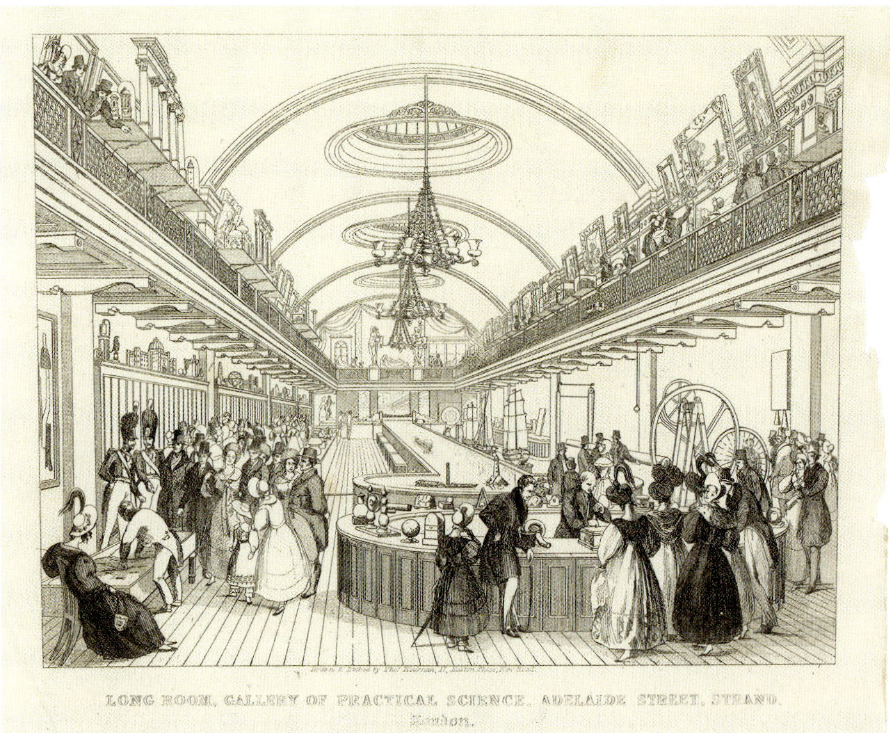

Fig. 3.4 | Thomas Kearnan, Gallery of Practical Science, Adelaide Street, Strand, engraving, 1834. British Museum, 1954, 1103.12. © Trustees of the British Museum.

Towards the end of September 1849 a curious letter arrived at 27 Argyll Street, the office of Lewis Vulliamy. What was curious about the letter, however, was that the writer introduced himself as Richard Day Jr (1815–1891) and offered his services to complete the model of Dorchester House. The following week a contract was agreed for the younger Day to complete the model started by his late father.[25] Correspondence between Day Jr and Vulliamy offer a glimpse of a model-maker's working life. Day Jr reported how his father's death had affected his ability to finish the model – his mother had been moved into new apartments, his father's personal effects had to be thrown away, and, crucially, modelling apparatus needed to be removed from his father's studio, some of which was being repaired and repurposed by Day Jr in his workshop at 42 Commercial Road in Southwark. A year later Day Jr moved to a new workshop on the New Kent Road, which he claimed caused further disruption as his tools and equipment were packed away for a week leaving him unable to continue with his work and therefore delaying the model's completion.[26]

The location of these workshops shows the complicated logistics of model-making in the rapidly expanding capital. With architects based in more upmarket locations for their clients, often in the West End, and model-makers in cheaper accommodation, often south of the river Thames, the physical distance between the office and the workshop could easily cause problems and delays. On one occasion Day felt he had to apologize to Vulliamy for not leaving a model at Dorchester House after a meeting because he was working on it in his studio. Day explained how travelling to Park Lane, 'causes such a loss of time, & I cannot work the hours there that I can at home'.[27] Day operated alone, without assistants, which reduced the speed at which he could complete projects. While Vulliamy had a team of architects engaged on the project at each stage, Day frequently worked on the model until the early hours of the morning. During a long period of work, from October 1849 until May 1857, Day made at least three major models for Dorchester House: a ¼-inch scale model of the house (begun by Day Sr in 1849), a larger model of the main facade, and a multi-tiered model of the interior with a central hall, staircase, and adjoining vestibules. (Fig. 3.5) These were supplemented by a series of smaller models made at various stages.

FROM LETTERS TO DRAWINGS

At the start of the project the scope and scale of the first model was undecided. A note from Robert Holford to Vulliamy in June 1849 questioned why a larger-scale model was not being produced by Day.[28] As a client Holford was highly educated, capable of understanding orthographic conventions and making his own copies of Vulliamy's drawings in order to offer suggestions to the design. In addition, Holford proposed that a fourth model should be made to solve a disagreement about the

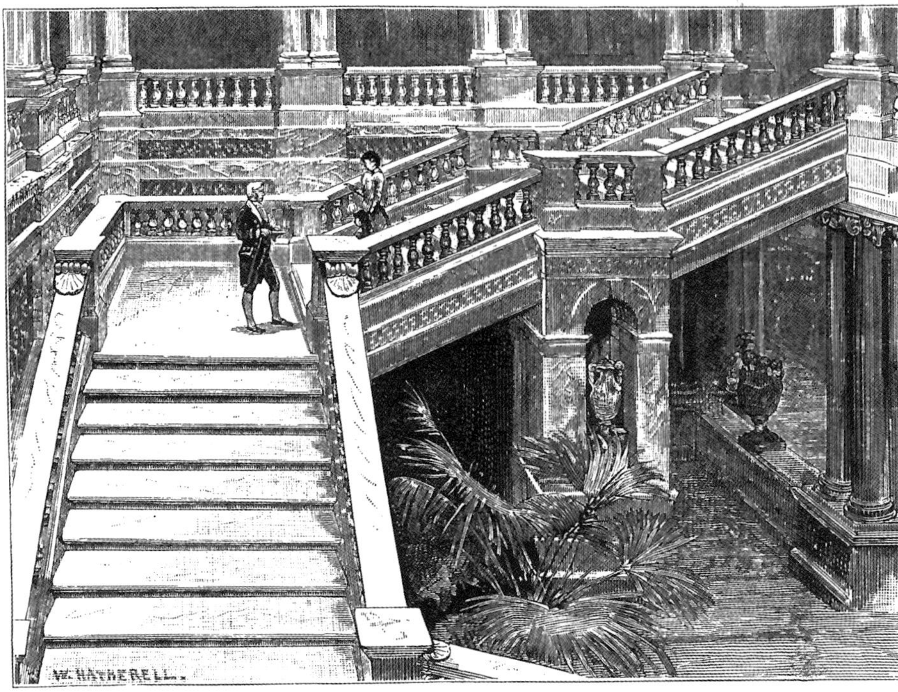

Fig. 3.5 | William Hatherell, View of the Staircase at Dorchester House, lithograph, 1883, in: Eustace Balfour, 'Dorchester House', *Magazine of Art* 6 (October 1883) 398.

leasehold of Dorchester House. In the margins of a letter Holford made a small sketch to outline to Day a rough block model to solve this dispute. This sketch suggests a model that included two possible options: one showing the relation between the boundary wall and the existing house, and the other showing the relation between the boundary wall and the proposed design.[29] (Fig. 3.6) It is unclear whether this model was ever executed by Day, but Holford's diagram shows how clients also conceived of models as explanatory aids to others.

In addition to spatial logistics, the business of model-making also included the organization of labour. Although he lacked a dedicated team of assistants like Vulliamy, Day collaborated with other skilled trades, subcontracting out portions of the work that he was unable to produce himself. Initially Day made slow progress on the first model. He was late on his promise to finish the first part by Christmas 1849 – its incompleteness, he claimed, was not his fault because the decorative figures were the responsibility of a friend, a sculptor in Liverpool working on St George's Hall.[30] It is possible that Day was working with William Grinsell Nicholl who not only carved the pediment and free-standing sculpture at St George's, but also produced the sculptural figures for C.R. Cockerell's now lost model for the Royal Exchange.[31] Day's schedule was often badly organized – no doubt a point of contention with Vulliamy's office, which kept highly detailed

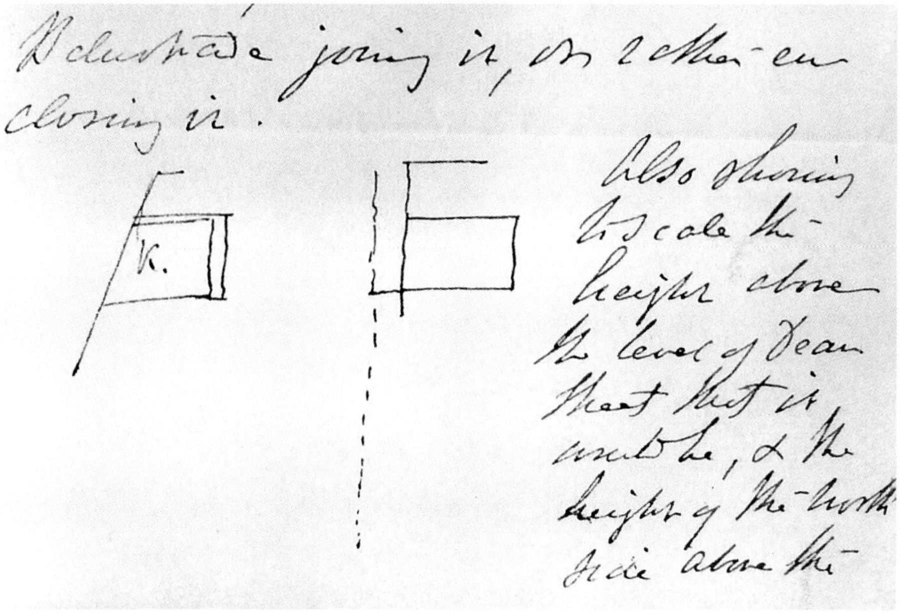

Fig. 3.6 | Robert Holford, Diagram in a letter to describe how a model should be made, 1850. RIBA Collections, VuL 1/2/5.

accounts of the work undertaken despite the small amounts of money involved (typically £3 or less; £240 in modern money).

After a year of work and several disputes with Day over money, Vulliamy's method of recording Day's work changed from a linear description of the work to a tabular system of labour. Every single action related to the production or alteration of the model was itemized by Vulliamy's employees. By way of contrast, Day's own records for each payment were far more concise. For instance, the work undertaken in the summer of 1850 was detailed over two pages by Vulliamy's office, where Day's account describes it in just thirty words. In one invoice Day explains how he would have asked for an advance on the work completed but he knew that Vulliamy preferred 'having the exact account of the works done'.[32]

These accounting practices relate to Vulliamy's family background as part of a transdisciplinary dynasty: Lewis Vulliamy was the son of the clockmaker Benjamin Vulliamy who also operated a tabular record keeping system. Unlike a linear system where each entry features a simple written description of the job or work to be performed (similar to Day's books), Benjamin Vulliamy's tabular system itemized the watches he was repairing into individual components (e.g., cylinder, wheel). Each listed component was detailed with a series of actions that described the specific activity happening to that portion of the watch (e.g., polishing, fitting, mending). This 'language of action' was the result of an emerging technical or operative culture within the economy of production. From one type of work to another in London, wider practices of economic management affected multiple aspects of society including the production of architectural models.

Despite discrepancies over their costs, one thing is clear about Day's models: they were not produced from a complete set of drawings. Instead their fabrication was a site of exploration where the model-maker made adjustments based upon conversations between architect and client. In the summer of 1850, the ¼-inch scale model of the house was reworked as the design progressed through discussions between Vulliamy and Holford.[33] Alterations were made to the facade, roofline, and details like the balustrade or profile of windows. Much of this work appears to have been made to the 'original' model (started by Day Sr), but other portions of the building may have been modelled to show options. Across several days in July 1850 Day modelled two possibilities for windows on the west facade of the building, which he followed with a much larger, one inch to one foot (1:12 scale) model of part of the lower storey of the facade. Models were also used to examine proposed changes to the location of the house. In August 1851, Day lowered the roadway of the carriage porch on the model and added moveable pathways to the porch from the corners of the building's east and west fronts, colouring them to differentiate from the rest of the model. Working back and forth between different scales, Day would use the models to test different designs and then present them to Holford. This iterative approach meant that work on one model to, say, explore the design for a facade, had a chain reaction as revisions would then be required on another. Day worked in this fashion, moving from scale to scale, model to model, from September 1849 (when he first wrote to Vulliamy) to July 1852. Then in the early autumn of 1852 Day began work on a new model, cast and carved in plaster, which included the staircase and surrounding rooms of Dorchester House. Over the five years it took to complete Day continued to make adjustments as new elements were examined and subsequently changed[34] (Fig. 3.7) The model was made in distinct sections enabling new components, such as options for the ceilings, to be applied to test different spatial possibilities.

Innovative as his methods were, the process was incredibly slow. While Day himself was often unwell – writing to Vulliamy, Jacob Wrey Mould (Vulliamy's assistant) or Clement Thomas (the clerk of works) to offer his excuses – the task of model-making appears to have been delayed by the techniques he used.[35] A letter written during the process of making the staircase model describes part of Day's working method. Day explained to Vulliamy how he had not fully assembled the staircase as his approach was to cast and carve each individual component before connecting them together. As a result, progress was often delayed as Day required drawings of particular portions, from tracings of plans to more decorative details, which Vulliamy and his assistants failed to deliver in a timely fashion. Another cause of delay was Holford's irregular presence in London. Unlike the drawings,

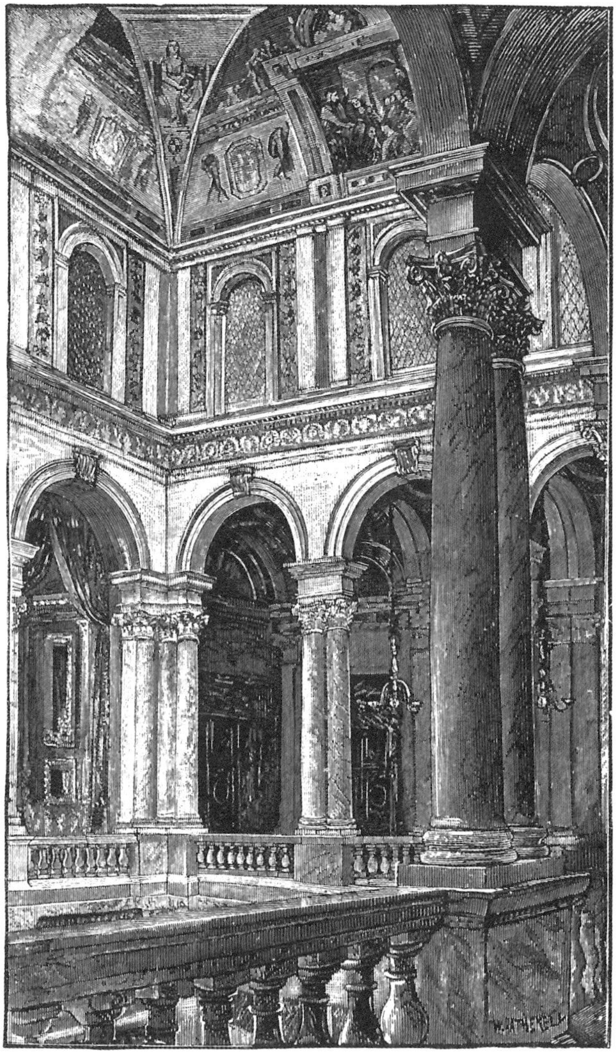

Fig. 3.7 | William Hatherell, View of Hall at Dorchester House, lithograph, 1883, in: Balfour, 'Dorchester House', 400.

which Holford had sent to his country residence where he would copy and return them, any discussion surrounding the architectural models required the attendance of all three men. From his letters, Day is often surprised by Holford's sudden appearance in London ('I did not expect Mr Holford would have been in London so soon or [I] would have had the lower part ready for his inspection') and often had to either delay presentation of the models or work faster to finish them.[36]

Despite the press attention related to the lack of clients for model-makers before his father's untimely death, the Dorchester House models were not Day Jr's only commissions. In December 1850, while working for Vulliamy and Holford, he was also making models for James Pennethorne and excused himself from work on Dorchester House.[37] (The model Day was working on may have been related to Pennethorne's work as architect to the Offices of Works, perhaps his design for the Museum of Practical Geology or the Ordnance Office, both of which Pennethorne was working on at the time. Interestingly, Dighton exhibited a model of the Public Record Office on Chancery Lane at the 1851 Great Exhibition, raising questions about how the market for model-makers operated or whether they competed against one another for commissions.) Later in March 1854 he excused himself again from work on Dorchester House to build a model for Decimus Burton. On another occasion, work on a different model for an unidentified competition forced Day to miss a meeting with Vulliamy and Holford. In April 1851 Day explained to Vulliamy that he had stopped work on the models for Dorchester House in order to prepare his models for display in the Great Exhibition.[38] There were additional long-term relationships with institutional clients that required his attention ahead of work on the models of Dorchester House – for instance, a model of an unknown subject for the Corporation of London (*c.*1853–54) became 'a longer job than I first thought'.[39]

Over time Vulliamy's office became accustomed to working with Day, writing several weeks in advance to warn him of Holford's arrival, but even when all three were in a room together there was still sometimes cause for confusion. For instance, in December 1850, Day responded to a note from Vulliamy who wanted to understand why the model had only four windows with pediments, rather than the six requested in his last letter. Day explained that these written instructions were contrary to the verbal discussions between the three during their last meeting.[40] When a simple note would not suffice, Day enclosed drawings of his own. On one occasion Day wrote to Vulliamy's office asking for a plan to be cut at a much higher level than normal drawing conventions would allow in order to represent the three-dimensional projection of a window and balcony. To illustrate exactly what he meant, he added a small sketch elevation of the stones above the window, annotated with a horizontal line ('A to B') to show the exact location where he required a plan to be drawn (Fig. 3.8).

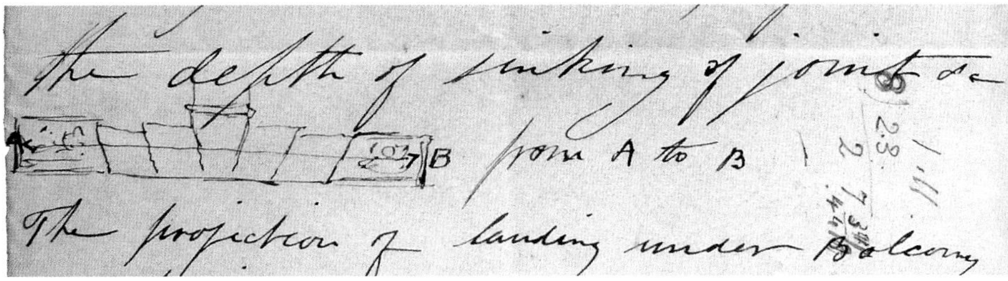

Fig. 3.8 | Richard Day Jr, Detail of letter showing diagram of measurements required for model, undated *c.*1850–52. RIBA Collections, VuL 13 1 38a.

FROM DRAWINGS TO MODELS

Issues with the translation of scale and dimensions emerged in the instructions sent by Vulliamy to Day. Day once had to apologize to the architect for the size of the sculptural panels he had attached to the ¼-inch model and noted, 'I am not aware that they are any larger than those sketches you gave me. I perceived that they were to inch scale so I made mine ¼ size of them.'[41] On another occasion Day questioned Vulliamy on the usefulness of a drawing, a pattern for a window and the above cornice, which lacked dimensions and a scale. He requested that in future all of the issued information 'be drawn to the scale I am at work upon & that there will be nothing of the ornament left to my taste', flattering Vulliamy was the author of a three-volume treatise on ornament.[42] There were instances when without the architect's drawings Day was unable to work. At one stage he explained to Vulliamy that he needed drawings for the ornament on the main cornice and balcony in order to continue while other parts of the model were drying.

In addition to these complications, the physical attributes of plaster also factored into the making and presentation of Day's models. Even the storage of the model at Dorchester House required particular environmental conditions. In December 1850 Day wrote to Vulliamy requesting that the clerk of works not remove the model from the room where it was stored. He also specified the temperature and lighting conditions needed to protect the model and ensure its correct appearance for their client:

> I hope you will not give orders to Thomas to remove the 1st model down to the room below during this weather as it will greatly affect the model, there should be a good Fire every day for at least a week previous; to drive off the damp. & perhaps you would arrange the sky light, so as to put the model in proper effect. Please excuse these suggestions but I know that the consequences would be ruinous to the model if placed in a damp room; it being nearly as absorbent as a sponge.[43]

Day's concerns were not unfounded. Over the course of the project there were several accidents involving the models. At one stage a portion of the parapet on a model was broken by a builder working on the new house. This was the same portion, Day noted, that had already been twice smashed and repaired when the model was moved from the previous house on the site. Day explained to Vulliamy how he had only partially repaired the model as the 'real' balustrade had now been completed to a different design, underlining how the models were part of an iterative and discursive process. Additionally, the process of modelling in plaster caused setbacks for Day himself. In a letter excusing his absence from the site, Day described to Vulliamy how a 'serious accident' happened to a model of the cornice which would take at least two days to repair.[44] Already behind schedule, he had been at work on the model all night and after putting it in front of the fire to dry, damaged it. Both the accident and Day's subsequent request for a fire to be lit in the room where the model was kept at Dorchester House show the importance of accelerated drying processes in the production of plaster models. Wet, recently cast plaster can be carved and worked into the required form and details can be added with tools, but this also means that the model is soft and weak. Recently cast plaster also retains the water mixed with the raw plaster and is therefore incredibly heavy until this water evaporates. At the same time, dried plaster can reabsorb moisture in the atmosphere, causing the model to soften again or, depending on the type of raw plaster used, crack at particular junctions.

In August 1859 the Science and Art department of the South Kensington Museum, which was acquiring contemporary specimens for public display, wrote to Vulliamy's office requesting models of Dorchester House 'which illustrate the appliances adopted in the construction and fitting of the edifice'.[45] By 1861 a model of the staircase and corridor at Dorchester House was on display in the museum's collection of Construction and Building Materials alongside models and prototypes of ventilators, lavatories, and zinc roofs.[46] It remained there until at least 1876.[47] Catalogues note the material of the model as 'marble and alabaster', suggesting that Day produced a second more decorative and final model of the staircase after March 1854, once iterations and adjustments to the design had been tested on the plaster version. It was absent from documents from 1876 to 1916, when it was named in lists of architectural models held in the storeroom of Southern Galleries of the Science Museum.[48] Unfortunately this was its last recorded sighting. The two other major models have also disappeared.

FROM MAIDSTONE TO WESTONBIRT

Following the completion of the models for Dorchester House in 1857, Day continued to work for Vulliamy and Holford between 1861 and 1871, making a total of seven architectural models related to the rebuilding of Westonbirt, Holford's country house in Gloucestershire. Built in a neo-Elizabeth or Jacobean Revival manner in warm yellow-brown ashlar from nearby Box, the house was built without a general contractor with Clement Thomas from Vulliamy's office directing independently employed tradesmen for each portion of the works. As Michael Hall describes, by the mid 19th century this was an unusual approach, but one that meant that a client was able to freely change the design, even during construction.[49] At Westonbirt, Holford ordered endless changes to Vulliamy's designs for the house, changes that were developed and tested through Day's plaster models.

Beginning with a model of the north-west tower in 1861, Day produced models of a bay window (1862), a 1:24 model of the house (1862–65), ornamental trusses for the central tower (1868), alterations to the north parapet (1868) and a model of the conservatory (1870). Translating the design from drawings and Day's proximity to the architect and client, two issues that had impacted the model-making process for Dorchester House, were increased due to Day's relocation to Kent in 1861.[50] By way of a biographical note, Ann Day (1821–76) moved with her husband to Maidstone. Day and his workshop were located at first at 20 Kingsley Road, Maidstone (1861–63), then 39 Kingsley Road, Maidstone (1863–67), before finally moving one street west to 14 Melville Road (1868–70). A year after her death, in September 1877, Day Jr married one of his neighbours, Caroline Dyson (1854–1930). The marriage register describes his occupant as 'School board inspector', but his father is listed as 'Richard Day, Architectural Modeller', and likewise the 1881 census notes Day Jr's occupation as 'Retired architect', which was subsequently upgraded to 'Retired modeller living on own means' in the 1891 census. At his death in October 1891 the value of his estate was £1011 15s., with Caroline Day the sole beneficiary.

Due to this relocation, drawings of the house moved in a triangular fashion, passing from architect's office to client, sometimes returned to Vulliamy or, on other occasions, dispatched to Day for model-making purposes. Frequently Vulliamy's assistants would write to Day, urging him to hurry his work and chasing the whereabouts of a particular drawing that needed to be returned to the office. Based outside the capital, Day and Vulliamy made careful arrangements to transport various models in and out of London. Early on in the design phase, Day offers to deliver the model of a bay window himself, explaining how he would like verbal instructions on how to begin the 1:24 model of the house as well as being paid in cash for the work completed so far.[51] In another letter, Day describes how the model of the house will be carefully packed away in a specially made softwood box and delivered on the 8.55 train from Maidstone Station that arrives at Charing Cross at 10.20.[52]

Howard Colvin once described how the improvements in communication and railway infrastructure in the nineteenth century allowed the newly professionalised architect to be based in London while personally supervising half a dozen buildings simultaneously, a situation which would have been impossible for his eighteenth-century predecessor.[53] At Westonbirt a complexity can be added to this reading as craftsmen like Day Jr were able to work remotely from workshops outside of the metropolis, while still being connected to networks of patronage that centred on London. Additionally, by thinking about architectural models from within the dynastic model-maker's workshop a host of new issues emerge. Following Richard Day Jr's work at Dorchester House and Westonbirt we see how the life of the model-maker in Victorian Britain included issues around sub-contracting, the effects of new record keeping systems on the production of models, and the practicalities of making and transporting large-scale plaster models across England.

NOTES

1. For a fuller history of architectural models in Victorian London see: Matthew Wells, *Modelling the Metropolis: The Architectural Model in Victorian London* (Zürich: gta Verlag, 2023).
2. A printed advertisement from the early twentieth century lists their sculptural work by programme (Hotel, Bank, Tomb, etc.) as well as the scale models for architects and engineers. The list is as follows: Liverpool Exchange (T. H. Wyatt), Admiralty and War Office (Leeming and Leeming), Barry Docks (John Wolfe Barry, Thomas Forster Brown, Henry Marc Brunel), Parthenon (James Fergusson), Harbour of La Guaira, Venezuela (Punchard, McTaggart, Louther & Co.), Mersey Docks (G. F. Lister), Tower Bridge (J. W. Barry), Putney Bridge (John Wolfe Barry and Henry Marc Brunel), Blackfriars Bridge (John Wolfe Barry and Henry Marc Brunel), Erechtheion (George Aitchison), Institute of Chartered Accountants (John Belcher), Model of the Alhambra, Crystal Palace (Owen Jones), Organ of St Paul's Cathedral (F. C. Penrose), Powerscourt (F. C. Penrose), Crystal Palace, Russia (Charles Barry), Models of the Houses of Parliament (Charles Barry), Eleanor Cross, Charing Cross (E. M. Barry), Temple Bar (Horace Jones), Auction Mart and General Credit Company, Tokenhouse Yard (G. Somers Clarke), the Rossetti Memorial (J. P. Seddon), Entrance to Burlington House (Sydney Smirke), University Observatory, Oxford (Charles Barry), Institute of Civil Engineers (Charles Barry), North Mymms (Ernest George and Harold Peto).
3. For a discussion of this and their effect on British architecture see Frank Salmon, *Building on Ruins: The Rediscovery of Rome and English Architecture* (Adershot: Ashgate, 2000), 73–5.
4. John Wilton-Ely, "The Architectural Models of Sir John Soane: A Catalogue," *Architectural History* 12 (1969): 10.
5. Susan Beattie, *The New Sculpture* (Yale: Yale University Press, 1983), 51–2; "Advert for James Mabey," *Kelly Building Trades' Directory* (1870): 47.
6. *County Hall: Survey of London Monograph 17* (London: The Athlone Press, 1991), 47.
7. *Post Office London Directory for 1845*, (London: Kelly's, 1845), 1269.
8. "Model of the Holborn Viaduct," *Builder*, 3 August, 1872, 602; Letter from Thomas Dibdin Dighton to William Henry Fox Talbot, 23 January 1830, London, British Library, Add MS 88942/2/26, l.
9. *The Exhibition of the Royal Academy – The Sixty-seventh*, No.958 (London: Royal Academy, 1832).
10. Account book, 1837, 113, Kent History Centre, U1776/E4.
11. Diaries of Edward Hussey, 1836–37, Kent History Centre, U1776/F1/16–17.
12. "Architectural Association," *Building News*, 21 March, 1899, 536.
13. Survey of London, *Volume 40, the Grosvenor Estate in Mayfair, Part 2 (The Buildings)* (London: London County Council, 1980), 273.
14. See for instance, Christopher Hussey, "London Houses: Dorchester House – I. London," *Country Life*, 5 May, 1928, 646-653; Christopher Hussey, "London Houses: Dorchester House – II. London," *Country Life*, 12 May, 1928, 684-689; David Watkin, "Holford, Vulliamy, and the Sources for Dorchester House," in *Influences in Victorian Art and Architecture*, eds. Sarah Macready and Frederick Hugh Thompson (London: Society of Antiquaries of London, 1985), 81–92.
15. Ingrid Roscoe, M. G. Sullivan, and Emma Hardy, *A Biographical Dictionary of Sculptors in Britain 1660–1851* (Yale: Yale University Press, 2009), 349.
16. *Royal Academy Exhibition LXIX*, no.1155 (London: Royal Academy, 1837), 56.
17. "Architectural Society," *The Gentleman's Magazine*, February, 1834, 209.
18. William Wilkins, letter to Board of Trustees, 10 September 1833, London, National Gallery [NG], 5/18/4. For a discussion of the exhibition see: "Architectural Exhibitions," *The Architectural Magazine*, March, 1834, 89.
19. Matthew Wells, "Architectural Models and the Rebuilding of the Royal Exchange, 1839–1844," *Architectural History* 60 (2017): 219–41.
20. "Day, the Architectural Modeller," *Builder*, 7 October, 1848, 490.
21. "To Correspondents," *Builder*, 6 July, 1850, 323.
22. "Architectural Models," *Builder*, 6 May, 1848, 225.

23. "Architectural Modelling in its Relation to the Architect, his Client, and the Public," *Builder*, 17 November, 1877, 1145-1146.
24. George Bailey, Diary entries for 29 July, and 5, 7, 9–10, 16 August 1847, London, Sir John Soane's Museum.
25. "Memorandum of understanding between Richard Day junior and Robert Holford," 1 October, 1849, London, RIBA, VuL 13/1/3.
26. Richard Day, letter to Lewis Vulliamy, undated, London, RIBA, VuL 13/1/19.
27. Richard Day, letter to Lewis Vulliamy, undated, London, RIBA, VuL 13/1/47.
28. Robert Holford, letter to Lewis Vulliamy, 14 June 1849, London, RIBA, VuL 1/1/3.
29. Robert Holford, letter to Lewis Vulliamy, 19 August 1850, London, RIBA, VuL 1/2/5.
30. Richard Day, letter to Lewis Vulliamy, 12 December 1849, London, RIBA, VuL 13/1/6.
31. Wells, "Architectural Models and the Rebuilding of the Royal Exchange, 1839–1844," 219–41.
32. Richard Day, letter to Lewis Vulliamy, 17 December 1853, London, RIBA, VuL 13/1/17.
33. Lewis Vulliamy, account book, entries for June 1850 and July 1850, London, RIBA, VuL 13/2/16.
34. Lewis Vulliamy, copy of payment receipt issued to Richard Day, 23 May 1857, London, RIBA, VuL 13/2/22.
35. For more on Jacob Wrey Mould and his life in the USA see: David Van Zanten, "Jacob Wrey Mould: Echoes of Owen Jones and the High Victorian Styles in New York, 1853–1865," *Journal of the Society of Architectural Historians* 27 (March 1969): 41–57; Francis R. Kowsky and Lucille Gordon, *Hell on Color, Sweet on Song: Jacob Wrey Mould and the Artful Beauty of Central Park* (New York: Empire State Editions, 2023).
36. Richard Day, letter to Lewis Vulliamy, 23 October 1852, London, RIBA, VuL 13/1/12.
37. Richard Day, letter to Lewis Vulliamy, 30 December 1850, London, RIBA, VuL 13/1/9; Richard Day, letter to Lewis Vulliamy, undated (*c*.1850–52), London, RIBA, VuL 13/1/23. *Great Exhibition of the Works of Industry of all Nations, 1851: Official Descriptive and Illustrated Catalogue*, 1851, II, p.830, 160.
38. Richard Day, letter to Lewis Vulliamy, 25 April 1851, London, RIBA, VuL 13/1/45. These consisted of five architectural models exhibited under his own name: the portico of the Parthenon, The Temple Church, the portico of the Pantheon at Rome, the Martyrs' Memorial at Oxford, and a window from St Paul's Church on Herne Hill. *Great Exhibition of the Works of Industry of all Nations, 1851*, 830, no. 161A.
39. Richard Day, letter to Lewis Vulliamy, undated (*c*.1853–57), London, RIBA, VuL 13/1/49.
40. Richard Day, letter to Lewis Vulliamy, 31 December 1850, London, RIBA, VuL 13/1/10.
41. Richard Day, letter to Lewis Vulliamy, undated (*c*.1850–52), London, RIBA, VuL 13/1/39.
42. Richard Day, letter to Lewis Vulliamy, undated (*c*.1850–52), London, RIBA, VuL 13/1/33.
43. Richard Day, letter to Lewis Vulliamy, 24 December 1850, London, RIBA, VuL 13/1/8.
44. Richard Day, letter to Lewis Vulliamy, undated, London, RIBA, VuL 13/1/35.
45. Science and Art Department, letter to George Vulliamy, 19 August 1859, London, RIBA, VuL/3/5/6.
46. Science and Art Department, *Catalogue of Building and Constructing Materials* (London, 1862), 49M.
47. Science and Art Department, *Guide to the South Kensington Museum,* 2nd ed. (London, 1866), 12; Henry Sandham, *Catalogue of the Collection Illustrating Construction and Building Materials* (London, 1876), 109-Y.
48. Science Museum, Lists of Architectural Objects in the Store Room of Southern Galleries Science Museum, 11 June 1916, London, Victoria & Albert Museum (V&A), MA/1/5851; Science and Art Department, *Catalogue of Building and Constructing Materials* (London, 1862), 22M.
49. Michael Hall, "A new term dawns: Westonbirt House, Gloucestershire," *Country Life*, 9 September, 2015, 99.
50. Vulliamy office files on tradesmen suppliers, Richard Day, London, RIBA, VuL/42/6.
51. Richard Day, letter to Lewis Vulliamy, 11 February 1862, London, RIBA, VuL 42/6/4.
52. Richard Day, letter to Lewis Vulliamy, 25 March 1867, London, RIBA, VuL 42/6/28.
53. Howard Colvin, *Biographical Dictionary of English Architects* (Yale: Yale University Press, 1954) 24.

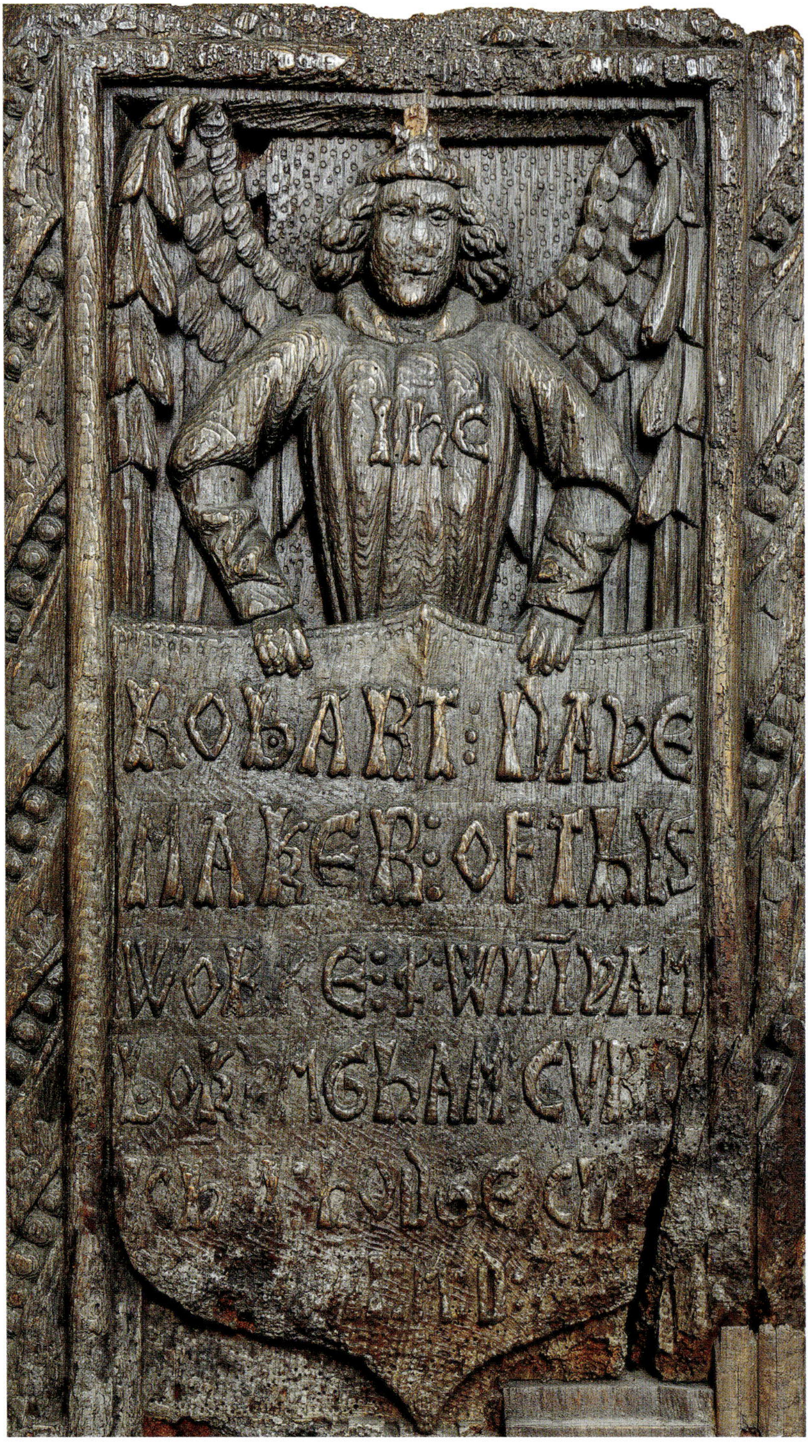

Fig. 4.1 | One of the 1523–54 bench ends at Altarnun, Cornwall, restored during the work there by Edmund and John Dando Sedding, 1865-67. Roy Reed.

4 · Sisters and Brothers: the Pinwill and Sedding Dynasties of Woodcarvers and Architects

HELEN WILSON

John Dando Sedding (1838–1891) is best known for his London architectural practice, seen as a cradle of the Arts & Crafts Movement, training the likes of Ernest Gimson, Ernest Barnsley, Charles Nicholson, and Henry Wilson. Yet he started his architectural career in Cornwall, a county he came to love and where he returned again and again to work after his move to London. His reason for exchanging a training in Oxford under GE Street for a small practice in Penzance in 1865 was to join his brother Edmund (1836–1868) who had moved there a few years earlier. Unlike John Dando, Edmund completed his training with Street and was generally considered the more talented of the pair. However, Edmund's location in Penzance, probably chosen for reasons of health, coupled with his death from tuberculosis at the age of 32, mean his work is now little known outside Cornwall. Yet he fostered and influenced his brother, allowing him to learn 'on the job', and within a short time the two forged a reputation that extended well into Devon and further afield. It was in Cornwall, working with his brother, that John Dando developed many of the ideas he was to carry into his highly successful London practice. Edmund's other great contribution to the world of architecture was through his son, Edmund Harold Sedding (1863–1921). Although he trained with his uncle in London, young Edmund chose to follow in his father's footsteps by moving to the West Country and in 1891 made his home in first Devon and then Cornwall. Thus this 'small but important dynasty' became 'the most accomplished ecclesiastical architectural name of the later nineteenth century in Cornwall'.[1]

The legacy of Edmund Harold extends further still in his championing of the fledgling professional ecclesiastical woodcarving company of Rashleigh, Pinwill & Co., established in 1890 by three sisters, Mary, Ethel and Violet Pinwill, in Ermington, Devon. The business became one of the most successful in the West Country, producing high-quality work for over 200 churches. Yet their emergence has been explained within rather narrow parameters, as one of a number of examples of 'Victorian feminine architectural adventures',[2] or as an 'experiment'.[3]

As this essay will show, the establishment of the Pinwill woodcarving company was far from frivolous; they formed a serious and successful business that flourished for over 60 years. Their achievements owed much to the milieu of Gothic Revival, the Arts & Crafts Movement and Anglo-Catholicism, and, of course, to their enormous talent and determination to succeed in a profession dominated entirely by men.

BEGINNINGS OF THE SEDDING ARCHITECTURAL DYNASTY

Edmund and John Dando Sedding were the eldest sons of eight children born to schoolmaster Richard and his wife Penninah.[4] From 1840, during their formative years, the family resided in Edensor, Derbyshire, a picturesque model village designed by Joseph Paxton for the 6th Duke of Devonshire on the Chatsworth estate.[5] Built between 1838 and 1842, the village was a work in progress for the brothers to observe. Growing up in an architect-designed village may have been a factor in the chosen careers of Edmund and John Dando, as well as the youngest son Arthur. The church was another significant dynamic in the upbringing of the Sedding children, with strong Anglo-Catholic leanings influencing their young lives and guiding their futures. Two of the daughters, Isabella and Christiana, joined an order of Anglican nuns, the Sisters of St Margaret's based at East Grinstead, Sussex, and played their part in beautifying God's house with their outstanding embroideries.[6] John Dando, in particular, was later known for his fervent support of radicals such as Fr Mackonochie, 'the martyr of St Albans' and Robert Brett, 'the pope of Stoke Newington', as well as Fr George Rundle Prynne in Plymouth.[7]

Whatever the reasons for their choice of career, the Sedding brothers were certainly fortunate in their training. Quite how it came about is not clear, but in 1852 Edmund travelled to Oxford to become architectural assistant to G. E. Street, and was followed there five years later by John Dando, by which time the Street office had been in London for two years. This highly professional and successful practice was the best possible start for these aspiring architects, a springboard for such future luminaries as Philip Webb, William Morris and R. Norman Shaw. The Seddings became enamoured by Gothic Revival and the new ideas of the Arts and Crafts movement, which they carried forward into their work.

After Edmund completed his articles with Street, he set up as an architect in Bristol and then London, finally moving to Penzance in 1862 where he began to build a practice.[8] Little is known about exactly what was undertaken by Edmund between his arrival in Cornwall and his brother's appearance in 1865. An obituary, however, lists St Stephen's in Launceston as a church on which he worked,[9] and a newspaper report of 1864 reveals he restored the chancel and aisle, including the removal of a vestry and the repositioning of the organ.[10] No other architectural work undertaken by Edmund during this period has yet come to light.

Meanwhile, the path to a professional practice for John Dando did not run smoothly. While he shared many fundamental architectural ideas with Street, their temperaments were opposed, and John Dando left as soon as the opportunity arose. That came in 1865 when he joined his brother in Penzance. By that time, Edmund had married Jessie Prockter, daughter of a local chemist, and their first child, Edmund Harold had arrived, with another on the way. John Dando lived with the growing family in a large, early nineteenth-century terraced house. A supportive relationship between the brothers enabled them to work closely together and their 'powerful work ethic'[11] established a successful architectural business that extended far into Devon, operating primarily as church restorers.

EARLY WORK OF JOHN DANDO SEDDING IN CORNWALL

It was during the years in Cornwall working with his brother that John Dando developed some of the ideas he later developed and that underpinned his London business. The pair earned a reputation for thoughtful and sensitive restorations, retaining as much ancient material as possible and pioneering the use of local materials, particularly polyphant, for new work. They regularly engaged trusted contractors, such as builder William Bone & Son of Liskeard,[12] who understood what was required. Yet the true extent of their work on churches during this period is not fully documented. As contemporaries of John Dando noted after his death, 'Of his country work, lying as it does in out-of-the-way parts of Cornwall and Devon, but little is known'.[13]

Those that are documented, but for which additional information is available in newspaper reports, include the notable church of St Nonna at Altarnun. Its interior 'of uncommon interest' was 'carefully restored' 1865–67 with new roofs for nave and chancel.[14] More detail on the extent of the restoration, which included the removal of the west gallery, repair of windows, and repointing of walls inside and out, is provided in a report of July 1867 that also states the ethos adopted:

> The desire throughout has been to make the restoration of such an interesting building in every sense a conservative one, and in no case has any ancient feature been disturbed without positive necessity. The remains of carved woodwork, for which this church is deservedly remarkable, have in all cases been religiously preserved and re-used.[15]

It appears that the wishes of the vicar and parishioners and the philosophy of the Seddings coincided precisely in achieving a sympathetic and sensitive restoration. Altarnun church is today revered not only for its Norman font, one of the largest in Cornwall, with bearded faces and traces of colouring, but also for its set of 79 bench ends, dating probably from 1523–54 (Fig. 4.1), thanks to the ethos adopted by the brothers, to preserve and re-use ancient woodcarving. The reputation thus earned served the Seddings well and they were engaged to carry out several other large projects, including at Ruan Lanihorne where the interior of this thirteenth-century church reflects their 'extensive but thoughtful restoration of 1866'.[16]

It is often assumed that John Dando only began to learn crafts for himself after his move to London in 1875 and his formative meetings with Ruskin, yet there is evidence that in Cornwall he took the opportunity to experiment with painting. Work at Gwithian to rebuild much of the body of the church was overseen by his brother 1865–67.[17] Refurbishment was also carried out, including a new reredos reported to be 'of oak, the central panel having a cross carved, painted, and gilded on a ground of dark green, the side panels being filled with angels and flowers, painted by Mr. John Sedding, a brother of the architect'.[18] At North Hill, the thorough restoration of the chancel by the brothers in 1868 is not documented, even by Snell (2006), and the discovery that the roof there was 'painted in floriated patterns by Mr John Sedding'[19] adds to the importance of this revelation (Fig. 4.2). A further example comes from Wendron, where both Edmund and John Dando are credited with restoring the nave and chancel roofs, rebuilding of the nave arcades and raising of the east window 1867–69.[20] The work included the installation of four-foot high panelled wooden screens marking off the chancel from the nave and aisles. These were described as 'now being decorated by the architect Mr. J. D. Sedding, as also the boarded roof over the sacrarium'.[21] It seems, however, this decorative work was a proposal that was not implemented, probably owing to the death of Edmund partway through the project. Nevertheless, these reports convey an important aspect of the work of John Dando in Cornwall and suggest he began his journey towards Ruskian ideals earlier than is usually noted.

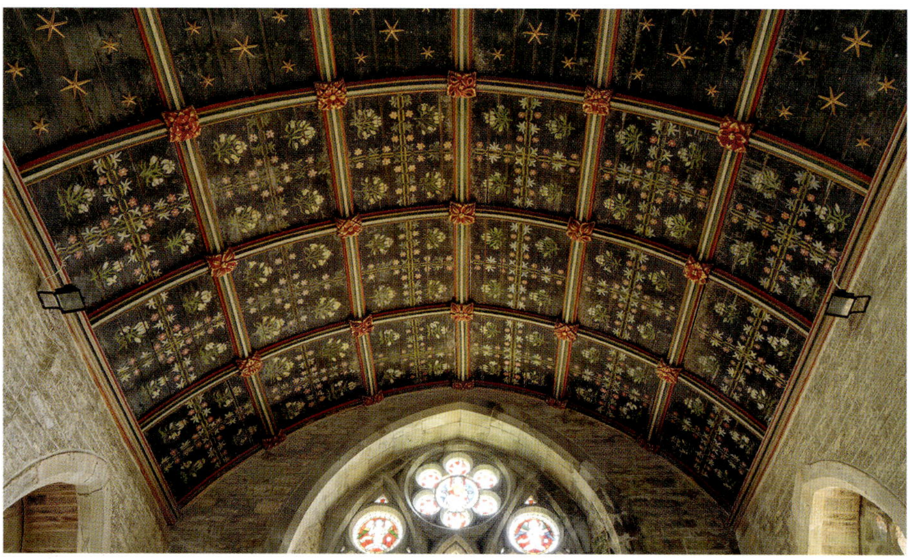

Fig. 4.2 | The Chancel roof at North Hill, Cornwall, painted by John Dando Sedding, 1868. Roy Reed.

All during their time in 'out-of-the-way' Cornwall the Sedding brothers maintained, and even strengthened, ties to family and friends, particularly those dedicated to the Anglo-Catholic cause. In the late 1850s and early 1860s they had been two of the most prominent workers at St Mary's Mission, Crown Street, Soho, designing and arranging furniture and decoration.[22] Isabella Sedding, through her brothers, was introduced to the work at St Mary's and went on to dedicate her life to serving God, being received in 1861 as a novice by the Society of St Margaret at East Grinstead, Sussex, the order of Anglican nuns established by John Mason Neale.[23] The artistic talents of Sister Isa (as she became) flourished at St Margaret's, inspired by the spirit of the Arts & Crafts movement to create designs of her own. She was described as having 'earnest dark grey eyes, out of whose steadfast depths the fire of the Sedding genius flashed'.[24] Her flair and commercial acumen led to her becoming head of the embroidery workroom, working on commissions from around the world. Isabella was followed to East Grinstead by her sister Christiana Bridget, who professed as Sister Bridget at the Mother House on St Margaret's Day 1868.[25]

THE MOVE TO LONDON

Through their work in Cornwall, the reputation of the Sedding brothers began to extend beyond the West Country and a significant engagement was to produce designs for a new church of St Martin, at Low Marple, Cheshire. But Edmund had not been a well man for some years; pulmonary tuberculosis finally claimed his life on 11 June 1868 at the age of only 32. He was laid to rest in the churchyard at Madron, overlooking Penzance and St Michael's Mount, in a tomb erected by his brother: 'a plain slab shaped in the old way, with a cross growing from a heart cut upon it'.[26] John Dando was left to carry on the practice in Penzance with several projects in hand. Those in progress he diligently completed to plan, such as at Bigbury, Devon, where the brothers were engaged to 'all but rebuild' the church.[27] The tower was retained, as were many of the medieval features, including the early fourteenth-century sedilia, piscina and tomb recess in the chancel, and the early fifteenth-century brass. The work began in 1868, continuing after the death of Edmund and was completed by John Dando in 1872, by which time he was described as 'of Bristol'.[28]

For the church at Low Marple Edmund had produced only sketches before his untimely death. John Dando took on this commission for the wealthy Anglo-Catholic family, the Hudsons, as his first independent work, which served to showcase his emerging individuality. He also developed an ability to engage expert craftsmen in his projects, including the likes of Edward Burne-Jones, Dante Gabriel Rossetti, Ford Madox Brown and William Morris.[29] As well as maintaining the Penzance practice, he also began to operate in Bristol, but as his reputation and confidence grew, it soon became prudent to make the move to London. Thus ended the first phase of the Sedding dynasty in Cornwall. Yet during his time in the county, John Dando grew to love its churches and developed such an affinity that he returned many times to carry out restoration work. His heart never left Cornwall nor his brother, to whom he owed so much. As his contemporaries later confirmed:

> The ideals and example of his elder brother Edmund had… much to do with Sedding's development. Edmund, if report does not err, was by far the more gifted of the two; he had much of the spirit of Rossetti in him, but, never strong, he went home before he had fully found himself. His ideals and influence survived, and had a new existence in the spirit of his brother John.[30]

Making the transition from provincial architect to prominent player, John Dando set up practice in London in 1874, first at 18 Charlotte Street and then at 447 Oxford Street, next door to Morris & Co. His practice is often described as the birthplace of the Arts and Crafts movement, and it was into this milieu that young Edmund entered to train as an architect under his uncle. Over just a few years in London, John Dando built a strong team of trainees and assistants, many of whom went on to forge enterprising and unconventional careers of their own. In the 'feverish activity' of the office, Edmund thrived and formed friendships with future artist-craftsmen, such as Henry Wilson, with whom he later collaborated, and Ernest Gimson, who went on to establish a radical Arts & Crafts workshop in the Cotswolds.[31]

DEVON AND THE EMERGENCE OF THE PINWILL SISTERS

A pivotal point in Edmund's career came when John Dando was commissioned by a wealthy proponent of the Arts and Crafts movement, Henry Bingham Mildmay of Flete, south Devon, to restore the churches at Holbeton and Ermington 1884–89.[32] Mildmay, a partner in Barings Bank, remodelled and extended Flete 1875–85, engaging the architect R. Norman Shaw, who may have recommended Sedding for the church work. Of the two churches, Holbeton was certainly favoured by Mildmay; he is purported to have spent a total of £25,000 on its restoration,[33] while Ermington received considerably less. The reason for this disparity undoubtedly lay with Mildmay's wife Georgiana (née Bulteel), for whom Flete was an ancestral home and Holbeton church where forebears, including her father, were buried. Associates of John Dando later wrote that he 'had the opportunity at Holbeton of showing what could be done with an old building when untrammelled by want of money'.[34] Indeed, so much of his time and energy was spent on the work at Holbeton[35] that Ermington was more or less left to Edmund to supervise. This was not necessarily to the detriment of Ermington; a fine, but restrained, restoration was achieved. Indeed, what may have seemed a less favourable situation became a transformative experience for all involved.

During the restoration at Ermington, Edmund visited to oversee progress and undoubtedly stayed at the vicarage with the incumbent, the Rev. Edmund Pinwill.[36] He had arrived in the village in 1880 with his wife Elizabeth and their seven daughters, to take up the post of Vicar of Ermington with Kingston.[37] Finding the church in a structurally unsafe state, the family endeavoured to raise funds to carry out repairs. After a great effort they succeeded in collecting sufficient resources and 'saved the church from inevitable destruction'.[38] Any further work to restore and embellish the building required funds beyond the reach of bazaars and fairs. Mildmay came to the rescue, providing the wherewithal for additional work on the fabric and to refurbish the church.

The restoration of both Ermington and Holbeton churches began in 1884 and a team of craftsmen arrived to carry out the work. They were not, however, from the company of William Bone & Son of Liskeard. By this time, John Dando had been appointed Architect to the Diocese of Bath and Wells and favoured more the Somerset firm of Charles Trask & Sons of Norton-sub-Hamdon.[39] Among the employees was the chief woodcarver, William Giles, who proved to be a crucial figure in the lives of three of the Pinwill sisters: this man was asked by Elizabeth Pinwill to teach woodcarving to her daughters Mary, Ethel and Violet. This may seem an extraordinary request, but the craft of woodcarving was then an acceptable 'accomplishment' for genteel young ladies, often taught by women in private classes,[40] as well as in girls' schools.[41] Yet Elizabeth Pinwill had rather more progressive plans for her daughters than for them to learn woodcarving as a mere pastime. It emerged in an interview with Violet Pinwill in 1909 that this request stemmed from a desire to present her daughters with a viable alternative to the inevitability of marriage and children or dependent spinsterhood:

> There being a family of seven daughters, the late Mrs Pinwill wisely decided that they would be the happier in having professions, and, while they were still in the schoolroom, she arranged for three of them to take lessons in wood carving.[42]

This is really quite remarkable. It reveals a woman of extraordinary foresight, who from the very beginning had the idea that her daughters, by learning to carve, might have a career before or even instead of marriage. Elizabeth must have been aware too that this was a profession entirely dominated by men, and yet she chose to encourage the girls to entertain that aspiration and to develop their artistic ambitions. The opportunity was grasped by all three, setting up their own workshop above the stables at the vicarage. By the time the restoration at Ermington was complete in 1889, the sisters were undertaking commissions for substantial pieces of work, executed with skill and flair. The first of these, an elaborate reredos for Chilthorne Domer, Somerset, was designed by Edmund, the carving work being carried out by the Pinwills with the assistance of William Giles. A charming

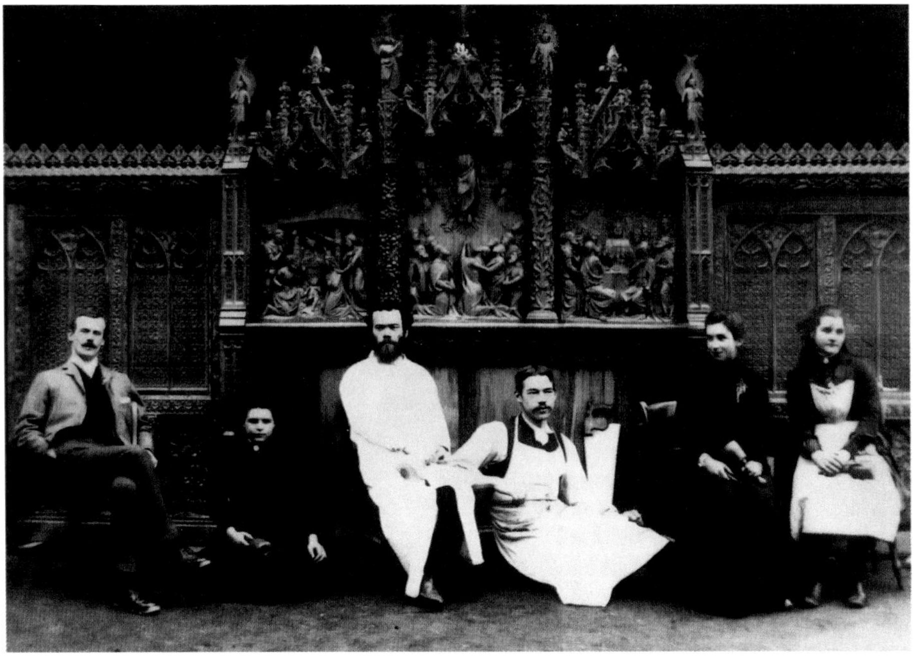

Fig. 4.3 | The Pinwill sisters with completed reredos for Chilthorne Domer, Somerset, 1889. *Left to right*: Edmund H. Sedding, designer; Ethel Pinwill; William Giles, carver; Harry Flashman, joiner; and Mary and Violet Pinwill. Ermington Church Collection.

photograph exists with the reredos in the background and Edmund, Mary, Ethel, Violet, William Giles the carver and Henry Flashman, a local joiner, seated before it (Fig. 4.3). It was after this that the sisters decided to take the next step and set up their own business. Mary, the oldest of the three and decidedly in charge, gave the company her middle name to create the business-like 'Rashleigh, Pinwill & Co'. This was a bold move and could only have come about with the support of their parents and the patronage of Edmund, who went on to produce challenging commissions for the sisters and their young company.

The emergence of the Pinwill sisters in 1890 as professional wood carvers is extraordinary and perhaps unique. Without the full context, it almost defies explanation, leading one local commentator to admire the Pinwills merely for their novelty value.[43] At an academic level, the phenomenon has been explained as one of a number of examples of 'Victorian feminine architectural adventures',[44] or as an 'experiment' conducted by John Dando.[45] While John Dando did encourage some women in artistic endeavours, his support was limited to close family members, such as his sister Isabella and his wife Rose, and then only in the eminently suitable skill of embroidery. The idea that the emergence of the Pinwill sisters was the result of an 'experiment' directed by John Dando neglects the pivotal role of Elizabeth Pinwill in initiating carving classes for her daughters with the express purpose of providing the pathway to potential careers. Most importantly, it denies the self-determination of the sisters to learn and hone their craft and to succeed in a profession dominated by men.

Edmund, on the other hand, was part of the second generation of the Arts & Crafts movement and more able perhaps to shirk off the shackles of gender roles and to see the potential of women as skilled craft workers, able and willing to raise that craft to the level of art. During his time at Ermington supervising the restoration of the church, Edmund undoubtedly spent many sociable hours with the sisters and their parents. One can easily imagine evenings spent in animated discussion on the exciting ideas of the Arts & Crafts movement. Edmund, a staunch Anglo-Catholic dedicated to the idea of beautifying God's holy places, and deeply in love with ancient churches, must have been impressed by these talented young women, their carving skills and artistry, and their willingness to use their gifts to create decorative ecclesiastical furnishings. Yet the decisive point for Edmund in his relationship with the sisters did not arise until sometime after they had established Rashleigh, Pinwill & Co.

THE DEATH OF JOHN DANDO SEDDING

On 7 April 1891 an event occurred that forced a re-evaluation of Edmund's professional ambitions and had the potential to change the trajectory of his life. His uncle John Dando was visiting the Vicar of Winsford, Somerset, just over the border from Devon, to discuss a restoration project there. He arrived apparently healthy on March 31 but fell ill the very next day.[46] A doctor diagnosed lung inflammation, and such was the seriousness of the situation it was advised that his wife Rose was telegraphed for and also a trained nurse. Rose duly arrived the following day, bringing along their baby daughter and close family friend the Rev. Edward Francis Russell.[47] Rose's sister Alice and her physician husband Oswald Auchinleck Browne also wished to be by her side and arrived in Somerset, staying in Dulverton.[48] Five days after Rose arrived in Winsford, on 7 April, John Dando died of pleurisy brought on by pneumonia at the age of 52.[49] Such devastating news reached Edmund while he was staying with the Pinwills at Ermington.[50] He could not have been in better company; but the grief and anguish were not to end there. Two days after the death of John Dando, his body was removed to London and Rose left the Vicarage intending to return home, accompanied by her sister Alice and her husband.[51] She was not well even before their departure and her companions found they could take her no further than Dulverton. On 15 April Rose died in Dulverton at the age of 44 from the same causes as her husband.[52]

The deaths of John Dando and Rose within such a short time of each other were devastating for their family and friends and also left their financial affairs, the custody of their four children and the longer-term management of the architectural business in question. Three days before he died, John Dando made a simple will in which he left his entire estate to Rose, naming no executors, but she died before accepting the Letters of Administration.[53] Rose also wrote a will two days before her death, naming her Executors and Trustees as the Rev. Edward Francis Russell and Oswald Auchinleck Browne.[54] Consequently, administration of the estate of John Dando was granted to the Executors named in Rose's will. They were to invest the residual capital and hold it in trust for all the Sedding children, and the Rev. Russell and Rose's sisters were appointed guardians. The missing piece in this settlement was the fate of the architectural business, which was left with work in hand and employees to consider. As we know, Henry Wilson, the manager (and partner in all but title) took the reins for several years following the death of John Dando, but this was surely not a forgone conclusion. In the context of the Sedding dynasty, some discussion of other possibilities is justified. In the immediate aftermath of the death of John Dando, it was inevitable that the day-to-day running of the practice should fall on the shoulders of Henry Wilson, but there were three Sedding family members who must surely have at least been considered for the role in the longer term.

The first of these was the youngest and sole surviving brother of John Dando, Arthur Edward Sedding. In or before 1871, he was taken on by John Dando as a pupil when the architectural practice was in Bristol.[55] Arthur made the transition to London when the practice was relocated there in 1875, and in 1881 stated his occupation to be that of an architect.[56] However, Arthur did not remain in the profession and when John Dando died in 1891, he was probably not seen as a strong candidate to inherit the mantle of his distinguished brother. The Sedding proclivity for creativity did, however, win the day, and in his late 40s Arthur trained in stained glass and then established his own business of 'Sedding & Co. Artists in Stained Glass' in Southwark.[57]

A similar story of craft being chosen over architecture characterised a second Sedding family member. As the eldest son of John Dando and Rose, George Elton Sedding was seen as heir apparent to the architectural business and the role of Henry Wilson was in 'maintaining the practice on behalf of Sedding's son George…'.[58] George, though, was only nine years old when his father died, and by the time he was old enough to start any training, Wilson had progressed his desire to establish his own business in metalworking, jewellery, sculpture and church furnishing, and abandoned architecture altogether. After briefly working with Wilson at the London office, George was apprenticed to him from 1901 to 1904 at his new premises in Kent. George became not an architect but a gifted art metal worker, later opening his own workshop near Oxford Circus.

The one surviving family member who trained in, and remained committed to, architecture was Edmund, yet his uncle's death presented a dilemma for him.

He could have continued to be part of the London practice, working with Henry Wilson on the unending opportunities presented by following in his uncle's footsteps. In the absence of any evidence to the contrary, it can surely be assumed that such a choice was open to him, and that Wilson would not have been averse to the idea. Indeed, it would have relieved Wilson of some of the burden of carrying the business forward on his own and perhaps he would have achieved his ambitions earlier if he had had the assistance of Edmund in managing the architectural work. Another option open to Edmund, however, was to eschew the London business altogether and take another path. At the time of his uncle's death, he had already worked with the Pinwill sisters by designing some of their early pieces for churches, and maybe that was enough to persuade him that his aspirations were more likely to be fulfilled in Devon and Cornwall than in London. Perhaps he was drawn by the idea that he could work there full-time, revisiting the past in restoring ancient churches, in the same way as his father had done, as well as playing a part in the future by acting as architectural patron to the new ecclesiastical woodcarving company of Rashleigh, Pinwill & Co. He chose to set up an architectural practice in Devon.

THE PINWILL-SEDDING COLLABORATIVE VENTURE

As early as May 1891, Rashleigh, Pinwill & Co. opened a workshop and office in Plymouth at Buckland Terrace and when Edmund chose to open his practice, these premises were the obvious choice, becoming the centre of the Pinwill-Sedding partnership. Their first major commission arrived in November 1891, when Edmund was commissioned to restore the late fifteenth- or early sixteenth-century chancel screen at Manaton, Devon. It retained most of its painted wainscoting but none of its fan vaulting or cornice, although significant portions of the arcade tracery and running ornament had survived.[59] These pieces were used by the Pinwills as templates for the recreation of the rest of the screen (Fig. 4.4). This was the first of several ancient screen restorations carried out by the Pinwills, who thereby learned from past masters to create the elaborate and symbolic carvings of the late medieval period.

When the Pinwill company relocated to 12 Athenaeum Street in about 1896, the Sedding architectural practice moved there too. Work progressed, with some prestigious design commissions obtained by Edmund, for which he engaged the Pinwills to carry out the woodcarving. Some were for churches where John Dando Sedding had worked earlier, such as the on-going refurbishment of the chancel at Plympton St Mary, Devon, begun by his uncle in 1886.[60] Now new choir stalls commissioned in 1897 by the Parker family of Saltram presented the opportunity for Edmund to express his evolving design ideas: overflowing with exuberant foliage and flowers, studded with birds and insects, yet still embracing traditional

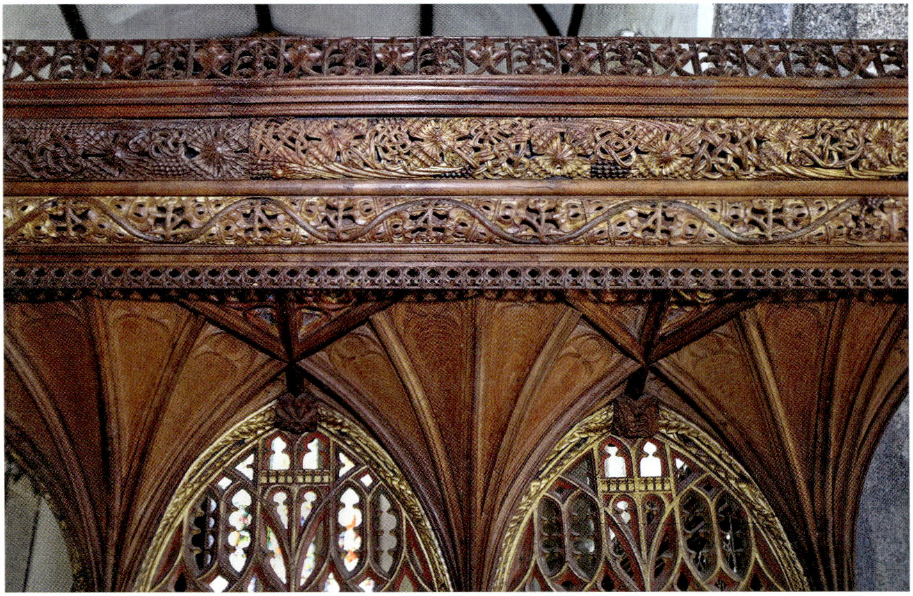

Fig. 4.4 | The cornice of the restored chancel screen at Manaton, Devon, designed by Edmund H. Sedding and carved by the Pinwill sisters, 1893, showing the original and the new work. Helen Wilson.

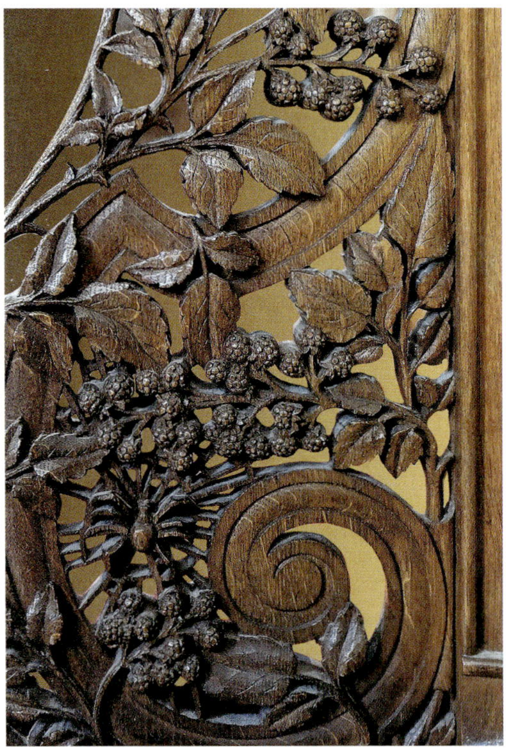

Fig. 4.5 | One of the bench ends at Plympton St Mary, Devon, designed by Edmund H. Sedding and carved by the Pinwill sisters, 1898. Helen Wilson.

forms (Fig. 4.5). It is truly innovative work for the West Country, particularly in a church, and illustrates how Sedding and the Pinwills were in the vanguard of art and fashion, leading a quiet revolution in Devon and Cornwall that is barely recognised, even today.[61]

The Pinwill-Sedding collaboration continued with the complete transformation of an entire church. A most remarkable restoration of the medieval collegiate church of St Carantoc, Crantock, Cornwall, was carried out between 1899 and 1907 to plans by Edmund, with the internal woodcarving executed by the Pinwill company.[62] The restoration was instigated by the Rev. George Metford Parsons, who possessed immense energy and fundraising skills. In Edmund he found his perfect architect – someone who was, by then, known for his sympathetic church restorations, his knowledge of medieval Cornish ecclesiological architecture and his commitment to High Anglican beliefs. Father George, Sedding and the Pinwill sisters together achieved one of the most ambitious Anglo-Catholic restorations in late Victorian Cornwall, and in the process created its 'entirely convincing medieval character'.[63] Possibly the most significant feature is incorporated into the parclose screen between the Lady Chapel and the chancel. A pair of hinged panels bearing the words *Misericordia Gratia et Pax* (Mercy, Grace and Peace) fold down to reveal a grill on which is carved a crucifix. On the opposite side of the screen, within the chancel, a seat is provided for a priest (Fig. 4.6). This is a confessional, one of very few in Anglican churches in the entire country and is symbolic of the strength of Anglo-Catholic conviction that lay at the heart of this restoration project.

During the time the transformation of Crantock church was taking place, the Pinwill company was also undergoing serious changes. In 1900, Mary, the eldest, married and bowed to convention by resigning from the business. By the end of 1907, Ethel decided to move away from Devon to work independently in Kingston on Thames, Surrey. This left Violet, the youngest, running the business single-handedly. With commissions increasing, she employed more and more carvers and joiners, and moved to larger premises near the town centre. Changes were afoot for Edmund too. In 1892 his growing reputation as a careful and insightful restorer of ancient churches led to a major commission in Cornwall to rebuild the church at Chacewater, with the restrained result evoking, said John Betjeman, a 'satisfying sense that Sedding here knew what effect he wanted to get; and got it'.[64] Perhaps it was this kind of rewarding employment restoring ancient churches that propelled Edmund to move to Cornwall, where his reputation ensured continued work in that sphere, or maybe he felt drawn anyway to the county of his early life and of his father's resting place. Whatever the reason, in early 1897, Edmund moved to Cornwall. There he became firm friends with Charles Stubbs, fourth Bishop of Truro,[65] and was eventually appointed Diocesan Architect, undertaking the design of extensions and new chapels for various institutions.[66]

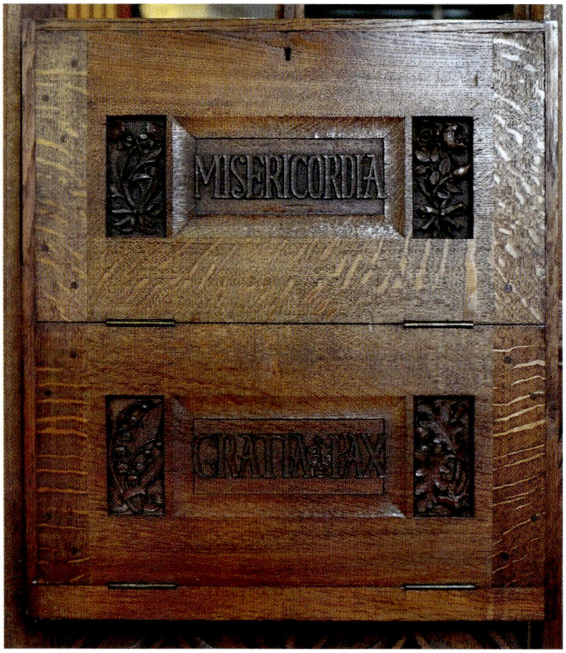

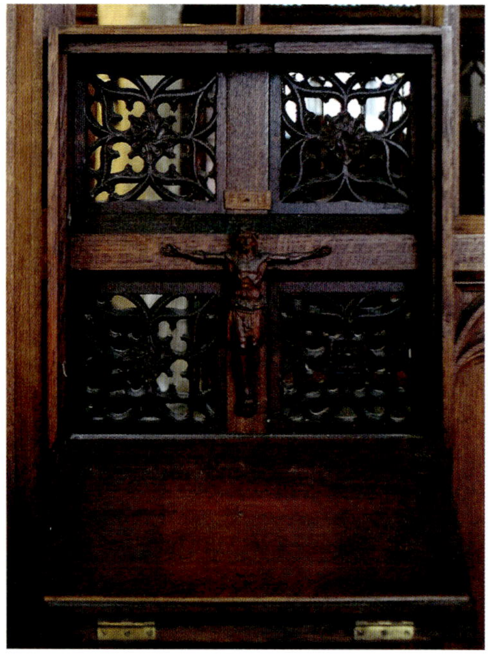
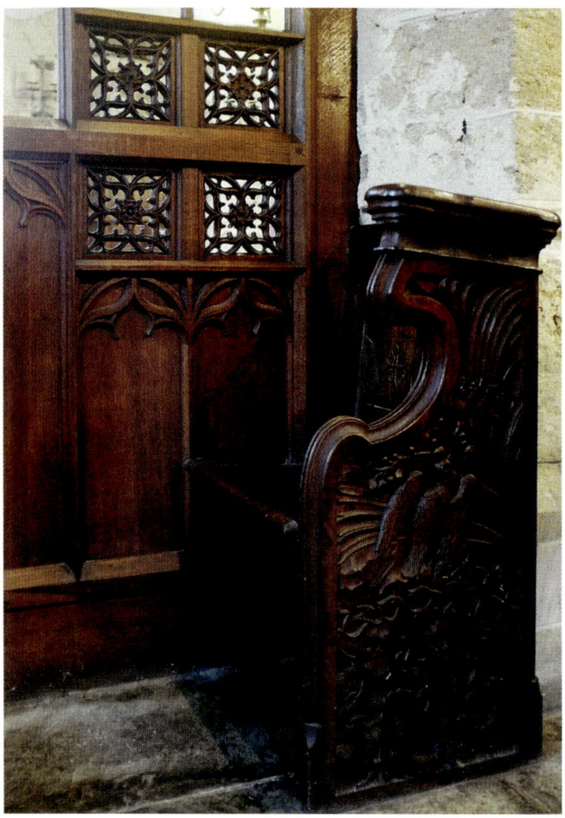

Fig. 4.6 | The closed and open confessional grill and priest's seat at Crantock, Cornwall, designed by Edmund H. Sedding and carved by the Pinwill sisters, 1899–1902. Helen Wilson.

Violet Pinwill continued working with Sedding, but increasingly gained commissions in her own right and began to prepare designs for clients. One of the most significant was the provision of 27 bench ends for Sheepstor Church, Devon, between 1914 and 1923.[67] It is clear from the Minutes of the Parochial Church Council that no architect was involved and that the designs for the bench ends were created by Violet. They are of two distinct sets: one carved with traditional symbols of the Passion and Biblical stories, the other, more unusually, illustrating scenes from the history of the Christian Church, including King John signing the Magna Carta, the voyages of St Patrick and Peter the Hermit preaching the First Crusade (Fig. 4.7), a most remarkable feat of inspired design and highly skilful execution.

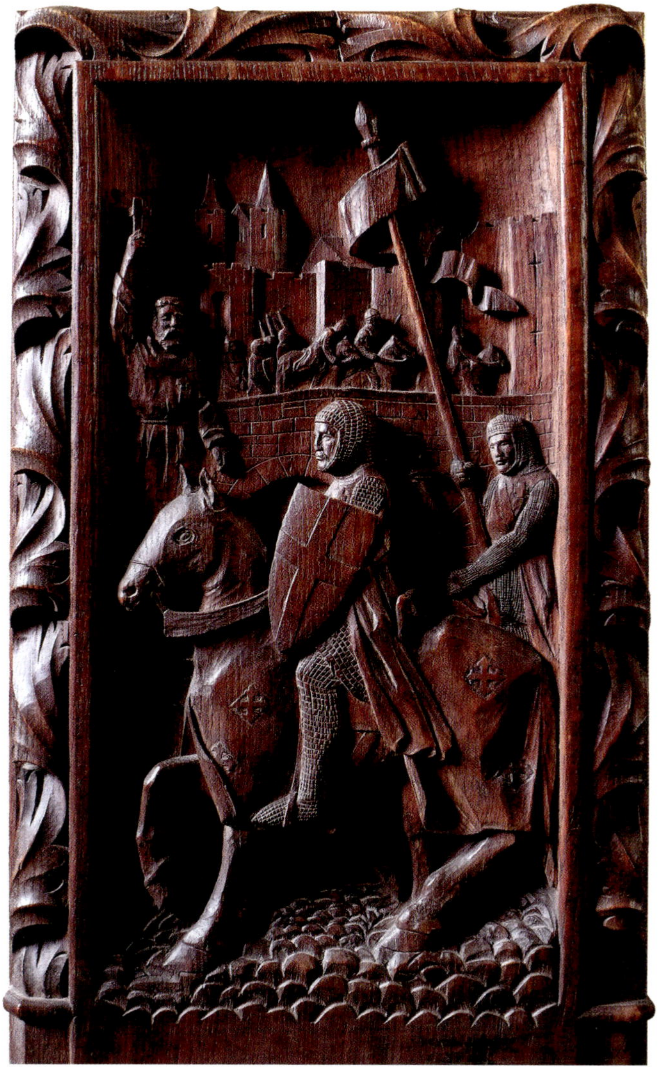

Fig. 4.7 | One of the bench ends at Sheepstor, Devon, designed and carved by Violet Pinwill, 1914–17. Helen Wilson.

It was from about 1910 that Sedding's ability to work independently as an architect was somewhat curtailed when his eyesight began to fail. His answer to the problem was to use someone else's eyes and he soon went into partnership with architect Reginald F. Wheatly (1879–1959). That partnership was dissolved by mutual consent in 1914 when Wheatly went to work abroad, and it was imperative for Sedding to take on another partner. Basil T. Stallybrass (1879–1922) came with impeccable credentials of a career imbued with the highest ideals of the Arts and Crafts movement. In 1899 the young architect had been taken on as Assistant by Detmar Blow, one of a group of architect-craftsmen who travelled from one building commission to another, known collectively as the Wandering Architects.[68] Despite the obvious limitations imposed by partial blindness, Edmund, in partnership with Stallybrass, continued to produce remarkable work including a baptistry at Bude Haven (1915)[69] and a Lady Chapel screen at Poundstock (1917),[70] both in Cornwall and with carving work by Violet Pinwill. As war spread over Europe, Sedding's eyesight deteriorated still further, and by 1918 he was almost blind.

In the later years of his life, despite his blindness, Sedding worked as hard as ever. Perhaps one of his greatest achievements during this period was again at Poundstock, where he is credited with a 'meticulous' restoration of the Gildhouse in 1919.[71] Yet Sedding's physical wellbeing declined further and by the early days of 1921 he had moved to The Hostel of God, Clapham Common, London. This institution, now known as Royal Trinity Hospice, was founded in 1891 to provide a home 'for the man who is neither curable nor incurable but simply dying',[72] and was an early forerunner of the hospice movement we know today. Patients were cared for by the Sisters of St Margaret's of East Grinstead, the order of Anglican nuns to which two of Edmund's aunts had belonged. There Edmund died of carcinoma of the stomach on 21 February 1921 at the age of 57. His crowning achievement was his work at Crantock, where he not only brought the fabric back to life but also designed a suite of furnishings, exquisitely carved by the Pinwill sisters, that exemplify Anglo-Catholic sensibilities. This is where he chose to be buried – where he felt closest to the ideals of his professional and spiritual life.

It was regrettable for the continuance of Edmund's architectural legacy that Basil Stallybrass, who was probably best suited to that role, died less than a year later. The architect who did most to perpetuate Edmund's legacy was Reginald F. Wheatly. Having returned to the UK, he settled in Truro and became a partner in Cowell, Drewitt and Wheatly, but also worked independently as architect to the Pinwill woodcarving business in Plymouth. Wheatly often reworked Sedding designs and, in the case of St Mary's, Newton Abbot, Devon, drew wholly on interior plans drawn up by Edmund before his death to complete the furnishing of the church 1925–26.[73] At Liskeard, Cornwall, the Lady Chapel was furnished (1927–37) to designs by Wheatly that owed a great deal to those of Edmund, and were expertly carved by Violet Pinwill and her employees (Fig. 4.8).[74] Yet Violet also increasingly created designs independently of Wheatly, not only continuing the legacy of Edmund Harold Sedding, but also developing her own sensitive style, most notably at St Martin-by-Looe, Cornwall, where the entire furnishings were replaced by Pinwill work from 1921 over several decades, with some remarkable bench end designs (Fig. 4.9).[75]

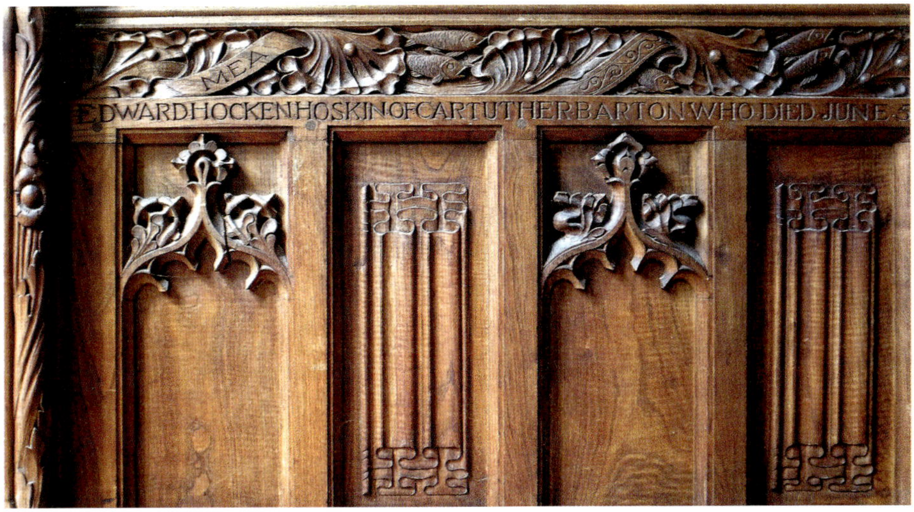

Fig. 4.8 | Bench front in Lady Chapel at Liskeard, Cornwall, designed by R.F. Wheatly and carved by Violet Pinwill, 1927–37. Helen Wilson.

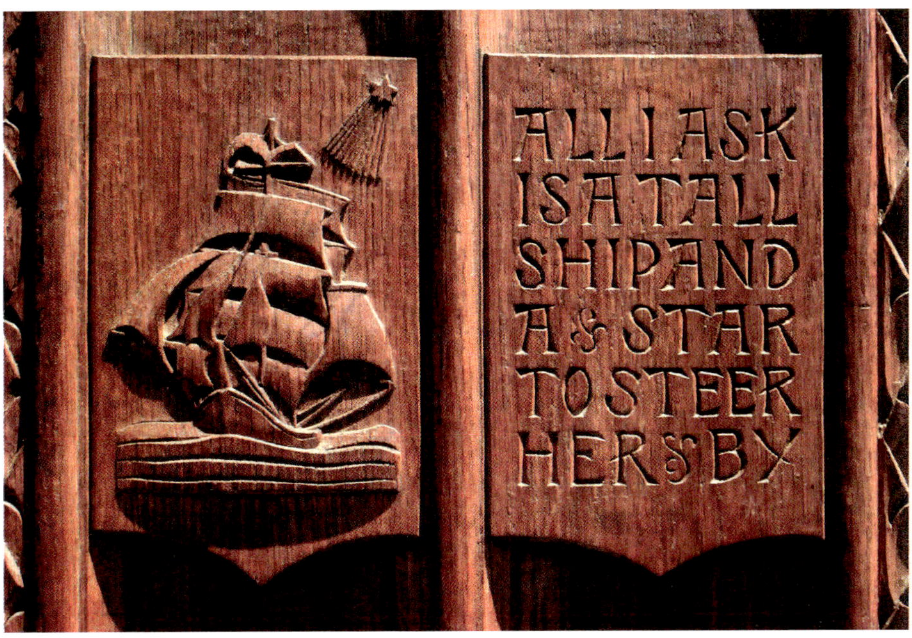

Fig. 4.9 | Bench end at St Martin by Looe, Cornwall, designed and carved by Violet Pinwill, 1931. Clare Pawley.

THE FINAL PHASE OF THE DYNASTY

At the height of the Pinwill business, probably just before the Great War, Violet employed nearly 30 carvers and joiners. That number declined as the demand for highly decorative church furnishings was curtailed by the ensuing depression and changing tastes. It might be assumed that all her employees were men, especially since the apprenticeship system was not open to girls, and so they probably were until after the Great War. During the war it had become necessary for women to take on occupations normally carried out by men. This was instrumental in changing not just the attitude of society, but also women themselves, who could see an alternative to their traditional roles as mothers and homemakers. Where Violet Pinwill and her sisters had led the way in 1890, other women now more readily and easily became professional woodcarvers. Indeed, the 1921 census reveals that Rashleigh, Pinwill & Co. employed women as Ecclesiastical Wood Carvers, namely, Phyllis Hunt (b. 1892) and Lilian Wells (b. 1886),[76] and probably others. They almost certainly learnt their initial skills at evening classes, which may even have been ones run by Violet, who taught woodcarving at Plymouth Technical School (later Plymouth Art College) for most of her career.

By the time war broke out again, Violet's business had contracted considerably. She relocated to much smaller premises in Plymouth in 1944 and was probably only employing two or three people by that time. Nevertheless, work did continue, and some significant pieces were created. One of the very last was for St Martin-by-Looe, Cornwall, the church she had helped beautify over several decades. This final commission was for a processional cross, and letters discussing its design and cost were exchanged in July 1956. The cross was duly made and delivered, but the next piece of correspondence was an invoice for £40, not from Violet but from accountants acting on behalf of executors winding up her estate after her death.

Violet was engaged in carving in her workshop on 29 December 1956, yet the next day she became ill and was taken to hospital. She died on 1 January 1957 at the age of 82, an event widely reported in newspapers across Devon and Cornwall, as well as in *The Times*. Her ashes are buried in the churchyard at Ermington, alongside her parents and other members of her family. Although work in hand was completed by one of her last remaining employees, Charles Gait, there was little call for the type of elaborate carving in which the company specialised and the Pinwill woodcarving business came to an end.

The Sedding architectural dynasty in Cornwall and Devon lasted from 1862 to 1921. All three members died at a relatively young age: Edmund at 32, John Dando at 52, and Edmund Harold at 57, and one wonders what more may have been achieved had they all lived longer. As it was, they left a lasting legacy in ancient churches, many being sensitively restored and some even saved from dereliction. All three developed a deep affinity for the West Country, and Cornwall in particular, with John Dando returning long after he had established his successful London practice. Edmund Harold, as part of the next generation and imbued in the Arts & Crafts movement, produced unique designs that combined naturalistic elements with traditional forms. He recognised in the Pinwill sisters an opportunity to develop a synergistic relationship in which these designs could be sympathetically interpreted. In becoming patron to the fledgling business of Rashleigh, Pinwill & Co., he helped to establish a women-led enterprise that became one of the foremost ecclesiastical carving companies in Devon and Cornwall. After his early death, his legacy was carried forward by Violet Pinwill, reinterpreting his designs and creating inspired new ones of her own.

Intriguingly, there is a dynastic aspect to the success of the Pinwills themselves. Probably the most influential figure in the establishment of the Pinwill company was their mother, Elizabeth. Given the paucity of professional women wood-carvers in the late nineteenth century, it is extraordinary that Elizabeth had such a vision for her daughters. While it may not have been at all unusual for Mary, Ethel and Violet to learn woodcarving, what was truly astonishing is that they achieved an ambition to become professionals and set up their own business. Such a confident step into the man's world of ecclesiastical carving may not have succeeded without the backing of the architect Edmund Harold Sedding, willing to act as patron to these remarkable young women and, most importantly, the inspired forethought of their mother Elizabeth, providing the opportunity for their training and fundamental support for their success.

NOTES

1. Peter Beacham and Nikolaus Pevsner, *The Buildings of England: Cornwall* (London: Yale, 2014), 76. I would like to thank Clare Pawley and Sue Andrew for inspiration, Peter Beacham OBE and Alex Woodcock for encouragement, and Anthony Lewis for logistical support.
2. Paul Snell, "John Dando Sedding and Sculpture in Architecture: The Fulfilment of a Ruskinian Ideal?" in *Ruskin & Architecture*, eds. Rebecca Daniels and Geoff Brandwood (Reading: Spire Books, 2003), note 64, 353.
3. Paul M. Snell, *'The Priest of Form' John Dando Sedding (1838–91) and the Languages of Late Victorian Architecture*, unpublished PhD thesis (University of Manchester, 2006), 217.
4. Helen M. Wilson, "The Architect Edmund H. Sedding and his Devon Churches," *Rep. Trans. Devon. Ass. Advmt Sci.* 148 (2016): 255–292. All further biographical information for the Seddings is taken from this paper, except where otherwise stated.
5. Kate Jordan, "A Benign Paterfamilias: John Dando Sedding, his Family and Followers," *Ecclesiology Today* 57 (2019): 6.
6. Kathryn Ferry, *The Old Convent East Grinstead: John Mason Neale, George Edmund Street and the Society of St Margaret*, (East Grinstead: Old Covent Estate Residents, 2021), 133.
7. A. Clifton Kelway, *George Rundle Prynne: A Chapter in the Early History of the Catholic Revival* (London: Longmans, 1905), 54.
8. Cyndy Manton, *Henry Wilson: Practical Idealist* (Cambridge, Lutterworth, 2009), 19.
9. "Death of Mr Sedding," *Oxford Times*, 27 June, 1868, 4.

10. "Local and District News Launceston," *Royal Cornwall Gazette*, 4 November, 1864, 8.
11. Jordan, "A Benign Paterfamilias," 6.
12. Bone & Son had been employed by G.E. Street in Cornish works during Sedding's time in his practice. Snell, "John Dando Sedding," 204.
13. J. P. Cooper and H. Wilson, "The Work of John Sedding, Architect," *Architectural Review* 3 (1897–8): 35. While we do now know more, thanks to the research of Paul Snell [notes 2 and 3], there is still more to be done.
14. Beacham and Pevsner, *The Buildings of England*, 92.
15. "Church Restoration in Cornwall," *Royal Cornwall Gazette*, 18 July, 1867, 5.
16. Beacham and Pevsner, *The Buildings of England*, 486.
17. Beacham and Pevsner, *The Buildings of England*, 231.
18. "Restoration of Gwithian Church," *Western Morning News*, 14 May, 1867, 4.
19. "Local News Launceston North Hill Church," *Royal Cornwall Gazette*, 9 April, 1868, 3.
20. Beacham and Pevsner, *The Buildings of England*, 696.
21. "The Restoration of St Wendron Church," *Western Morning News*, 9 January, 1869, 2.
22. Mary Schoeser, *English Church Embroidery 1833–1953* (London: Watts & Co., 1998), 51.
23. Ferry, *The Old Convent*, 133.
24. Mother Kate, cited in Schoeser, *English Church Embroidery*, 113.
25. Kathryn Ferry, personal correspondence with the author, 6 May 2022.
26. Cooper and Wilson, "The Work of John Sedding," 128.
27. Bridget Cherry and Nikolaus Pevsner, *The Buildings of England: Devon* (London: Yale, 1991), 180.
28. "Bigbury," *Western Times*, 6 May, 1873, 5.
29. Jordan, "A Benign Paterfamilias," 7.
30. J. P. Cooper and H. Wilson, "The Work of John D. Sedding," in *Edwardian Architecture and its Origins*, ed. A. Service (London: Architectural Press, 1975), 277.
31. Annette Carruthers, Mary Greensted and Barley Roscoe, *Ernest Gimson: Arts & Crafts Designer and Architect* (London: Yale, 2019), 33–5, 38.
32. Cooper and Wilson, "The Work of John Sedding," 128, 130, state work began at Holbeton in 1884 and concluded at Ermington in 1889, but whether the work in the two churches was carried out simultaneously or consecutively is debatable.
33. Snell, *'The Priest of Form'*, 214, note 95 states that the sum of £25,000 has yet to be proven.
34. Cooper and Wilson, "The Work of John Sedding," 267.
35. Snell, *'The Priest of Form'*, 214–215.
36. John Dando Sedding, on the other hand, stayed at Flete while in south Devon. Snell, *'The Priest of Form'*, 215.
37. Helen Wilson, *From 'Lady Woodcarvers' to Professionals: The Remarkable Pinwill Sisters* (Plymouth: Willow Productions, 2021). All further biographical information for the Pinwills is taken from this publication, except where otherwise stated.
38. Edmund Sedding, "Ermington Church," *Transactions of the Exeter Diocesan Architectural and Archaeological Society*, Third Series, vol. 1, part 1 (1894): 58–9.
39. Snell, *'The Priest of Form'*, 213.
40. For example, Miss Agatha Middleton of The Studio, Southernhay, gave notice of her classes in Wood Carving and Art Work in the 'Scholastic' advertisements in *Devon and Exeter Gazette*, 9 July, 1892, 1.
41. For example, Exeter High School for Girls lists wood carving as among classes provided for girls not preparing for examinations in the "Education" advertisements in *Western Times*, 19 April, 1898, 1.
42. "The Misses Pinwell's [*sic*] Woodcarving," *The Queen*, 21 August, 1909, 357.
43. David Young, *More… Cobblestones, Cottages and Castles* (Exeter: Obelisk, 1992), 20–22, within a chapter entitled 'Curiosities'.
44. Snell, "John Dando Sedding," 353.

45. Snell, *'The Priest of Form'*, 217.
46. *West Somerset Free Press*, 11 April, 1891, 8.
47. Census 1891 Winsford, London, TNA, RG12/1868 Fo. 113; Russell was 'one of the devoted band who... for many years made St. Alban's, Holborn, the most conspicuous centre of the High Church party in London.' *The Times*, 9 November, 1925, 14.
48. Census 1891 Dulverton, London, TNA, RG12/1868 Fo. 115.
49. General Register Office copy Death Certificate 1891(2Q) Sedding, John Dando, 52, Dulverton 5c 235.
50. Census 1891 Ermington, London, TNA, RG12/1721 Fo. 95.
51. *Western Times*, 21 April, 1891, 5.
52. General Register Office copy Death Certificate 1891(2Q) Sedding, Rose Catherine, 44, Dulverton 5c 236.
53. Administration (with will) of estate of John Dando Sedding proved 8 June 1891.
54. Will of Rose Catherine Sedding proved 16 May 1891.
55. Jordan, "A Benign Paterfamilias," 12; Census 1871 Bristol, London, TNA, RG10/2537 Fo. 18.
56. Census 1881 Bloomsbury, London, TNA, RG11/321 Fo. 42.
57. Kelly's Post Office Street Directory London 1908, 444 (accessed via www.thegenealogist.co.uk).
58. Manton, *Henry Wilson*, 62, 84.
59. Wilson, *From 'Lady Woodcarvers' to Professionals*, 60.
60. Cherry and Pevsner, *The Buildings of England*, 685.
61. Wilson, *From 'Lady Woodcarvers' to Professionals*, 65–66. Despite the importance of this work, Cherry and Pevsner, *The Buildings of England*, 685, neglects the contribution to the furnishings of the chancel by Edmund H. Sedding and the Pinwills.
62. Wilson, *From 'Lady Woodcarvers' to Professionals*, 66–75.
63. Beacham and Pevsner, *The Buildings of England*, 166.
64. Cited in Beacham and Pevsner, *The Buildings of England*, 150.
65. Their mutual admiration led to Sedding penning an affectionate biography: Edmund H. Sedding, *Charles William Stubbs, D. D. Fourth Bishop of Truro* (Plymouth: Brendon, 1914).
66. Helen M. Wilson, "The Architect Edmund H. Sedding," in *What is Unique About Cornish Buildings? Proceedings of the 2019 Cornish Buildings Group Conference*, ed. Paul Holden (Donington: Shaun Tyas, 2023), 228–9.
67. Wilson, *From 'Lady Woodcarvers' to Professionals*, 183–6.
68. Michael Drury, *Wandering Architects: In Pursuit of an Arts and Crafts Ideal* (Donington: Shaun Tyas, 2016), 1, 119, 133, 152–5.
69. Wilson, *From 'Lady Woodcarvers' to Professionals*, 157–8.
70. Wilson, *From 'Lady Woodcarvers' to Professionals*, 163–5.
71. Beacham and Pevsner, *The Buildings of England*, 460.
72. "The History of Royal Trinity Hospice," Our History, Royal Trinity Hospice, accessed 25 August, 2023, www.royaltrinityhospice.london/our-history.
73. Wilson, *From 'Lady Woodcarvers' to Professionals*, 194–200.
74. Wilson, *From 'Lady Woodcarvers' to Professionals*, 208–10.
75. Wilson, *From 'Lady Woodcarvers' to Professionals*, 186–91.
76. Census 1921 Plymouth, London, TNA, RG15/10591/0591-0592; Census 1921 Plymouth, London, TNA, RG15/10606/0599-0600.

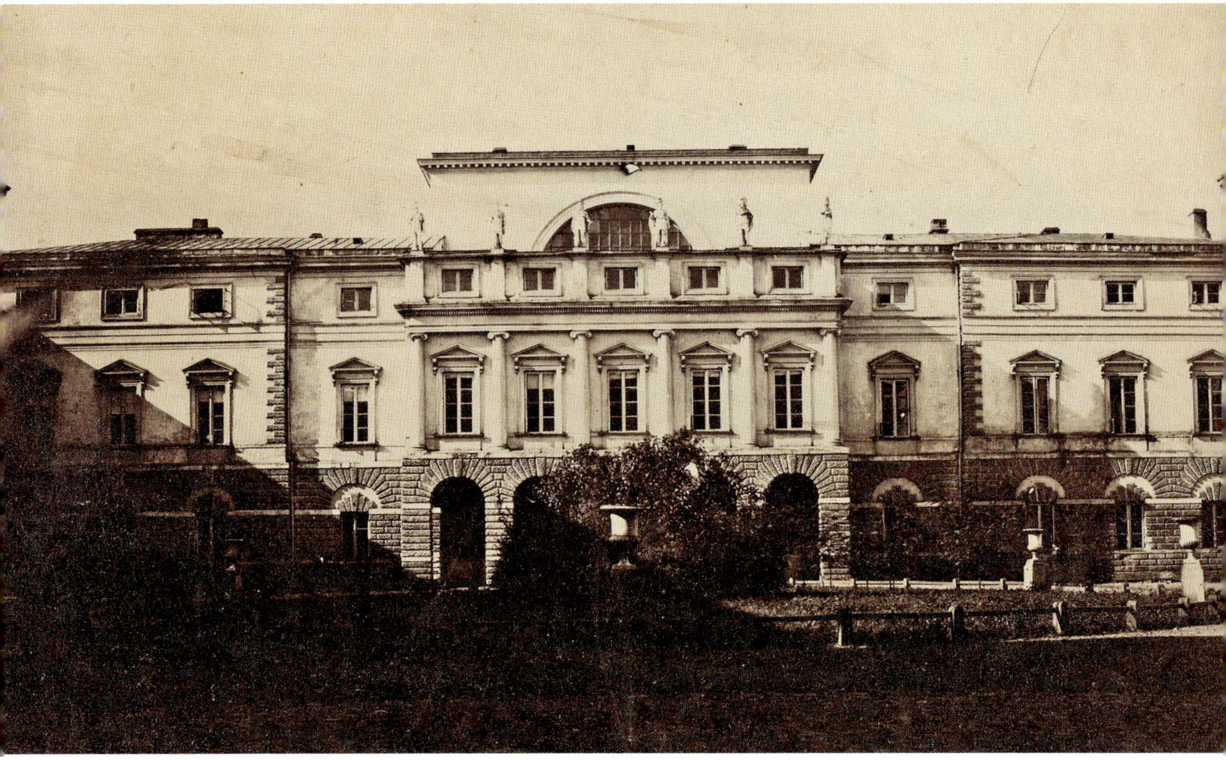

Fig. 5.1 | Pac Palace in Warsaw, ca. 1870, photograph by K. Brandel, National Museum in Warsaw.

5 · Classicism and Legitimacy: The Marconi Dynasty of Architects in the Kingdom of Poland

MIKOŁAJ GETKA-KENIG

In the history of Polish architecture of the long 19th century, the two generations of the Marconi family had a special place. Their active participation in the development of the classical idiom was one of the family's most significant and acclaimed contributions (despite the fact that the family's patriarch ironically started his Polish career designing a big neo-Gothic house). The architectural heritage of classical antiquity and its early modern (Italian) interpretations found in Enrico, Leandro and Władysław Marconi not only keen followers, but also talented innovators. However, their spectacular and lasting success in attracting attention of Polish elite clients, interested in their classically-oriented designs and eager to pay for their execution, owed much to specific socio-cultural circumstances in which this family of Polonized Italians had an opportunity to prosper for almost a century.

Such clans of Italian immigrant builders were a well-known phenomenon in the early modern Polish state (the Polish-Lithuanian Commonwealth). They exerted great influence on local architecture in the 17th and 18th centuries, offering a direct link with Italy and Italian interpretations of the ancient classical heritage.[1] Thus, the career of the Marconis in the 19th century may seem to have been no more than yet another incarnation of that old and entrenched tradition. However, it should be stressed that the Marconis' professional success occurred in a very different situation. It was not only the political context that changed (the partitioning of the former Commonwealth between neighbouring superpowers of Russia, Prussia and Austria). It was also the fundamental transformation of the local architectural culture that no more supported that traditional career model, characterised by informal structures and clannish relationships. Although the originator of the Marconi dynasty in Poland, himself a descendant of builders, started his work as an aristocratic protégé, thus in a very traditional way, he was forced to swiftly adapt to the bureaucratisation and professionalisation of architecture (or building practice in general) as a vocation in order to thrive. His sons, entering the architectural job market thirty years later, represented the already fully-fledged new model of the profession. Even if their respective reputations were built to some extent on the memory of their celebrated father, they also managed to make a name for themselves, independently achieving recognition and fame.

However, the Marconis' success consisted not only in their patriarch's adaptation skills or mastery of the classical architectural vocabulary (derived not only from the heritage of Rome and Greece, but also the Florentine Renaissance, Palladianism, or even early Christian architecture), but also in a continuous demand for classicism among members of the Polish social elite. For their clients the classical idiom proved to be an important instrument of legitimacy in the period of incessant change during the long 19th century. Note that Barbara Arciszewska once argued that Palladianism flourished in early Georgian Britain as a response to 'the collapse of traditional pre-modern foundations of authority'.[2] In that case, it was not a random coincidence that the wide popularity of the allegedly timeless classical idiom occurred in Britain simultaneously with the advent of 'modernity' in local politics, economy, culture and society. In Arciszewska's discussion, 'modernity' as a historical phenomenon and context for her analysis of the rise of Palladianism was defined by 'certain salient characteristics of the "modern"', such as 'rationality, individualisation, the emergence of capitalism, bureaucracy and imperialism along the development of the civic society and increase of the disciplinary powers of the nation state'.[3]

In the case of Poland, the process of 'modernisation' defined in this manner was much more observable in the 19th rather than 18th century. The collapse of the centuries-old Polish-Lithuanian Commonwealth, an aristocratic 'republic of nobles' partitioned by its imperialist neighbours in 1795, triggered a series of political, social, economic and cultural changes that affected and consequently eroded the traditional Polish community. Such typically 'modern' phenomena as bureaucracy, capitalism or nationalism, whose development was supported or provoked by the imperial domination of Russia, Prussia and Austria (as well as temporarily France, during the Napoleonic Wars), led to many protracted political and social tensions, often intertwined with each other. They found their symbolic expressions also in contemporary architecture, both public and private, including classically informed undertakings in which the Marconis took part as designers. They were professionally active between 1820s and 1910s in the Russian-controlled part of the former Commonwealth, mainly in the so-called Kingdom of Poland (Congress Poland). Established in 1815, it was originally an autonomous territory centred on Warsaw that only in the early 1870s became effectively incorporated into the Romanov Empire. Even then, however, it remained distinct as an area socially, economically and culturally dominated by its Polish population. It was there, in that (rather poor) substitute for the former Polish state, where the confrontation of modern changes and traditional identities proved especially fruitful with regard to the development of classicism as an architectural instrument of social legitimacy.

ENRICO MARCONI (1792–1863)

Enrico Marconi, to architectural historians better known under his Polish name of Henryk, was born into a well-to-do Italian family of builders and artists. The Marconis originated from Mantua, but later they settled in the Papal States. Enrico's father, Leandro Marconi (1763–1842), was both an architect and painter of wall and theatre decorations, who ended up as professor of ornaments at the Academy of Fine Arts in Bologna. It was Leandro who also was Enrico's first teacher, supervising his early efforts in architectural drawing. Then, Enrico studied independently engineering (at a university) and architecture (at an academy of fine arts) in Bologna. He got his first job as teacher of drawing in a grammar school in Lugo, but simultaneously tried also to gain experience as professional designer. After four years of teaching, he decided to focus solely on architectural practice. He participated in competitions in Bologna and then Rome, where he moved in order to study ancient classical monuments. In Rome, he met an agent of Count Ludwik Michał Pac, a rich Polish aristocrat. The agent offered him employment in his master's service, and Marconi grasped the opportunity, arriving in the Kingdom of Poland in the summer of 1822. His first task was to finish the construction of Pac's new country house in the village of Dowspuda near Suwałki, originally designed by another Italian, Pietro Bosio.[4]

Count Pac was by no means an ordinary landowner. That scion of one of the grandest magnate families of the former Polish-Lithuanian Commonwealth represented the old aristocracy that could hardly come to terms with the rise of political centralism that characterised the Kingdom already in the early years of its existence. In that case, that administrative transformation coincided with the national efforts to restore the old Polish state. The consecutive incarnations of 'resurrected' Poland, namely the Napoleonic Duchy of Warsaw and post-Napoleonic Kingdom of Poland, were politically dependent on European superpowers. It was the Russian emperor in the Kingdom's case. Therefore, the bureaucratic and centralised regime, imposed first by Napoleon, and then solidified by the Romanovs, was seen by many as a foreign and alien novelty that was at variance with the centuries-old heritage of Polish republicanism.[5] Since the latter system mostly benefitted the magnates, it was especially opposed by such aristocrats as Pac for whom his ancestors' bygone political role and influence were a source of pride and self-esteem. The new country mansion was intended to represent his noble nonconformity. Since he wanted to link the glorification of his own family past with the contemporary political discourse in order to legitimize the former, he wanted to associate his residence with Britain. In the 19th century, the British constitutional monarchy and its elitist political culture was an object of permanent veneration among blue-blooded Poles, sharing also some similarities with the pre-partition Polish-Lithuanian political regime (such as a bicameral parliament). Pac's choice was the Gothic Revival style that was strongly associated then with British architecture as well as indicative of the passage of time.[6]

Marconi accepted the offer despite his little knowledge of medieval architecture. He needed to study it in Warsaw libraries, where he found sufficient sources.[7] It was a daring challenge for someone who was trained only in classical architecture, although Marconi managed to carry out the task successfully. It paved him the way to another commission in which he took full advantage of his classical background. It was the building of Pac's palace (Fig. 5.1) in Warsaw, the very centre of the Kingdom's political regime that the count so much disliked. It seems that it was not a coincidence that both residences were designed by Marconi in such different styles, since their architectural forms resulted from different contexts. In the 1820s, the Gothic was seen as an antithesis of classicism and was rather unusual in public, especially urban spaces in the Kingdom. The prominently exposed Warsaw palace conformed thus to the classical standards of palatial architecture, consequently engaging in a symbolic rivalry with the official architecture of the state. After 1815, the Polish (but controlled by the Romanovs) government of the Kingdom invested a lot of money in new edifices of ministries and other central offices that were built in the spectacular neoclassical style. Many of them were designed by Marconi's compatriot, Antonio Corazzi.[8] The monumental ensemble of Pac's palace, its grand scale, vast courtyard and Palladian façade, suggested that the owner wanted to compete with the state in terms of magnificence. The main entrance was articulated with a semi-circular gate that was adorned with a large bas-relief representing the Roman Consul Flamininus declaring liberty to Greek cities during the Isthmian Games.[9] The event was a notorious example of political hypocrisy, thus the sculpture can be interpreted as an expression of Pac's own political attitude towards the very idea of national 'resurrection' of Poland under the Russian emperor.

Despite his association with Pac and his artistic political statements, Marconi's talent soon found recognition of the Kingdom's governing elite. Already in the late 1820s, he started an official career of government builder that lasted until his death, and garnered him the chivalric Order of Saint Stanisław (3rd class).[10] Nevertheless, he did not cease to work for private clients, especially aristocrats and affluent landowners to whose eyes and minds his mastery of classical architectural vocabulary proved especially pleasing, and responsive to their expectations. Among his clients, there was Count Andrzej Zamoyski, a keen propagator of agricultural modernisation, highly acclaimed as a leader of progressive landowners in the Kingdom of the mid-19th century, but also a keen businessman, willing to invest in new sources of income such as rental property.[11] In 1843, Marconi designed his new mansion in

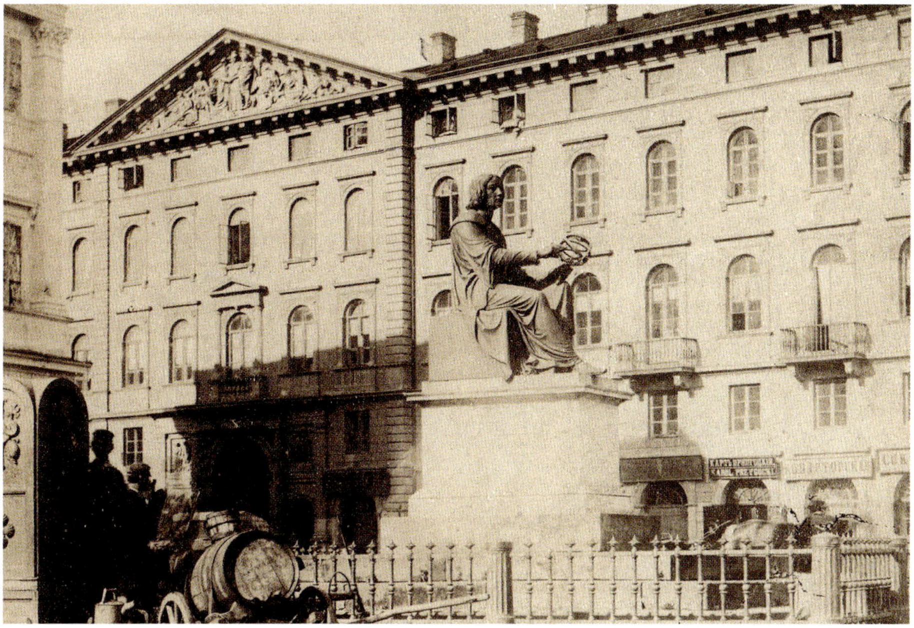

Fig. 5.2 | Zamoyski Tenement House in Warsaw, ca. 1870, photograph [photographer unknown], National Museum in Warsaw.

Warsaw, situated in the very centre of the city. The actual residence of the comital family was hidden behind a much bigger tenement house (Fig. 5.2) facing the street of Krakowskie Przedmieście, one of the main arteries of contemporary Warsaw.[12] That front building had no local precedent in terms of size and urban context. It was not an outbuilding or a side wing that could also provide accommodation for rent (like in the case of Pac Palace and many older residences), but a dominant element of an architectural complex that literally overshadowed the proper residence of its noble owner. The tenement house had a truly palatial façade, inspired by Palazzo della Cancelleria in Rome, but also distinctly classicized by the addition of a pediment, a central portal reminiscent of Roman triumphal arches and figural bas-reliefs. In fact, the tenement house had much richer external decoration than the count's family house. It was a novel mode of aristocratic representation in Warsaw. The count was represented as a self-sufficient man of business rather than a mere patrician and heir to his family's status.

Zamoyski served also as president of the Society of Land Credit (*Towarzystwo Kredytowe Ziemskie*), an association of landowners specializing in giving loans to its members under the pledge of their property as security for debts. The development of modern agriculture in the Kingdom owed much to the Society. Its members belonged to local economic elites of landowners who championed not only innovations in farming, but also industrialization of landed estates. Although the Society had been established already in 1825, it managed to afford its own building only in

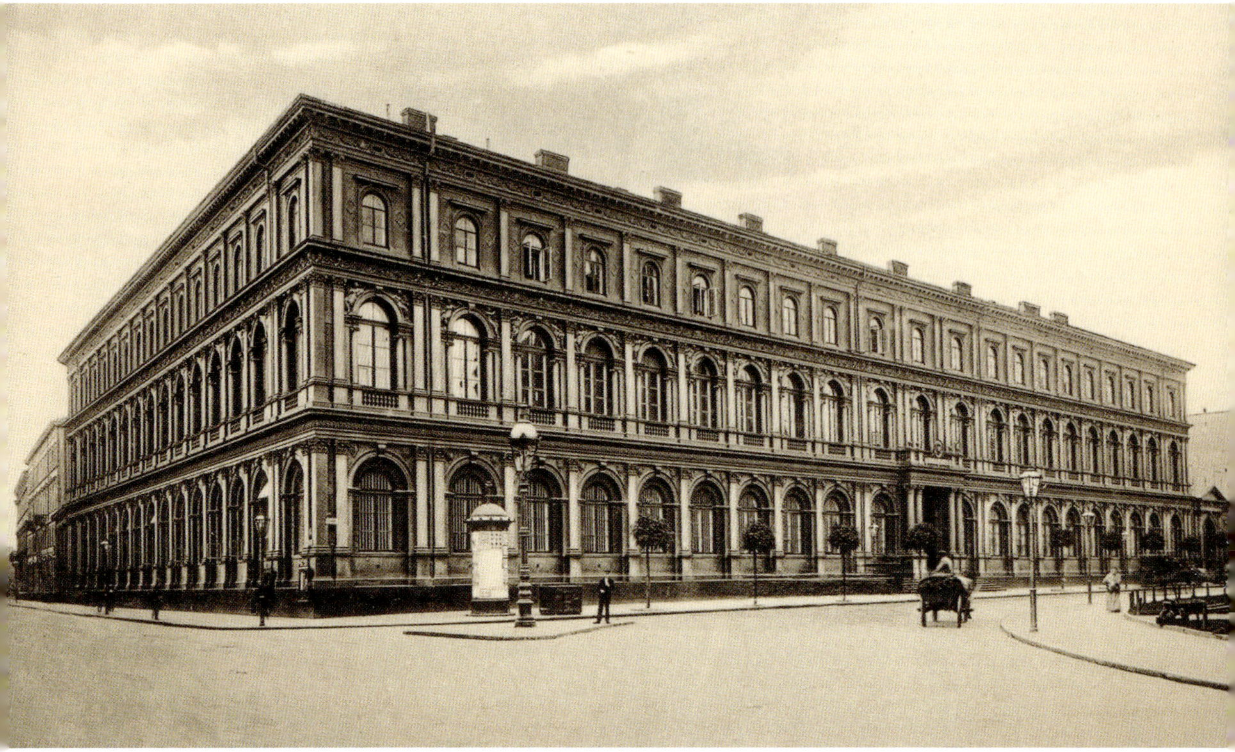

Fig. 5.3 | Building of the Society of Land Credit in Warsaw, ca. 1913, photograph [photographer unknown], National Museum in Warsaw.

the 1850s.[13] The new edifice (Fig. 5.3) manifested the social and economic significance of the progressive landed class. Marconi, whom the Society commissioned to design its headquarters, chose the Marcian Library and New Procuracies in Venice as a source of inspiration. In that context, those architectural epitomes of the Venetian Republic's greatness could bring to mind associations with the pre-partition Polish-Lithuanian 'republic of nobles'. Members of the Society saw themselves as successors to the old Polish nobility as it was evidenced by large-scale frescos in the building's assembly hall. One depicted Poland's king Casimir the Great granting the first Polish codification of laws to nobles in 1362, and another was a scene showing the Russian Emperor Alexander I (first ruler of Congress Poland) presenting landowners with the Society's statute in 1825.[14]

Marconi was also responsible for designing the building of the *Europejski* Hotel or Grand Hotel of Europe (Fig. 5.4). It was the biggest and most luxurious hotel of the mid-19th century Warsaw, whose façades were inspired by the Renaissance palaces of Rome (Palazzo Caetani, Palazzo Farnese) and Venice (Palazzo Corner).[15] It was owned by a company initiated by Count Aleksander Przezdziecki and founded together with Counts Władysław, Zygmunt and Ksawery Pusłowski.[16]

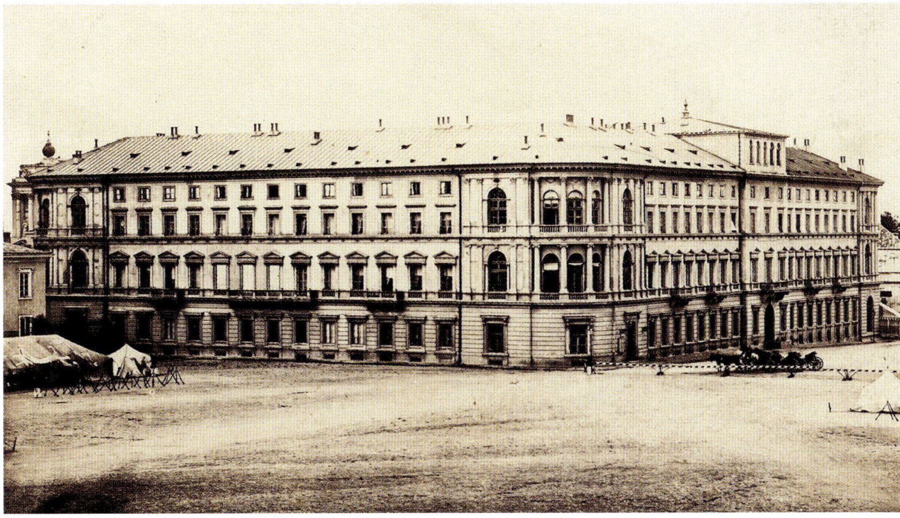

Fig. 5.4 | Europejski Hotel in Warsaw, ca. 1862, photograph by K. Beyer, National Museum in Warsaw.

Like Zamoyski, they all successfully engaged in non-agricultural ventures in order to diversify and secure their economic base. The new hotel was above all intended to meet the expectations of rich foreign businessmen who visited Warsaw in order to invest their money in local commercial enterprises. It was a place where they could not only sleep and eat, but also meet with potential business partners, negotiate agreements, or throw parties.[17] The palatial architecture of the building visually legitimised that characteristic lifestyle of the modern men of business, responding to their social aspirations and longing for respectability, but also providing the old elite with an alternative source of income.

In that period, the architectural patronage of the aristocracy encompassed also new parish churches that were built in Warsaw's developing districts. Despite the constant population growth of Warsaw at the turn of the 18th and 19th centuries, virtually no new Catholic church (but one) had been built there since the first half of the 18th century. However, the period between the November Uprising (1830–1) and the Crimean War (1853–6) was tormented by the proliferation of revolutionary activity that reversed that trend. From the perspective of the social and political elite, churches were essential to provide the burgeoning, predominantly Catholic population with sufficient pastoral care that was seen as a fundamental instrument of moral instruction and social order. That goal could be achieved by private aristocratic donations such as the one of Countess Klementyna Małachowska nee Princess Sanguszko. She co-founded (with the state's aid and many smaller contributions from aristocratic donors) a new church of the old and vast parish of Saint Andrew (Fig. 5.5).[18] Marconi's design was inspired by early Christian basilicas such as San Paolo fuori le Mura and Santa Maria Maggiore in Rome.[19]

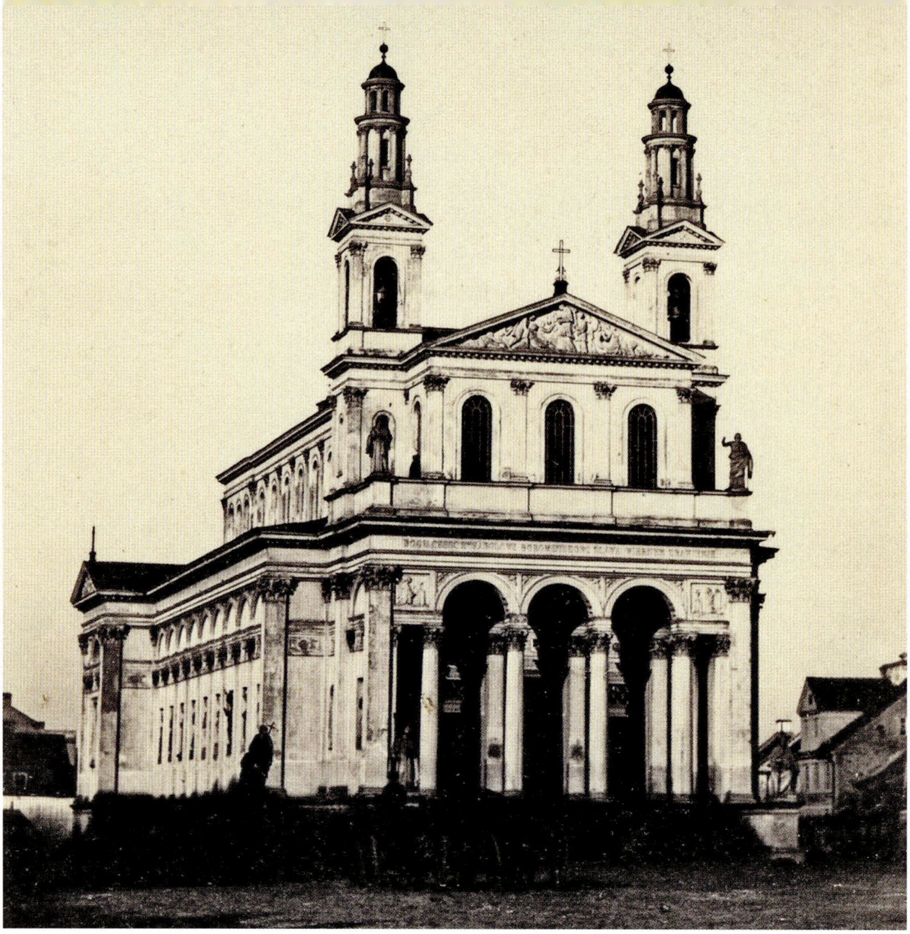

Fig. 5.5 | St Charles Church in Warsaw, ca. 1862, photograph by K. Beyer, National Museum in Warsaw.

The church's late classical architecture had its genesis in the dedication to Saint Charles Borromeo, requested by Małachowska. Its characteristic (and then quite unusual) form represented the ideal of ecclesiastical architecture that was promoted by the saint cardinal as a true expression of Christian spirit. It was the architecture of spiritual rebirth and a visual weapon against secularisation that was not without unwanted political implications. Note that the church was seen by contemporaries as a symbol of the Russian liberal attitude towards Catholicism under the Orthodox Emperor Nicholas I. Above the entrance, there was also an inscription underlining the fact that it was built during his reign.[20] The building was thus a product of the cooperation between the Polish Catholic elite and the Russian government, aimed at the preservation of the established order that benefitted both sides.

Marconi himself longed for social recognition as architect and citizen of Warsaw. His designs for the upper class made him relatively wealthy, thus he could afford a house that definitely surpassed average living standards for the contemporary middle class. In the 1840s, he designed the so-called *Casa Marconi*.

That spacious family mansion, inspired by Palazzo Sacchetti in Rome, consisted of four pavilions that were centred around an inner courtyard. The pavilions were linked by wings articulated by Serlian windows.[21] The scale and architecture of Casa Marconi was a manifestation of its owner's professional success and also his ambition to belong to the city elite. It was not, however, situated in Warsaw's centre (where the aristocracy and aspiring non-noble elite tended to live), but on its outskirts. Land was probably much cheaper there, but it seems that it was not the sole motivation for Enrico to choose the area. Concurrently, Marconi designed also the first Warsaw train station, known as the Viennese Station (*Dworzec Wiedeński*).[22] It was operated by the state-owned Warsaw-Vienna Railway (*Kolej Warszawsko-Wiedeńska*) that connected the capital of the Kingdom with the Habsburg capital.[23] In designing the building, Marconi apparently had in mind a model of Palazzo Pitti in Florence (although its façade was articulated with pilasters instead of characteristic rusticated arcades).[24] It was the earliest train station in the Kingdom, and second earliest in the Russian Empire. Moreover, during its construction, it was the only station connecting Russia with the rest of Europe. The building was thus an ultimate symbol of the Kingdom's dynamic development and its leadership in the field of technological progress in the Russian-dominated part of Europe. Casa Marconi stood directly opposite the station. It seems that it was not a random coincidence. Marconi apparently wanted to associate his name (and his historically-oriented designs) with civilisational progress, epitomized by the novel mode of transport.

LEANDRO MARCONI (1834–1919)

Enrico Marconi was married with Margaret (in Polish: Małgorzata) Heiton who was of Scottish extraction. Her father, originally from Selkirk, worked as gardener in Pac's service in Dowspuda. Enrico and Margaret had five sons and one daughter. Two of them – Leandro and Władysław – followed in their father's footsteps. Leandro, named after his paternal grandfather, was born in Warsaw in 1834, thus over a decade after his father's arrival in the Kingdom. He attended a 'real school' (*gimnazjum realne*) in Warsaw that was a secondary school dedicated specifically to the training of future technicians and engineers. Leandro did not attend a university or polytechnic (all Polish institutions of higher education in the Kingdom were abolished after the anti-Russian November Uprising of 1830), but trained in Enrico's studio.[25] It is unknown whether he ever visited his paternal homeland. Nevertheless, the Italian architectural legacy played an important role in his professional life, greatly influencing his own architectural output.

Due to his substantial inheritance that made him financially independent, Leandro was not as prolific as his father. He was an elite architect of residential buildings, working for a selected clientele of aristocrats and rich capitalists (of

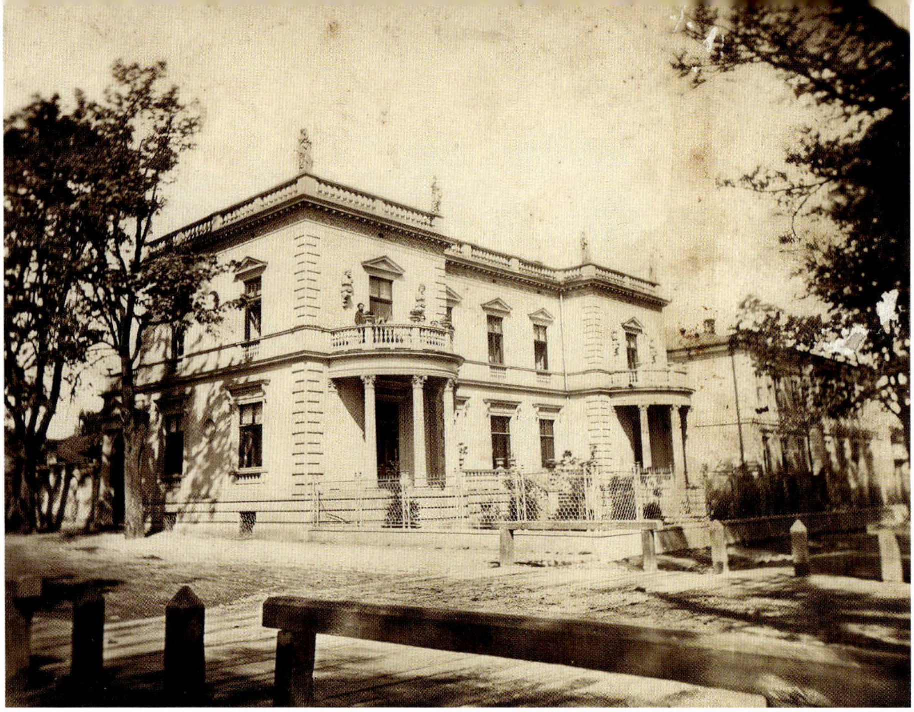

Fig. 5.6 | Rau Villa in Warsaw, ca. 1875, photograph by K. Brandel, National Museum in Warsaw.

middle-class background).[26] In 1865, he designed an urban villa (Fig. 5.6) for Wilhelm Ellis Rau, a German-born industrialist and banker, future co-owner of the big engineering company Lilpop, Rau and Loewenstein. He represented the second generation of foreign entrepreneurs who were responsible for the Kingdom's quick industrial development in the second and third quarter of the century.[27] The relatively small mansion was built in the fashionable area of the Baths Garden (*Łazienki*), a former residence of the last king of the Polish-Lithuanian Commonwealth, later acquired by the Romanovs (it was then their main seat in Warsaw). The villa by Leondro was situated next to an earlier house, built in 1852 for Rau's business partner Stanisław Lilpop.[28] Its architecture testified that its owner was not only wealthy, but that he also belonged to the cultured elite. Its elegant, symmetrical form, with direct citations from ancient classical monuments (such as semi-circular colonnades in the main façade, reminiscent of the Temple of Vesta in Tivoli) and neoclassical exterior decoration (copies of ancient busts and statues as well as bas-reliefs with allegories of the owner's favourite occupations: mechanics, painting, architecture and sculpture),[29] alluded to the social ambitions of that upstart millionaire.

On the same street, but closer to the imperial residence, there was also another villa designed by Leandro in the style evocative of Poggio a Caiano or other Medici villas in Tuscany. The building (Fig. 5.7) was originally built in the 1850s (by Julian Ankiewicz for Aniela Bławacka), and later substantially rebuilt by Marconi in 1876 for Countess Emilia Sobańska nee Countess Łubieńska, wife of Feliks Sobański.[30]

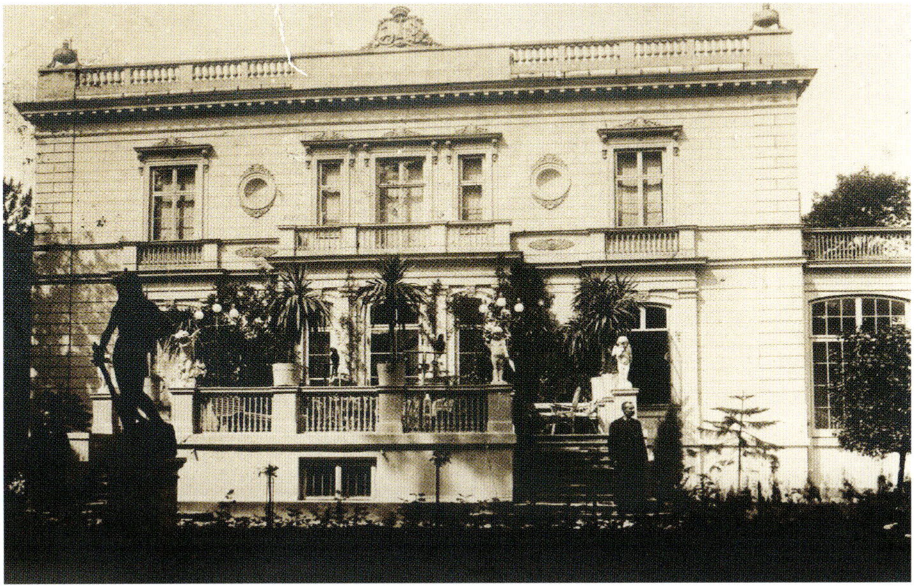

Fig. 5.7 | Sobański Villa in Warsaw, before 1906, postcard, National Library in Warsaw.

The Sobański family belonged to the richest Polish landowners in the Ruthenian part of the Russian Empire (formerly part of the Polish-Lithuanian Commonwealth), although they joined the ranks of the true aristocracy only in the mid-19th century. Unlike Rau, the Sobańskis had already achieved a secure elite status in the period of the villa's building, supported by their immense riches and relations with such well-established and old families as the Łubieńskis. The intended association of their mansion with the cultural heritage of the Renaissance was reinforced by a modern copy of Donatello's David, placed in front of the main façade, with David's face directed towards the street (and thus easily visible from outside by passers-by).[31] It seems that it was not only an evidence of cultural sophistication, but also a very subtle political message. The Sobański and Łubieńskis represented the same group of aristocrats as Zamoyski or Przezdziecki. They preferred to focus on their private wealth and in this way contribute to the repressed nation's economic development. They generally abstained from supporting patriotic radicals. Nevertheless, their Polish identity remained strong. In this case, Donatello's vision of the triumphant David trampling on his enemy's severed head could be interpreted as a symbol of the future Polish victory over a long-standing oppressor. However, it seems that the house originally lacked more direct references to Poland or Polishness in its external decoration. Only in 1912 did Emilia's son and successor adorn the main façade with busts of medieval kings of Poland: Casimir the Great and Vladislaus Jagiełło (two monarchs who started the Polish expansion towards Ruthenia). By this, he openly engaged the villa in the visual discourse of Polish patriotism.[32]

In the second half of the 19th century, such rich people as the Sobańskis and Raus shared not only a tendency to build their residences in the same area of Warsaw, but they also often engaged in the same economic ventures. It was the case of the Commercial Bank (*Bank Handlowy*) that proved to be the main source of credit for Polish entrepreneurs in the late 19th century, and a pillar of industrial development of the Kingdom.[33] The Bank was founded by Leopold Kronenberg, a banker and industrialist of Jewish descent (converted Calvinist) whose daughter married Zamoyski's nephew.[34] It was an ultimate example of how Warsaw's self-made men and aristocratic families became closely interconnected with each other during that period. Leandro Marconi designed the Warsaw headquarters of the Bank, not only a place of busy work, but also a space of representation. It was a two-storey corner building in the old centre of Warsaw, near Kronenberg's and Zamoyski's palaces. The pediment of its entrance façade held a clock face flanked by cornucopias, a salient allegory of the capitalist regime of work, lauded as a source of universal wealth. The side façades were inspired by such Renaissance Italian palaces as Palazzo Farnese in Rome or Palazzo Pitti w Florence.

WŁADYSŁAW MARCONI (1848–1915)

The youngest son of Enrico, Władysław, also chose to follow his father's example by becoming a professional architect. Born in Warsaw in 1848, he attended the real school in Warsaw, like his other brothers. He did not, however, have an opportunity to study and practice architecture under his father who died when he was only fifteen. Thus, he graduated from the Imperial Academy of Fine Arts in Petersburg. As a student, he won several medals for his architectural designs. On his return to Warsaw, he actively participated in many local initiatives. He was especially interested in the fate of old historical monuments. He co-founded the Society for the Protection of the Monuments of the Past (*Towarzystwo Opieki nad Zabytkami Przeszłości*).[35]

In the case of Władysław, his family's characteristic predilection for the heritage of Italian classical architecture found its most spectacular expression in a design for Bristol Hotel (Fig. 5.8) in Warsaw. The building stood opposite his father's Europejski Hotel. The constant development of Warsaw as the Kingdom's metropolis and commercial hub at the turn of the 20th century made it necessary to provide native and foreign visitors with new modern and luxurious facilities. However, unlike Europejski Hotel, built half a century before, Bristol Hotel was sponsored not by aristocrats or foreigners, but affluent Polish investors of middle-class background – lawyers, managers, engineers and middle landowners. It was a sign of the times, since there had been previously few Polish capitalists (except blue-blooded landowners) who could invest in such ventures. The company was led by the world-famous pianist Ignacy Jan Paderewski, also a businessman.[36]

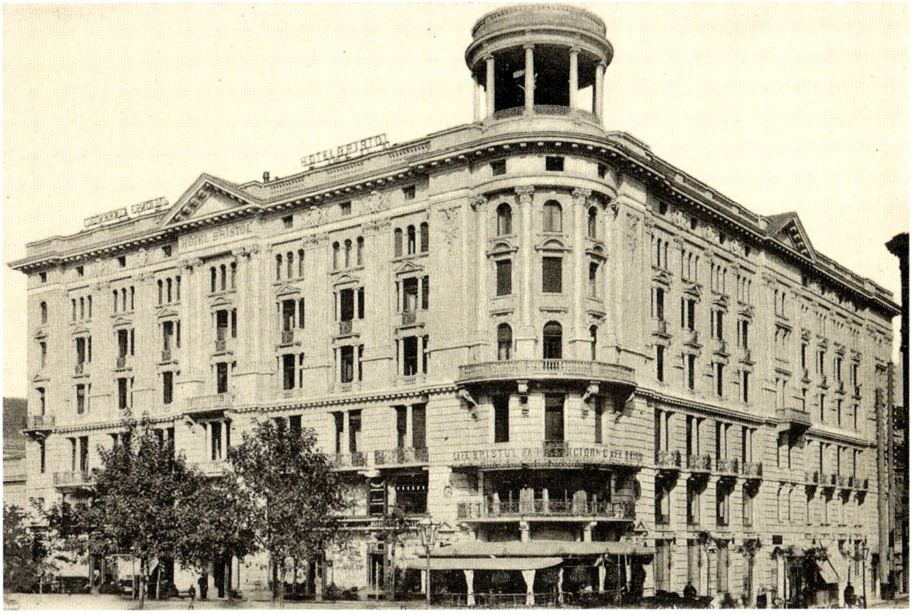

Fig. 5.8 | Hotel Bristol in Warsaw, before 1914, postcard, National Library in Warsaw.

The original Art Nouveau design of the exterior was provided by Tadeusz Stryjeński and Franciszek Mączyński. The proposal was, however, rejected by the owners. The fashionable, but still rather unconventional design was expected to deter potential clients whose tastes could be more conservative. Too much was at stake to risk such an innovation. Therefore, Władysław was invited to redesign the project by adding column, pediments and other classical ornaments to the original structure (although the interior was designed in the Vienna Secession style).[37] The classical exterior of Warsaw's Hotel Bristol evidenced that even at the beginning of the 20th century classicism was still a powerful instrument of legitimacy and social recognition.

Like his brother Leandro, Władysław also had an opportunity to contribute to the architectural development of the Baths Garden area. Ca. 1910, he designed a neo-Renaissance villa for Stefan Dziewulski (Fig. 5.9), built on the site of the former villa of the Princes Lubomirski, not far from Rau's house (already then occupied by Princess Radziwiłł).[38] Dziewulski was not an industrialist or aristocrat, but a barrister and economist with a penchant for academic studies and social activism.[39] He belonged to a specific social class known as the intelligentsia (Polish: *inteligencja*). It was a status group that encompassed university-educated professionals such as teachers, journalists or academics. It played a very important role in the Polish political and cultural life in the long 19th century, albeit disproportionate to its relative economic weakness (when compared to capitalists or great landowners).[40]

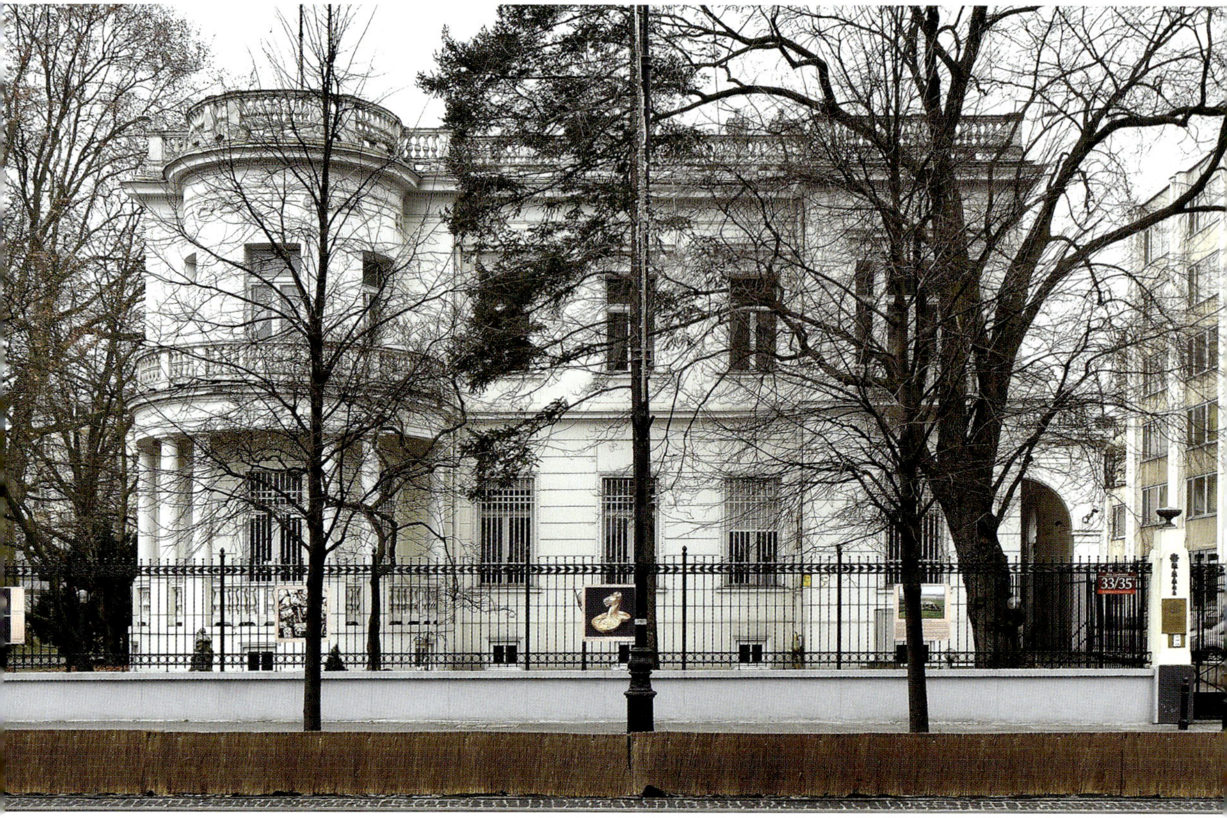

Fig. 5.9 | Dziewulski Villa in Warsaw, 2017, photograph by A. Grycuk, from: Wikipedia Commons.

Like many other families of that social status, the Dziewulskis had distant noble roots, but Stefan's parents were landless and his father earned his living as teacher. Stefan owed his unusual economic elevation to his wife Antonina Natanson, an only daughter and heiress of a rich banker. Their Warsaw mansion, sharing some characteristic similarities with Rau-turned-Radziwiłł Villa, was not only a symbol of his spectacular social rise, but it also hinted at the intelligentsia's aristocratic complex and a sense of inferiority. The architecture of the villa, designed during the heyday of the Art Nouveau, was strikingly traditionalist in both external form and decoration, and apparently intended to perfectly harmonise with its much older architectural neighbours.[41] Like Bristol Hotel in Krakowskie Przedmieście, the house of the Dziewulskis was not intended to stand out in that elite neighbourhood.

Władysław designed also country houses. The most spectacular commission of that kind came from the Karski family for whom Marconi rebuilt their old manor house in Włostów near Sandomierz (Fig. 5.10).[42] At the turn of the 20th century, the Karskis belonged to the highest echelons of the Kingdom's landed elite, although

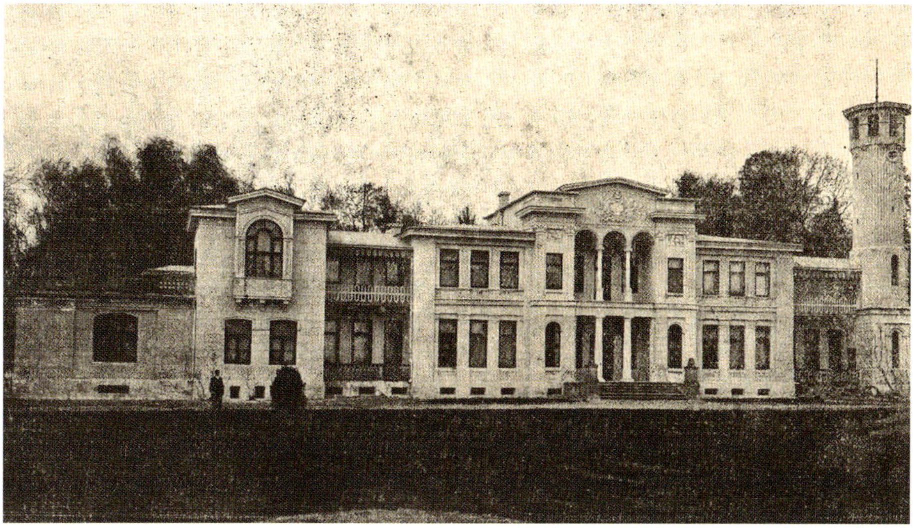

Fig. 5.10 | Karski Palace in Włostów, ca. 1915, from: J. Wiśniewski, Dekanat sandomierski, Radom 1915.

– like the Sobańskis – they managed to enter the ranks of the (though untitled) aristocracy only in the previous century. Unlike the Pacs or Zamoyskis, they were devoid of famous ancestors from the pre-partition period. However, the site, on which they wanted to erect their new stately home, had its own history that proved to be a source of prestige for its owners. In the 17th century, there was a parish of the Polish Brethren (also known as Arians) in Włostów. That protestant movement, started already in mid-16th century, was an important, although ill-fated phenomenon of the Polish Reformation and, more generally, the Polish Renaissance culture.[43] The Karskis were Catholic, but they apparently appreciated that their estate was part of Poland's history, since they renovated an old granary house, standing next to the future palace, already in the mid-19th century. According to a legend, the granary originally served as an Arian church (remarkably, it was renovated in the neo-Gothic style probably because of the owner's intention to emphasize its old age).[44] The palace itself was an example of an eclectic design, in which the predominance of the Renaissance mixed with Baroque and Gothic. Its picturesque façade was dominated by the family's large coat-of-arms directly above the entrance, an ultimate emblem of their highly cherished noble status.

CONCLUSION

The history of the Marconi architectural family and their classical designs is a good example of how the socio-cultural context determined the development of Polish architecture in the long 19th century. Their classical designs, inspired by different historical sources of inspiration, responded to the Polish elite's preoccupation with social change after the collapse of the Polish-Lithuanian Commonwealth.

The popularity of the classical idiom among the Marconis' cultured elite clientele, both native and naturalised, was motivated not only by its prestigious historical background but also more general associations with permanence and stability. In all the above-mentioned examples, the crucial issue was legitimacy. All those buildings existed because of their initiators' ambitions and aspirations that were either progressive and challenging established norms, or conservative and born out of fears of status decline during the period of modern transformation. The heterogenous classicism of the Marconis engaged in those discourses of the national elite's insecure status and identity by providing them with more or less specific historical connections. The longevity of the problem resulted in the prolonged demand for the Marconis' services as providers of classical designs.

NOTES

1. See Wojciech Tygielski, "The Italian presence in early modern Poland. Its cultural and civilizational consequences," in "Italien–Mitteldeutschland–Polen: Geschichte und Kultur im europäischen Kontext vom 10. bis zum 18. Jahrhundert," ed. Wolfgang Huschner, Enno Bünz, Christian Lübke, special issue, *Schriften zur sächsischen Geschichte and Volkskunde* 42 (2013): 761–76; Callogero Bellanca, "Architecture from 17th to 18th centuries in Poland," in *Architectural Conservation Studio, ed.* Callogero Bellanca (Roma: Sapienza Università Editrice, 2019), 159–176.
2. Barbara Arciszewska, *Classicism and Modernity: Architectural Thought in Eighteenth-Century Britain (*Warszawa: Neriton, 2010), 477.
3. *Ibid*., 24.
4. Stanisław Łoza, *Henryk Marconi i jego rodzina* (Warszawa: Instytut Urbanistyki i Architektury, 1954), 8–10.
5. See Jarosław Czubaty, *The Duchy of Warsaw, 1807–1815. A Napoleonic Outpost in Central Europe* (London: Bloomsbury, 2014); Frank W. Thackeray, *Antecedents of Revolution. Alexander I and the Polish Kingdom, 1815–1825* (Boulder: Columbia University Press, 1980).
6. See Mikołaj Getka-Kenig, "Pałac Andrzeja Deskura w Sancygniowie a problem upamiętnienia wielkich rodaków na elewacjach rezydencji ziemiańskich w Królestwie Kongresowym," *Rocznik Historii Sztuki* 44 (2019): 54–57.
7. Łoza, *Henryk Marconi*, 10.
8. Daniel Beauvois, "Le developpement d'une capitale. Varsovie, 1815-1830," Revue d'Histoire Moderne & Contemporaine, 18, no. 1 (1971): 94; Mikolaj Getka-Kenig, "Architektura i prestiż nowoczesnego urzędu. Przypadek budynków ministerialnych w Warszawie, stolicy konstytucyjnego Królestwa Polskiego (1815–1830)." in *Urzędnicy i urzędy w społeczeństwie XIX wieku*, ed. Alicja Kulecka (Warszawa:WUW, 2017), 39-49. See Aleksander Łupienko, *Order in the Streets. The Political History of Warsaw's Public Space in the First Half of the 19th Century*, trans. Jarek Garliński (Frankfurt am Main: Peter Lang AG, 2020).
9. Aldona Bartczakowa, *Pałac Paca* (Warszawa: PWN, 1973), 68.
10. Łoza, *Henryk Marconi*, 12.
11. See Maciej Janowski, *Polish Liberal Thought before 1918*, trans. Danuta Przekop (Budapest: CEU Press, 2004), 118.
12. Stefan Kieniewicz, *Między ugodą a rewolucją. Andrzej Zamoyski w latach 1861–1862* (Warszawa: PWN, 1962), 11–12.
13. Łoza, *Henryk Marconi*, 37.

14. Łoza, *Henryk Marconi*, 52.
15. Andrzej Rottermund, *Hotel Europejski* (Warszawa: PWN, 1972), 46.
16. *Ibid.*, 26.
17. *Ibid.*, 30.
18. Piotr Krasny and Michał Kurzej, "Kościół św. Karola Boromeusza na ulicy Chłodnej w Warszawie," in *Święty Karol Boromeusz a sztuka w Kościele powszechnym, w Polsce, w Niepołomicach*, ed. Piotra Krasnego and Michała Kurzeja (Kraków: DodoEditor, 2013), 127–128.
19. *Ibid.*, 136.
20. *Ibid.*, 146–147
20. Łoza, *Henryk Marconi*, 41–42.
22. Łoza, *Henryk Marconi*, 36.
23. Sławomir Łotysz, "89mm from Europe. Mediating Railway Mobility on Russia's Western Peripheries," in *Peripheral Flows. A Historical Perspective on Mobilities between Cores and Fringes*, ed. Simone Fari, Massimo Moraglio (Newcastle upon Tyne: Cambridge Scholars Publishing, 2016), 105.
24. Krzysztof Stefański, *Architektura XIX wieku na ziemiach polskich* (Warszawa: DiG, 2005), 72–73.
25. *Ibid.*, 53–54.
26. *Ibid.*, 54.
27. Jerzy Kubiatowski, "Rau Wilhelm Ellis," in *Polski Słownik Biograficzny*, vol. 30, ed. Emanuel Rostworowski (Wrocław: Ossolineum, 1987), 646–7.
28. Jadwiga Roguska, "Warszawska willa przemysłowca Raua," in *Podług nieba i zwyczaju polskiego. Studia z historii architektury, sztuki i kultury ofiarowane Adamowi Miłobędzkiemu*, ed. Zbigniew Bania et al. (Warszawa:PWN, 1988), 459–460, 464.
29. *Ibid.*, 462.
30. Tadeusz S. Jaroszewski, *Księga pałaców Warszawy* (Warszawa: Interpress, 1985), 145; Jarosław Zieliński, *Atlas dawnej architektury ulic i placów Warszawy*, vol. 1 (Warszawa: TOZ, 1995), 70.
31. Zieliński, *Atlas*, 71.
32. *Ibid.*, 71.
33. Zbigniew Landau and Jerzy Tomaszewski, *Bank Handlowy w Warszawie S. A.: zarys dziejów 1870-1995* (Warszawa: Muza, 1995).
34. Andrzej Żor, *Kronenberg: Dzieje fortuny* (Warszawa: PWN, 2011), 206.
35. Łoza, *Henryk Marconi*, 57-58.
36. Ewa Pustoła-Kozłowska and Jacek Pustoła, *Hotel Bristol* (Warszawa: PWN, 1985), 39.
37. *Ibid.*, 33–34.
38. Tadeusz Stefan Jaroszewski, "Architektura rezydencjonalna wielkiej burżuazji warszawskiej w latach 1864–1914", in *Sztuka XIX wieku w Polsce. Naród – miasto* (Warszawa: PWN, 1979), 182.
39. "Stefan Dziewulski," in *Polski słownik biograficzny,* vol. 6, ed. Władysław Konopczyński (Wrocław: PAU, 1948), 176–177.
40. See Jerzy Jedlicki, Maciej Janowski, Magdalena Micińska, *A History of Polish Intelligentsia*, vol. 1–3 (Frankfurt am Main: Peter Lang, 2014).
41. Jaroszewski, *Architektura rezydencjonalna*, 182–183; Zieliński, *Atlas*, 74.
42. Łoza, *Henryk Marconi*, 59; Juliusz Karski, "Włostów – dzieje pałacu i miejscowości oraz znaczenie jego mieszkańców od początku istnienia do upadku," in *Dwór polski. Zjawisko historyczne i kulturowe*, ed. by Tadeusz Stefan Jaroszewski (Warszawa: SHS, 2000), 498.
43. See George Huntson Williams, ed., *The Polish Brethern: documentation of the history and thought of Unitarianism in the Polish-Lithuanian Commonwealth and in the Diaspora 1601–1685,* vol. 1–2 (Cambridge: Scholars Press, 1980).
44. Jerzy Łoziński and Barbara Wolff, *Katalog zabytków sztuki w Polsce*, vol. 3, no. 11 (Warszawa: IS PAN, 1962), 119.

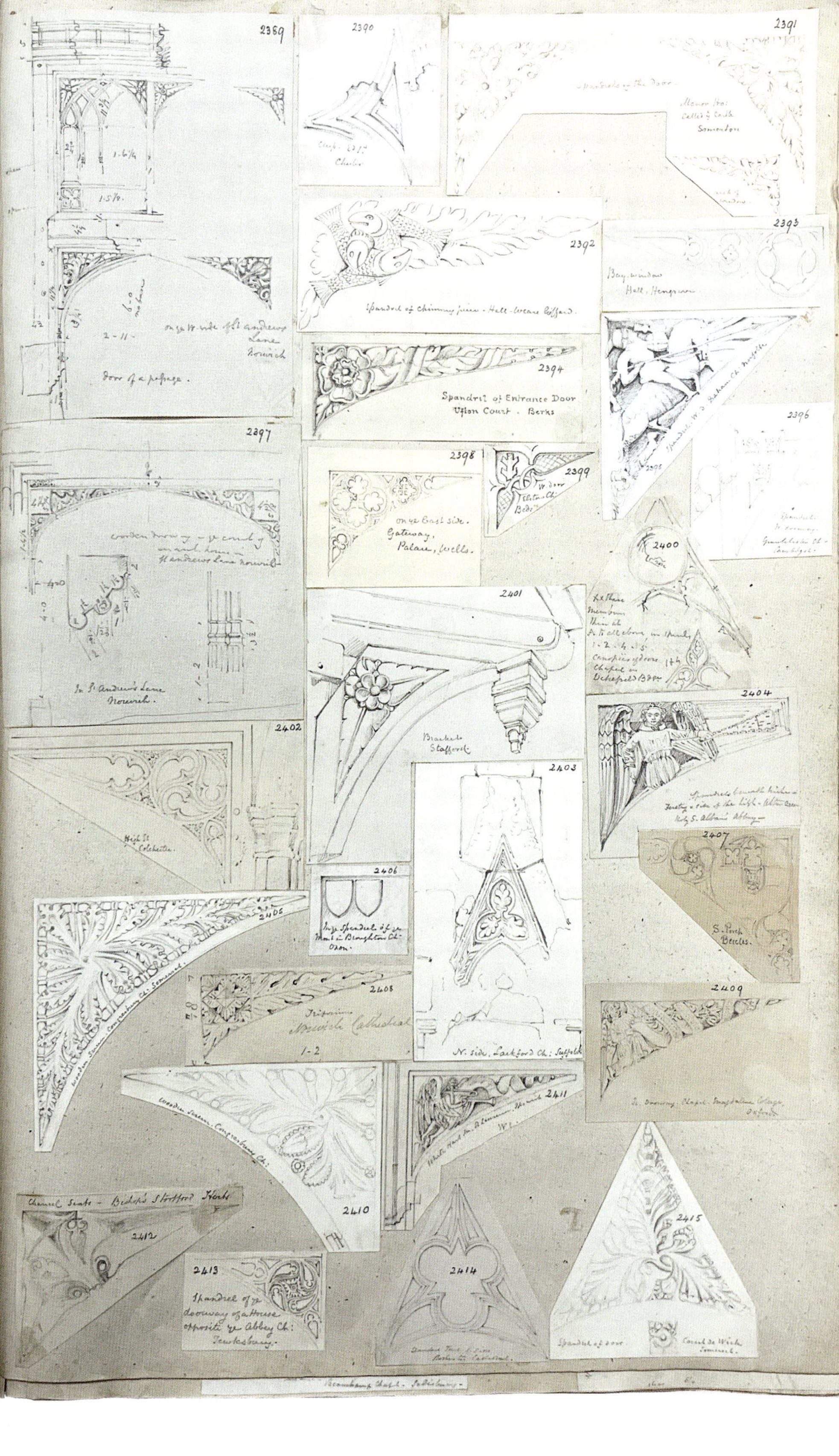
2389
on ye W. side of St Andrews Lane Norwich
door of a passage
2390
2391
Manor Ho: called ye Castle Somerton
2392
Spandrel of chimney piece - Hall - Weare Giffard.
2393
Bay window Hall, Hengrave
2394
Spandril of Entrance Door Upton Court . Berks
2396
2397
In St Andrew's Lane Norwich
2398
on ye East side. Gateway, Palace, Wells.
2399
2400
2401
Brackets Stafford
2402
High St Colchester
2403
N. side, Lackford Ch: Suffolk
2404
2405
Wooden Screen. Congresbury Ch: Somerset
2406
2407
S. Porch Beccles.
2408
Triforium Norwich Cathedral
2409
2410
Wooden Screen. Congresbury Ch:
2412
Chancel Seats - Bishop's Stortford Herts
2413
Spandrel of ye doorway of a house opposite ye Abbey Ch: Tewksbury.
2414
2415
Spandrel of door

6 · Fables and Gables: the Buckler Dynasty of Architects and Antiquarian Draughtsmen

JOSHUA MARDELL

The Bucklers gloried in the archaic. As Sir George Gilbert Scott described his Gothic kinsmen in 1866: 'The bent of their minds for three generations has been in the mediaeval line'.[1] He was referring to three generations of architects, antiquaries and artists, all impassioned actors in the late Georgian and Victorian Gothic Revival, namely: John Buckler (1770–1851), his son John Chessell Buckler (1793–1894), and his son in turn, Charles Alban Buckler (1824–1905). George Buckler (1811–1866), the youngest son of John, was also an architect and antiquarian, who became an informal archivist and chronicler of his family, helping (self-consciously or otherwise) to construct a dynastic identity.[2] In the process of researching this cadre of Gothic purists, I came to realise that they were much more than the sum of their parts. They exemplified the obsessive desire to create an architectural dynasty, and according to the romantic claim of George Buckler, 'worked together in perfect harmony without any confusion of labour'.[3] Hence, *The Catholic World* in 1872 remarked that 'it may be said with peculiar significance [that John Chessell] has let his mantle fall on the heir [Charles Alban] to his name and art.[4] What follows is an economical attempt to confront those peculiar hereditary claims, and examine how the Bucklers passed on their patrimony, how they constructed an idea of themselves as a family unit, and how they functioned as a social group of relatives within a larger profession.

The Bucklers, reactionary and anti-bourgeois, mythologised pre-capitalist stability. The medieval period offered an uncompromising view of a stratified social structure that appealed to conservatives (as well as later radicals, like William Morris). The Bucklers' choice of the Gothic can be seen as an expression on the part of the architects and their patrons to reinforce/reintroduce a feudal order of society much divorced from the social order under increased attack over

Fig. 6.1 | One page from the Bucklers' (mixed authorship) portfolios of architectural elements or 'mendums' [memoranda], this one showing a collection of specimens of medieval and neo-medieval spandrels, nd. London, British Library, Add MS 36430, f. 130.

the dynasty's lifespan, especially in the wake of the French Revolution, the Swing Riots (in which agricultural workers rose up in protest against agricultural mechanisation in the 1830s) and industrialisation. One way of considering the Buckler dynasty, then, is as a fail-safe against insecurity, as one (symbolic) manifestation of what Martin Bressani described as nineteenth-century architects' 'Romantic attempts at recovering the unity of an idealised past… [by] experimenting with architecture's capacity to create totalised worlds'.[5]

The Bucklers have not received much scholarly attention, and have consequently not occupied a significant place in the narrative of canonical architectural history. Yet they independently or collaboratively fulfilled a century's worth of commissions in the revived styles of English domestic and ecclesiastical architecture across the UK.[6] They were polemical figures in building conservation debates. They were industrious topographical draughtsmen who left behind an invaluable source for the archaeological record. It behoves us, therefore, to address this lacuna in our knowledge. While sparing vignettes outlining the careers of each Buckler will follow, to rediscover and frame the family and their significance, there are several areas which first need to be addressed: the fabulist aspects of the Bucklers' self-construction; their establishment of intellectual capital, or authority, as seen in the 'forbidding bulk' of their archive; and the networks of patronage that sustained them.[7]

The Bucklers produced a family history, *Bucleriana* (1886).[8] The proverb for its frontispiece is telling: 'the glory of children are their fathers'. It is suggestive of the centrality of the family unit in their life and work, a disposition commonly held in the nineteenth century; Eric Hobsbawm, for instance, noted the dominance of the 'small-scale family enterprise' or 'patriarchal family autocracy'.[9] If families are constructions, dynasties are yet more acutely self-constructed. Such constructions have to be maintained and perpetuated. The Bucklers' self-construction always had something of the heroic about it. It was akin to a fable.[10]

The most obvious example is their common adoption of the double-entendre of their family name – a small round shield, whose verb form means 'to shield, defend, protect'. It is used, for instance, as one of the chosen epigrams in *Bucleriana*:

> The Crown is He to guerdon,
> The Buckler to protect,
> And he Himself the Mansion
> And He the Architect.

This comes from Bernard of Cluny, the twelfth-century Benedictine monk, but was put into the popular hymnbook by the ecclesiologist Revd. John Mason Neale (1818–1866), who read it as 'a bitter satire on the fearful corruptions of the age' in contrast to the peace and glory of heaven.[11] It fits, therefore, with that other popular trope of the nineteenth century, 'contrasts' – as the Bucklers must have meant it, between a Gothic tradition and a profession that was heroic and one that was increasingly alien, and contemptible.[12] The Bucklers as defenders of medieval buildings, of forms of practice and no less of their reputation as individuals and as a dynasty, is a pertinent analogy.

The antiquary M.H. Bloxam identified John Buckler as among the most erudite of the early nineteenth-century professors of Gothic Architecture in 1836, before gothic knowledge was common knowledge among architects.[13] Evidence of the Bucklers' development of knowledge can be found in their archive, primarily at the British Library.[14] The collection was as much a means of educating the members of the dynasty as it was motivated by the practical means to produce buildings in a revived style. Dynastic self-consciousness was critical to its formulation, development and arrangement.

Just as the family entomologist (and miniature painter) William Buckler (1814–1884), sought to find order in the natural world, with his expertise in winged insects, the Buckler architects sought to find order in the man-made world, with their expertise in medieval architecture.[15] The dynasty's main portfolios at the British Library are ordered along typological lines (Fig. 6.1). They are demonstrative of the Bucklers' nurturing of the specialised antiquarian knowledge that informed their intellectual consciousness and architectural production, in addition to establishing their voice, position and reputation. A case in point is the use of the archive by John Chessell and Charles Alban when, in 1843, they (unsuccessfully) entered a competition held by the Yorkshire Architectural Society to restore the Wayside Chapel in Wakefield. In their submission, they had at their disposal the advantage of 'memoranda collected within the last thirty years during which period [they] have had opportunities for examining [the Bridge-Chapel], and of preserving with the pencil, the perishing forms of its architectural enrichment' (Fig. 6.2).[16] Their submission was labelled 'Fidelitas', reminiscent of the Buckler family's motto (*fidelitas ad mortem*), faithful unto death – in this case, this meant faithfulness to the Gothic tradition as inherited by their forefathers.

Dynasties were to a large extent created by their patrons. The Bucklers benefited mostly from a late eighteenth-century model of aristocratic patronage, and that of the Church of England and the universities.[17] As Joseph Mordaunt Crook pointed out, 'the noble patron and the family practice remained key factors long after British architecture is popularly supposed to have gone over to the "goddam bourgeoisie"', or, we might add, to the building committee.[18] Patrons of architecture seemingly had a stake in dynasties, as though a hereditary aristocracy saw excellence through pedigree. The Bucklers owed much of their early work to conservative aristocratic patrons, including proud-pedigreed old Catholics, and the ancient colleges of Oxford and Cambridge (among other lay patrons).

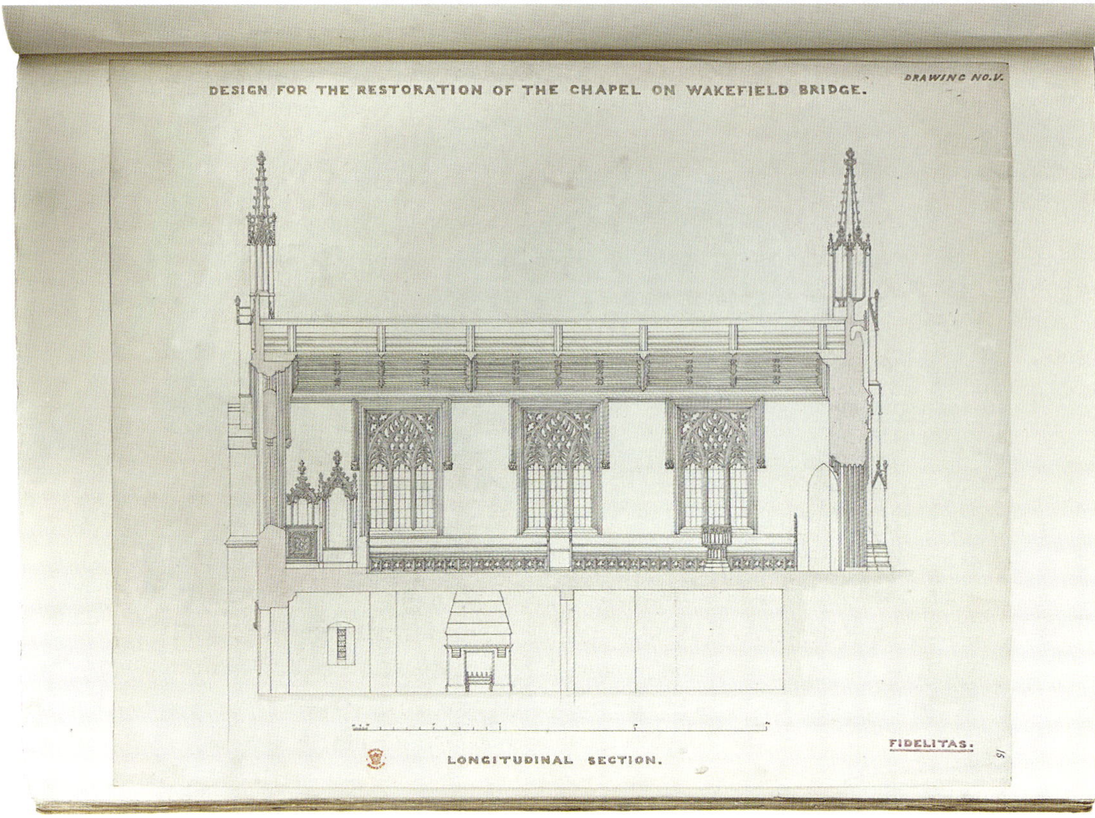

Fig. 6.2 | John Chessell and Charles Buckler, design for restoration of chapel on Wakefield bridge, West Riding of Yorkshire, *c.* 1843. London, British Library, Add MS 36402.

The Bucklers give the impression, at times self-consciously and quasi-aristocratically, that commercial gain was accessory to the value they placed on the relationship with their patrons, a relationship threatened by increased professionalism (as lamented more famously by Norman Shaw, T. G. Jackson, and (later) C. F. A. Voysey).[19] They viewed architecture not as a profession but as a duty and a calling – or they performed as though they did. A case in point is Charles Alban's seeming reluctance to take his salary when building the Catholic church at Exton Park, Rutland for the 2nd Earl of Gainsborough: 'The State of my Exchequer reminds me that I shall be obliged to ask of your Lordship the favour of £50… always reluctant to make any claim whatsoever.[20]Meanwhile of the works of heraldry that he carried out at Exton, 'I regard them as extra=professional'.[21] In Simon Bradley's words, Buckler was 'tugging his forelock in a sychophantic way'.[22]

In short, the Bucklers were invested in a model of patronage akin to that of the architect-gentleman. Or gentlewoman: Frances Jerningham, Lady Stafford, was reminiscent of the typical early eighteenth-century patron, so 'au fait with the latest canons of taste' that she assisted John Chessell conspicuously in the designs for the first phases of Costessey Hall, Norfolk, discussed below.[23] As artist-architects, the Bucklers flattered their patrons by drawing their country seats and, as thoroughgoing antiquarians, by producing pedigrees for them. In short, the Buckler dynasty resembled a 'Fable', a fiction invented to aggrandise the dynasty that was thereafter sustained by both those within and those who supported it. That fiction established and maintained 'Authority', and this 'Fable of Authority' enabled the Bucklers to secure a 'Patronage' that shared their stakes in historicising place, blood and buildings.

JOHN BUCKLER (1770–1851)

The dynasty's *paterfamilias* was born into a family of cordwainers, or upmarket shoe-makers, in Calbourne on the Isle of Wight. Our story really begins, however, in Oxford, 1785, when the fifteen-year-old John Buckler made a decisive move to Magdalen College to assist the Steward, Richard Barnard Fisher. He had known the Fishers from his birth place, including Col. George Bulteel Fisher, an amateur draughtsman who first encouraged his artistic pursuits. As Buckler recalled, 'at just eight years old I began to scratch and scrawl'.[24] His first exhibited architectural drawings at the Royal Academy depicted his college, and his view of it from the River Cherwell was subsequently published. Flanking the arms of the college founder, Bishop William Waynflete, and encircled by the Garter, is Buckler's dedication to the college Fellows and its President: his antiquarian employer, the Revd. Martin Routh (1755–1854). Over his sixty-three years as President, Routh took a considerable interest in architecture, and was the first President of the Oxford Society for the Promotion of Gothic Architecture. Thus, although Buckler served as the college bailiff (and factotum) until his retirement in 1849, Routh's encouragement enabled him to develop a prominent career as a topographical draughtsman and architect. Buckler recalled how he 'employed all his leisure time when engaged at the College in that pursuit'.[25]

The historian William Dunn Macray, a Fellow of Magdalen, remembered Routh as a 'quaint and venerable figure never seen by his study fire without wig, gown, bands, cassock and silver buckles invested with all the tradition that had gathered around him' – whimsical legend has it that he was the last man in England to wear a wig, a sign of his archaicism.[26] Oxford, then, was the appropriate breeding ground for the establishment of an antiquarian dynasty. One commentator's observation in this respect was most pertinent:

> No wonder that the spirit of medieval days should have descended on this favoured family [the Bucklers], since their dwelling place for a long time was the matchless old city of Oxford. There is a magic in that name that has a creative artistic suggestion in its very sound.[27]

John Buckler journeyed the country, assiduously recording its medieval architectural inheritance, enabled by widespread antiquarian patronage, such as that of Thomas Lister Parker, for whom he and John Chessell drew 'Castellated and Domestic Architecture of England and Wales' (n.d.) (Fig. 6.3), or Thomas Dunham Whitaker for whom Buckler and J. M. W. Turner drew *A Series of Views of the Most Picturesque Scenes in Richmondshire* (1843).[28] This appetite was inherited by his children, leading John Harris to describe the family as 'peripatetic in their artistic thirst'.[29] Buckler is perhaps best remembered today for his aquatint engravings of the cathedrals and abbey churches of England and Wales, which he began self-publishing in the 1790s, benefiting from a market spawned by patriotism.[30]

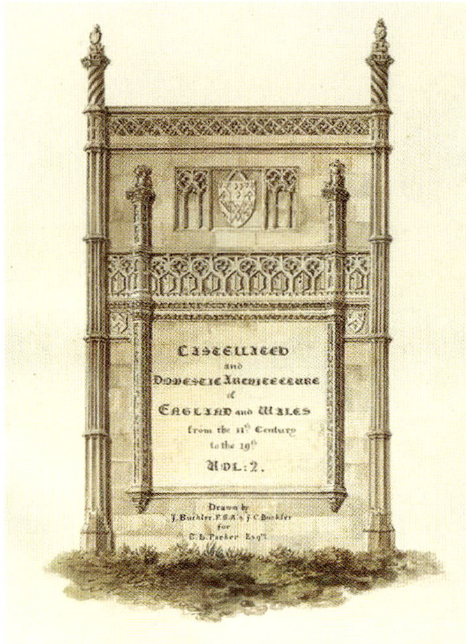

Fig. 6.3 | John Buckler and John Chessell Buckler. Title Page of 'Castellated and Domestic Architecture of England and Wales from the 11th Century to the 19th', vol. 2. for T. L. Parker, nd. New Haven, Yale Center for British Art, nd., B1991.40.1.

A fellow of the Society of Antiquaries of London from 1810, he belonged to a radical and romantic clan nominally led by the antiquaries John Carter, Richard Gough and Sir Richard Colt Hoare that helped revive the Gothic and develop a new scientific form of archaeology.[31] The strict historicism stemming from the Carter school remained the most potent 'theory' to the Bucklers; the other key strand was their preference for 'conservation' (as we would now understand it) over 'restoration'.[32] The Bucklers usually set out to conserve as much medieval (albeit seldom *post*-medieval) fabric as possible, rather than destroying traces in favour of an imagined medieval design.

John Buckler designed several 'castellated' mansions from the 1820s onwards, most notably Pool Park (Denbighshire, 1826–1829) for the 2nd Baron Bagot (Fig. 6.4), an early example of a neo-Elizabethan country house, with half-timbering (of plaster) to the upper storey, and Halkyn Castle, Clywd, a simple essay in Tudor Gothic (1824–27) replete with hood moulds, mullioned and transomed windows, castellated turrets, towers and stacks built for the 2nd Earl Grosvenor, later Marquis of Westminster, Tory and then Whig MP. Buckler occasionally designed 'monastic' houses, such as Sundorne Castle, Shropshire (1820), on the site of Haughmond Abbey, and Abbey House Glastonbury (1829–30), constructed with a view over the ruins of Glastonbury Abbey.[33] Buckler's corpus includes only a handful of churches, including St. John the Baptist at Pentrobin, Flintshire (1843), early in its adoption of ecclesiological ideas of style and internal decoration. It was built at the expense of Sir Stephen Glynne, Tory politician and antiquary who would later become the Vice-President of the Ecclesiological (late Cambridge Camden) Society. In line with his interest in the Oxford college founders, Buckler was also responsible for Bishop Waynflete's Chantry Chapel at Winchester Cathedral (1828); Waynflete (sometime Bishop of Winchester and Lord Chancellor) had founded Magdalen College in 1458.

Buckler's 'good health and spirits' enabled him to live 'far beyond the limits of the span assigned by the Psalmist to mortality', as one obituarist put it following his death aged eighty-one in 1851.[34] In fact, all three generations of the dynasty enjoyed a considerable longevity advantage over many of their contemporaries.[35] This meant that not only did each of our protagonists have long careers, but they overlapped with one another in adulthood, and so, professionally. Furthermore, one key mechanism for the success of an architectural dynasty, and the maintenance of a commitment to the Gothic, was the pupillage system of architectural education, owing to its 'efficient transmission of an inherited bias towards some particular style'.[36] The Bucklers' training was inter-dynastic and autodidactic. John Chessell had been John Buckler's 'only assistant and companion from early in this century', and Charles Alban was in turn his father's only pupil, as we see in his portrait, looking younger than the 15 or 16 years when one would typically begin pupillage (Fig. 6.5).[37]

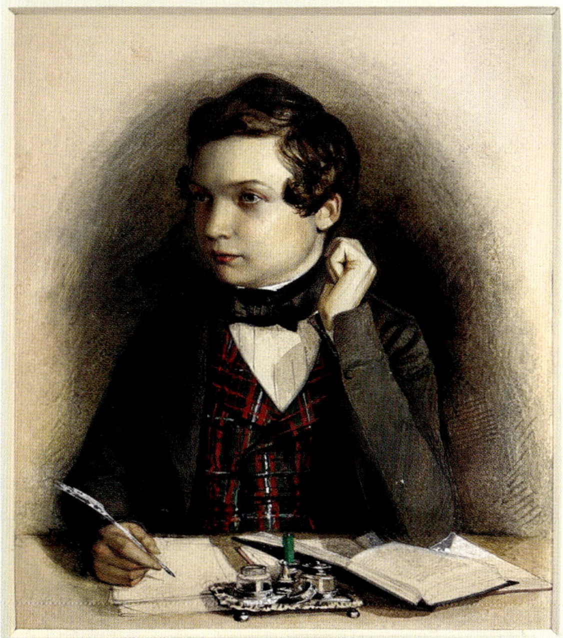

Fig. 6.5 | Portrait of C. A. Buckler, watercolour by Thomas Hollis, n.d., *c.* 1830s. London, British Library, Add MS 37120, f. 2.

While taste-based partisanship, exaggerated through journalistic fantasy as the 'Battle of the Styles', might have clarified the appeal of a dynasty to clients, the Bucklers show that being Gothicists was not merely a formal or advantageous choice, but a whole identity, for it was in Gothic architecture 'where religion loves to dwell'.[38] John Buckler turned away from design, however, preferring 'the study of architecture as an artist'.[39] When he was asked, on his retirement in 1849, to give an 'account of the collection of sketches over the last half-century', he did so only with fulsome apology, concluding, after a couple of paragraphs: 'I am afraid I shall have tried your patience… I have never said so much about myself before[,] I hope you will excuse garrulous old age'.[40] Resisting biography, the Bucklers presented themselves as objective and neutral agents.[41] John Buckler died in 1851.

JOHN CHESSELL BUCKLER (1793–1894)

John Chessell established his own reputation as a topographical artist on the back of his father's name, initially through the reappropriation of his published prints of cathedrals into a new context, as the market for the antique widened, necessitating cheaper circulation. While the more direct patronage which his father had enjoyed was no longer available, he actively joined the wave of antiquarian-topographical publications after the Battle of Waterloo (by John Britton, E.W. Brayley, J. P. Neale and others). This culminated in *Views of the Cathedrals of England and Wales* (1822), with an accompanying letterpress, that bestowed on its author 'a kind of hereditary claim on the admirers of Cathedral antiquities'.[42] His surveys of medieval buildings were still more meticulous than his father's. He also (unlike his father) contributed to the promotion and development of the Gothic Revival through narrative publications.[43] He felt, in particular, that domestic typologies had been neglected in the discourse, and specifically 'that the investigation of any perfect house of remote antiquity would prove a subject of considerable interest'.[44] While the sources were largely assembled by 1810, when John Chessell was aged 17, his *An Historical and Descriptive Account of the Royal Palace at Eltham* was not published until 1828.[45]

John Chessell built a substantial practice as an architect, including designing the picturesque Perpendicular palace, Toddington Manor (1819–1840), for Charles Hanbury-Tracy, 1st Baron Sudeley. He was a major beneficiary, moreoever, of Catholic patronage, albeit Buckler himself was a protestant. His largest commission was the rambunctious Costessey Hall, Norfolk (*c.*1825–1870), for the Stafford-Jerningham family – a palimpsest of Tudor Gothic details, described by John Claudius Loudon as no less than 'the richest Gothic building in England' (Fig. 6.6).[46] Chris Brooks found it astonishing, 'its red-brick ranges running every which way about the base of a massive tower'.[47] In commissioning Buckler to rebuild their seat, the Stafford-Jerninghams sought to both legitimise lineal descent following Catholic Emancipation (albeit building commenced before the passing of the Catholic

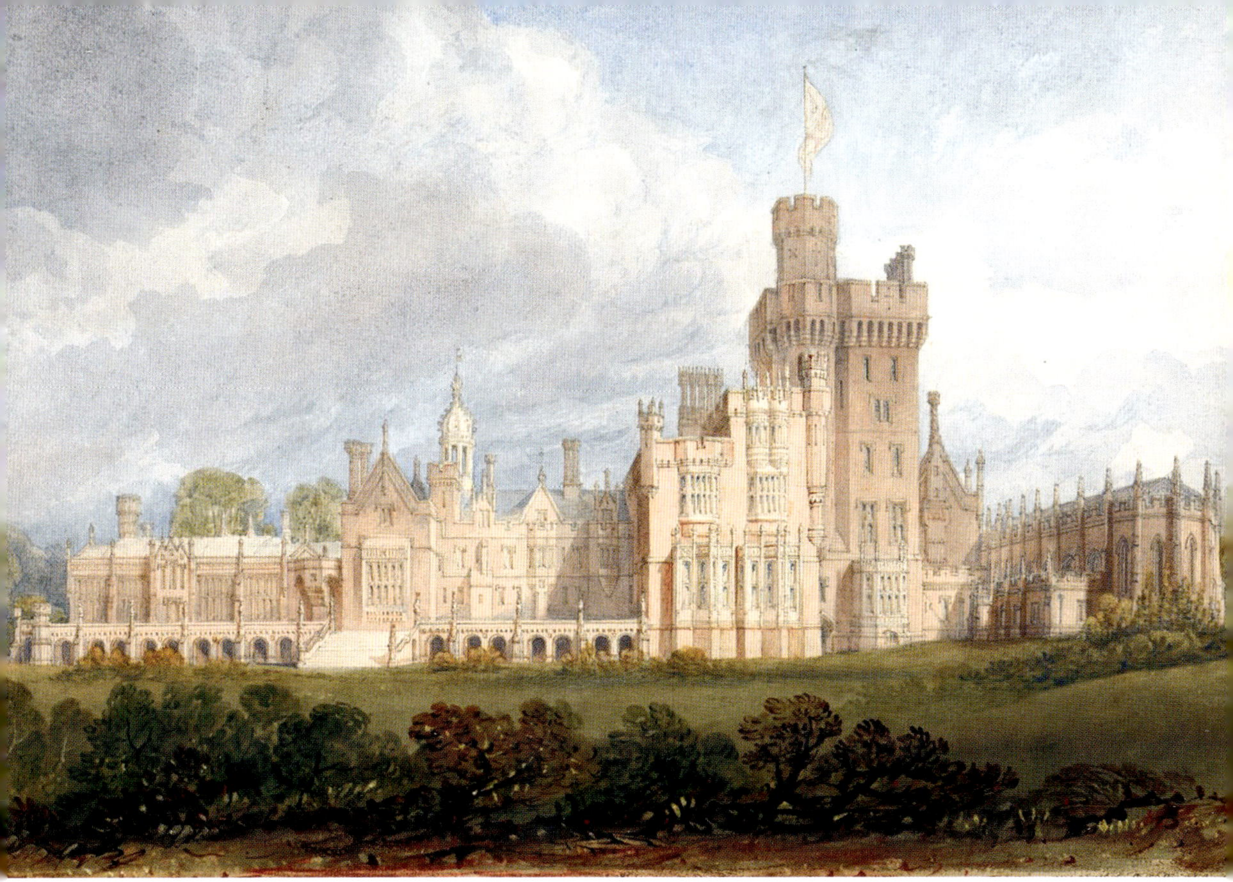

Fig. 6.6 | John Chessell Buckler, Costessey Hall, Norfolk, 1831. Graphite, pen and brown ink, and watercolour. New Haven, Yale Center for British Art, B1975.2.363.

Emancipation Act in 1829), and to maintain power among their own religious community as the working-class and poor (especially Irish) Catholic population was rapidly expanding. Respecting the existing medieval inheritance, John Chessell carried out much more reticent re-edifications at the fifteenth-century moated manor house, Oxburgh Hall (1826–*c.*1865), in the same county, for the Stafford-Jerningham's Catholic relatives, the Bedingfelds. In short, John Chessell can be seen as having partook in what Crook called the 'battle for the re-conversion of England'.[48] This is reminiscent of the titular antiquary in Walter Scott's novel who, with the help of the heralds, helped to preserve the recusant Glenallan aristocracy, 'the reestablishment of dying houses [and] the restoration of dynasties'.[49]

John Chessell accompanied his inherited skills and Gothic predilection with a rhetoric and force of his own. He was an impassioned preservationist (and gadfly) who so often 'agitated in defence of … old buildings'.[50] With a disposition rooted in the Carter school of his father's generation, he discussed architecture in a relentlessly acidic, moralising tone, over a decade before A.W. N. Pugin wrote *Contrasts* (1836). A case in point is Buckler's strongly worded pamphlet aimed at preventing the demolition of the Old Quadrangle of Magdalen College, Oxford, in 1822.[51]

The outrage voiced by Buckler and others mostly saved the cloister of the north range from destruction, with the demolished parts quickly rebuilt in a manner advocated by Buckler and his father. While published anonymously, Oxford readers would have been very familiar with Buckler's distinctive 'haughty tone of challenge'.[52]

A contingent narrative in *Observations* can be found in overlong footnotes in the book that offered the vestiges of John Chessell's thoughts on Gothic architecture, such as:

> The only style of Architecture in which embellishment resigns all her charms to utility, is the ancient Grecian; that where use and ornament claim an equal share of the patron's bounty… is what we falsely call 'Gothic'.[53]

As Rosemary Hill put it: 'His [John Chessell's] writings are full of ideas that Pugin was credited in the twentieth century with inventing, such as the precept that a building should express its various functions in its different elements.'[54] There is a rationalist strand conditioning Buckler's thinking here, at a time when rationalist theory was not being widely (or consistently) disseminated through publications in the UK; albeit such an inclination was not further developed by Buckler subsequently.[55]

John Chessell briefly worked in collaboration with his brother, George, when in 1839 he was invited to enter a competition, along with E. M. Foxhall, A.W. N. Pugin and J. J. Scoles, to design the new Catholic church of St. George's, Southwark, which was to accommodate growing numbers of Catholic worshippers owing to the influx of Irish immigrants to working-class districts in Walworth.[56] Although the commission eventually went to Pugin, the *Gentleman's Magazine* praised 'the truly English [design] of the Messrs. Buckler', for a key strand of their oeuvre was their all but unwavering Anglocentrism as designers.[57]

All three generations had a long-lasting preference for the Perpendicular on the one hand – so much of it survived, and was the subject of many of their drawings – and the Early English, on the other. By mid-century, both styles were squeezed out on either side by the fashionable 'Middle Pointed'.[58] The Bucklers stayed with them. Their interest in concepts of stability could act as a welcome foil against the more general focus on differentiation within the Revival when attitudes as to the meaning of Gothic, or its best means of adoption, were ever prone to equivocation – even extreme confusion and anxiety.

John Chessell also had many commissions from Magdalen, Jesus, Brasenose and Oriel colleges in Oxford, and from Magdalene College in Cambridge.[59] In 1864, for instance, while Thomas Deane was overseeing the erection of the Meadow Buildings at Christ Church and William Butterfield those at Merton, John Chessell was 'faithfully' and 'with great care' restoring the early sixteenth-century gateway and tower over at Brasenose.[60] While George Gilbert Scott's chapel at Exeter

College (1856–9) and Deane and Woodward's University Museum were being erected (1855–60), John Chessell and Charles Alban contemporaneously built a wholly unassuming new front to Jesus College. At Oriel, the Bucklers' restoration of the gateway in 1864 was so much a facsimile that one can discern no difference between it and the gateway in Loggan's print of 1675. They also quietly restored the most characteristic and memorable motives at Oriel: the shaped gables topping the elevations of the front and middle quadrangles (Fig. 6.7).[61]

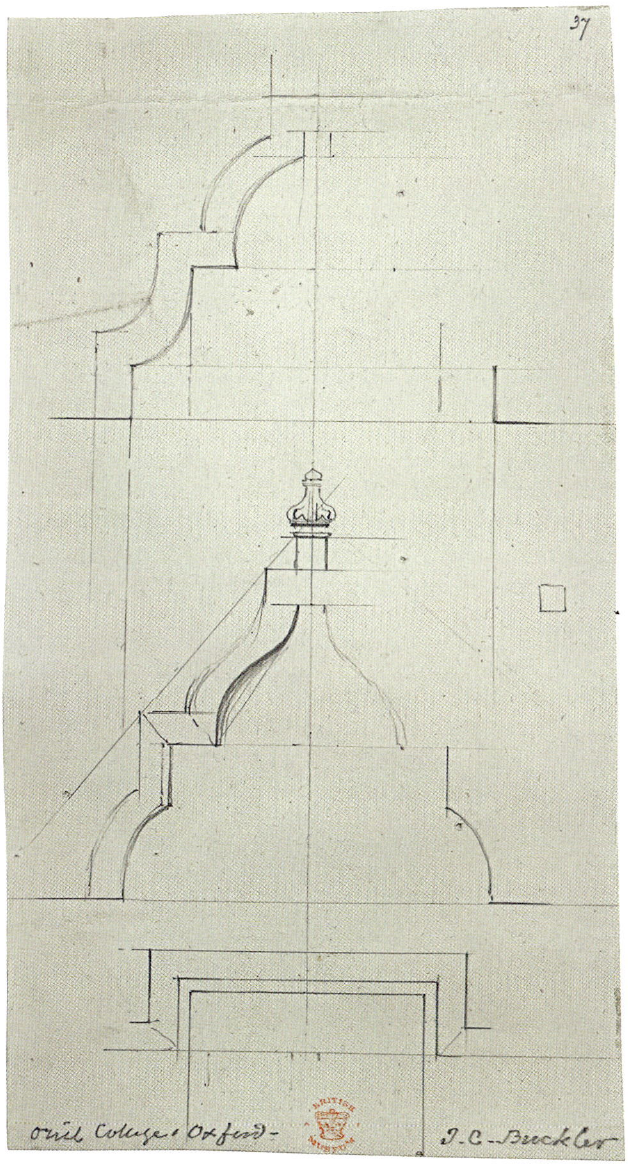

Fig. 6.7 | John Chessell Buckler, undated sketch of gables at Oriel College, n..d. London, British Library, Add MS 36423, f. 37.

The nature of Bucklers' work in Oxford might be seen in line with the eighteenth-century 'medievalizing spirit' at the colleges, mostly 'cosmetic in character'.[62] Buckler was working in a tradition spanning from the early nineteenth-century when many colleges had begun to confront the decay of their facades, especially those faced in Headington stone, matching the refacings with new stone (and sometimes upgrading to ashlar, such as Corpus Christi, in 1804). Rather than 'innovating', Buckler was continuing an Oxford artisan tradition albeit with a greater degree of knowledge of style, and a greater readiness to expunge 'impure' post-medieval forms in favour of the Perpendicular collegiate vernacular.[63] If the wealth of tradition in the ancient institutions often relied on the associative power of Gothic, John Chessell helped 'maintain' it in a nuanced, at times a literal way, in work characterized by its humility that, was concerned less with newness, as with existing buildings' more enduring temporalities. This aligns with Hilary Sample's understanding of what she calls 'maintenance architecture', which she claims 'represents an investment in the persistence of architecture – both as an image and as an ideal'.[64]

Outside of Oxford, John Chessell in 1834 painstakingly recreated the fifteenth-century chancel fittings and Perpendicular tracery at St. Mary Adderbury, Banbury (Oxon., a living of New College, Oxford). The historian Edward Freeman approved of the work, later observing that 'nothing could be more creditable to the restorers'.[65] Yet, 'maintenance architecture' aside, there were more destructive instances. At St. Mary the Virgin, Iffley (Oxon.), the otherwise pro-'Perp.' John Chessell, with the assistance of Charles Alban, replaced the existing Perpendicular window on the west front. He reinstated the Norman oculus window based on traces of one that survived in the fabric.[66] Furthermore, where John Chessell, often in collaboration with Charles Alban, undertook church restorations enabled by grants from the Incorporated Church Building Society, to increase the 'sittings', to allow for a larger congregation, much medieval fabric was removed. For instance, although retaining much of the Norman fabric, and the twelfth- century west tower at St. Mary the Virgin, Dover (1843–4), the Bucklers' additions left in their wake a considerable loss of medieval fabric.

Buckler was employed as cathedral architect to Lincoln Cathedral from 1859–66. His authority was questioned and substantially diminished when he was widely accused of a damaging practice of 'scraping' the surface of the building, which failed to please the Ruskin generation of purists who argued against any interference with ancient buildings.[67] Their complaints surfaced in the *Ecclesiologist* magazine, and were led by George Gilbert Scott. Buckler, in response, wrote an angry book – *A Description of the Restorations of the Exterior of Lincoln Cathedral* (1866) – to avouch his (and the dynasty's) reputation (Fig. 6.8). It was a work of passionate invective and incautious criticism that should be seen as part of an enduring tradition of the

Fig. 6.8 | Photograph of John Chessell Buckler, *A Description and Defence of the Restoration of the Exterior of Lincoln Cathedral* (Oxford: Rivington, 1866), with the arms of the Diocese of Lincoln. Joshua Mardell.

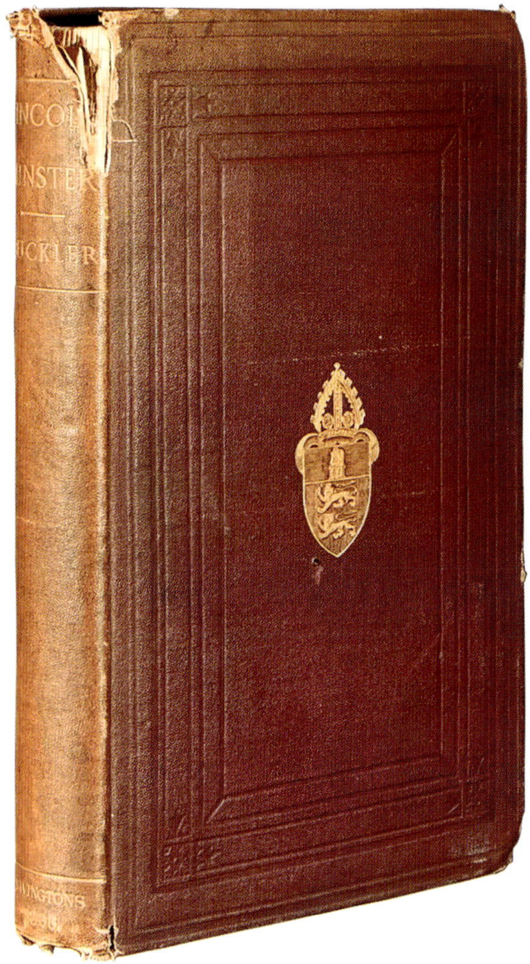

architectural protest book. John Chessell received very few design commissions after 1866 (Longridge Towers, Berwick-on-Tweed, 1876, was an exception, when John Chessell was 85 years old), but he was still drawing, with a steady hand and clear eyesight, into his nineties. He died in his centennial year in 1894.

CHARLES ALBAN BUCKLER (1824–1905)

Charles Alban was profoundly affected by the ultra-reactionary religious and architectural events in the city of his birth, subsequently known as the Oxford Movement. He had already been nurtured into a Catholic milieu through his father's patronage, and perhaps as an inevitable consequence of the Bucklers' stubborn medievalism, it was unsurprising that he converted to Roman Catholicism in 1844. It was only then that Charles adopted the name 'Alban' after the first English martyr, or, as he and his father wrote in their history of St. Alban's abbey church (later cathedral), that 'illustrious Protomartyr [who] gave glorious testimony of steadfastness in the Faith'.[68]

Working only occasionally in partnership with his father, Charles Alban started his own practice in 1856. Benefiting from the re-establishment of the Catholic Hierarchy (1850), he focused on designing new Roman Catholic churches and chapels, beginning with the new Sodality chapel at Stonyhurst College, a school and centre of the Jesuit order in England. Cardinal Wiseman, the first Post-Reformation Cardinal and Archbishop of Westminster, keenly encouraged converts' missionary roles, together with the development of missions in small parishes, and it was mostly these small missions that Buckler served. His school-chapel and teacher's house at Shifnal in the Staffordshire estate of Baron Costessey, who sponsored its construction, is a case in point. It is built of roughly hewn, locally-quarried red sandstone ashlar, sparingly punctured by simple cusped lancets. Inside, a plain open roof sits on plain corbels. In spite of its humility, work of this kind was not insignificant in the context of its production. For instance, when Charles Alban added a mere north aisle to the church of the Holy Cross in Leicester (1879), crucial in the revival of the English Dominican Province, it was a very great occasion; Cardinal Manning opened it, escorted from the railway station by the League of the Cross.[69]

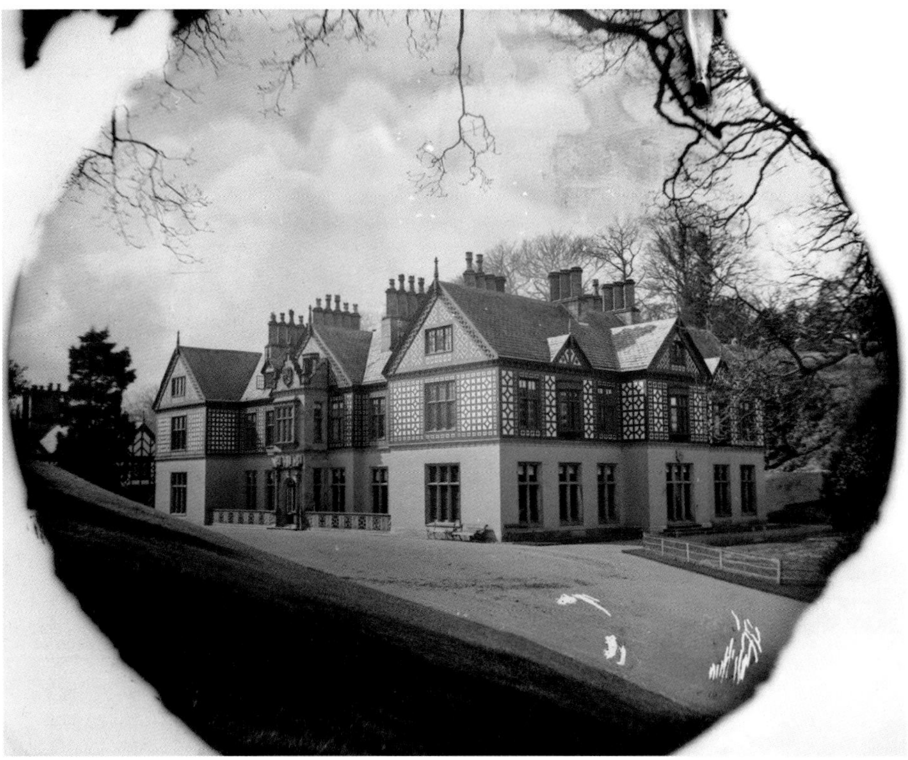

Fig. 6.4 | Pool Park, Ruthin, Clwyd (John Buckler, 1826–29). Negative, glass and wet collodion, 1875. The National Library of Wales.

Charles Alban – reminiscent of the humble work of his father at Oxford – built many modest small Catholic missions around the country, many of them in urban settings. His oeuvre was thus described by Bryan Little as 'straightforward and unassuming'.[70] Or perhaps 'primitive' is a suitable term – 'primitive' in the Ruskinian sense of a reduction of elements, simplified masses, and an emphasis on abstraction.[71] Small commissions adopting the Early English very often meant plate tracery, primitive foliation and cusping, rough masonry, an absence of decorative mouldings, bare outlines and simple plans. They also meant humble gabled belfries and saddle stones rather than soaring spires. The conventual chapel he built for the Sisters of Mercy at Battersea (1868–69) is a case in point. All of stock-brick, even the plate-tracery and dressings exhibited, as Buckler himself put it, 'a tone of holy poverty'.[72] Conversely, Charles Albans's largest ecclesiastical (and conventual) commission was the capacious auditory church of Our Lady of the Rosary and St. Dominic, Haverstock Hill (1874–1883) (Fig. 6.9). A grand symbol of the mission of the

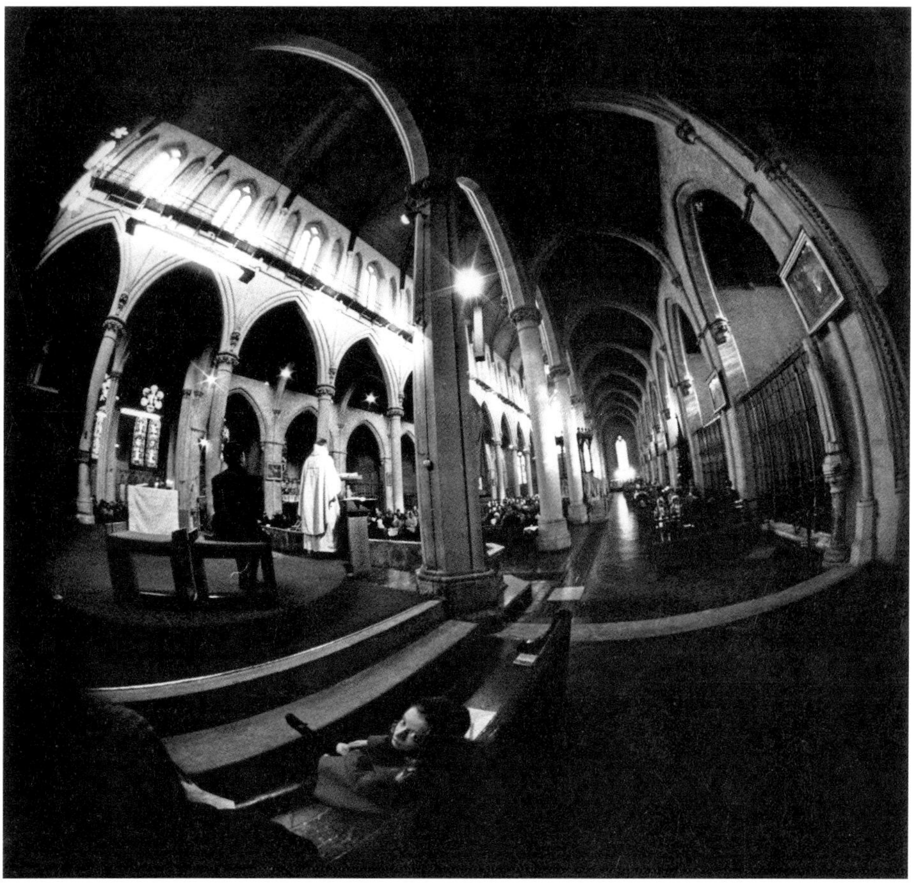

Fig. 6.9 | Fish-eye lens view of the sanctuary during Mass at the Church of Our Lady of the Rosary and St Dominic, Hampstead, by Peter Baistow, 1969. London, Architectural Press Archive/RIBA Collections.

revived Dominican Order, a high altar and fourteen lateral chapels are dedicated to the mysteries of the rosary, a devotion central to Dominican worship that was promoted by Pope Leo XIII in 1883.

In line with our dynastic theme, a brief digression will be made to allude to a further case of 'Scott versus Buckler' here. St. Dominic's, which opened in 1883, received criticism from George Gilbert Scott Jnr (1839–1897), the eldest son of George Gilbert Scott. He complained of aesthetic, liturgical and, especially, structural shortcomings, namely, the lack of ties in the construction of the wooden barrel-vaulted roof. His section drawing of the lean-to aisle's transverse arch shows him making calculations of weight and span, revealing his suspicions of shearing (Fig. 6.10) In his magazine, *The Sacristy*, Scott Jnr claimed that 'nothing but a miraculous interposition on the part of Providence – or of St. Dominic – can keep the building on its legs'.[73]

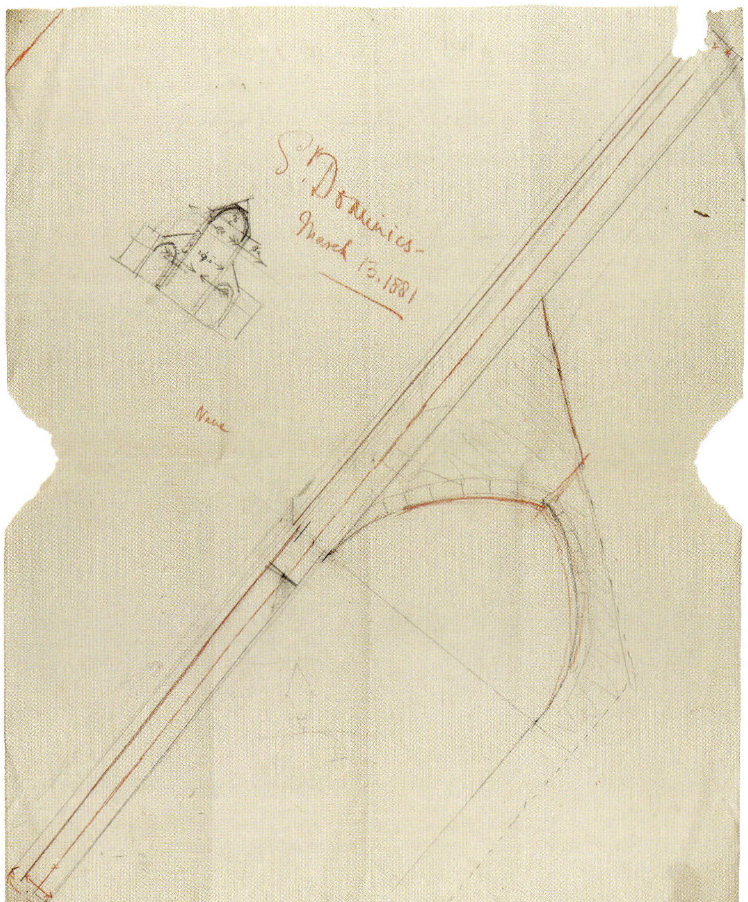

Fig. 6.10 | George Gilbert Scott Jnr., Our Lady of the Rosary and St Dominic, sketch sections, 1881. London, RIBA Collections.

Mirroring his father's defence against Scott Snr's accusations of 'scraping', Charles Alban sent an impassioned defence to the *Sacristy* which published his letter.[74] Meanwhile, Frederick Wallen, district surveyor of St. Pancras, undertook a structural survey concluding that, while 'the design was a daring one [that] approached the limits of absolute safety', the question of the building's stability rests with the architect.[75] Mild concern notwithstanding, there was no shortage of calumny in the way such concern was raised by Scott Jnr. Fr. Reginald Buckler wrote to Scott Jnr in defence of his brother Charles Alban, angry that the issues he raised publically were 'calculated to embitter [Charles Alban] & put him strongly on the defensive. Especially joined to knowledge of what occurred some years back between your father & mine, in reference to the works at Lincoln Cathedral'.[76]

Such calumny likely had to do with professional jealousy; Scott Jnr had converted to Rome in 1880 and may have been envious of a commission to design one of the largest Catholic churches in the capital. Moreover, from an earlier generation than Scott Jnr, Charles Alban would have been used to relying on experience, his qualification as an architect sufficient enough for his judgment. He may have felt disinclined to have to justify his decisions, such as rectifying the building's forces, to the Board of Works. Frank Jenkins summarized this change of disposition:

> Beside developments in the purely professional aspects of his work, the nineteenth century saw a growing complexity in the technical questions with which the architect had to contend. New types of building, new materials, increasingly involved building legislation… [that] had profound effects on his methods of practice.[77]

John Chessell, aged 88, visited Haverstock Hill and, predictably, dismissed any evidence of structural instability. He held that 'the novelty, merit, & elegance of the design, vex the critics'.[78] Beyond dynastic rivalry, in this case, the Buckler dynasty is turning against, or being victimized by, increasingly professionalized expertise, press scrutiny and bureaucracy.

Charles Alban's *magnum opus* was the rebuilding of Arundel Castle, Sussex (1874–1901), the Gothic fortress of Henry, the 15th Duke of Norfolk, England's premier Catholic nobleman. Buckler adapted a free and expansive group of (mostly) thirteenth-century precedents. To realise his project, Buckler patronized many old firms, Puginian in origin and inspiration (e.g. metalware and stained glass by Hardman and Powell's, Minton tiles, wrought ironwork by Hart, Peard & Co., and Crace fabrics). At Arundel, unlike the muted works aforementioned, Buckler constructed extraordinary, almost abstract spaces – heavy and geometric, including a neo-feudal Baron's Hall.

It seems appropriate that the Duke should have employed for his architect someone imbued with a strong sense of the dynastic – the Howards, as Catholic recusants, had long been 'faithful to an exiled dynasty and a proscribed faith'.[79] Indeed, the Fitzalan-Howard family's rich pedigree was the overriding inspiration for the iconography and armorial decoration at Arundel that Buckler carried out, from Fitzalan acorns and oak leaves, to the Howard lion. Even in modern apparatuses and electric devices, such as speaking tubes and bell-pulls, the family remained the over-riding inspiration (Fig. 6.11). As Buckler likely understood, in celebrating the re-establishment of Roman Catholicism in England, the careful conservation of the medieval family chapel at Arundel was no less important; an 1867 court case had recently determined that the 14th-century Fitzalan Chapel in the Castle grounds had remained uninterruptedly Catholic since the Reformation. Charles Alban meticulously incorporated surviving medieval fabric in his conservation of

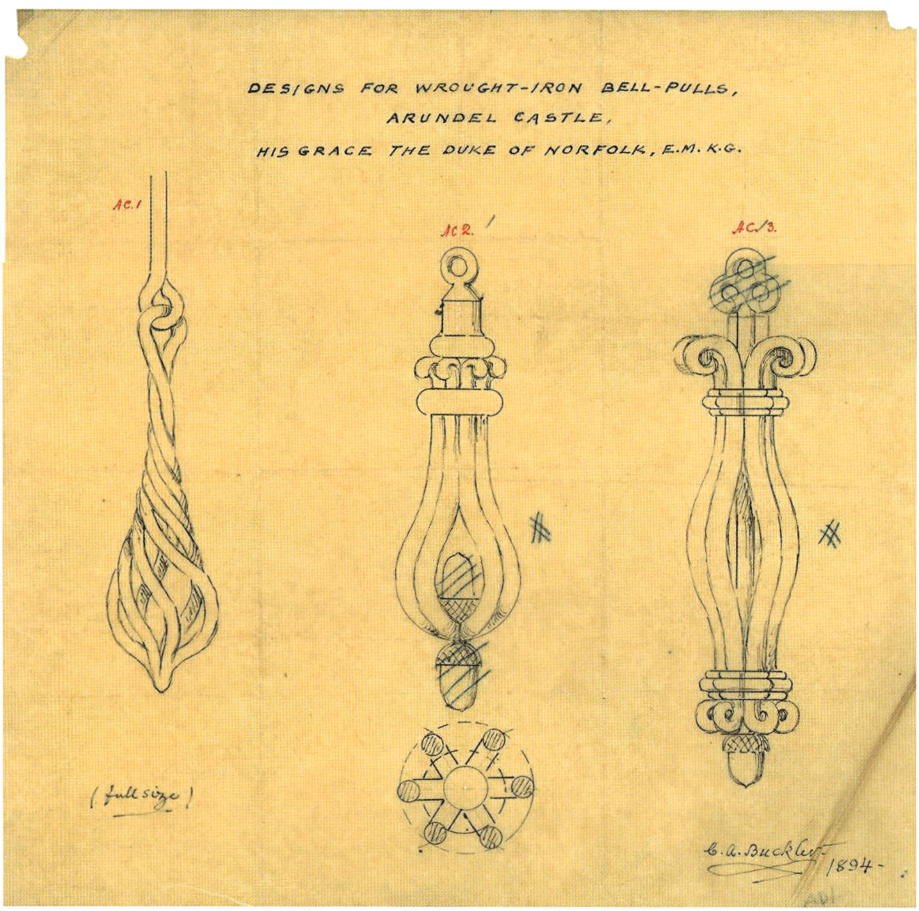

Fig. 6.11 | Charles Alban Buckler, 'Designs for Wrought-iron Bell-pulls', Arundel Castle, Sussex, 1894. Arundel Castle Archive, AD/19/47.

the choir stalls at the chapel's east end in 1885.[80] As Charles Tracy put it in 1986, 'anyone could be forgiven for assuming the furniture is entirely the product of 19th century historicism', yet, it was 'an enlightened act of restoration' of much surviving medieval fabric, carried out 'at a time when it was fashionable to swep away traces of the old and start again according to some imagined design'.[81]

The Duke (and Earl Marshall) appointed Charles Alban Surrey Herald of Arms Extraordinary in 1880; he is depicted in full regalia in stained glass at the church of St. Edward the Confessor, that he had built for the Catholic Salvin family, at Sutton Park, Surrey, where he was also buried with his wife, Mary. As though honouring his sense of knight errantry in his pursuit of Gothic, bound up with his obsessive cult of chivalry, and his profound Catholic religiosity, Buckler became a Donat of the First Class of the Sovereign Military Order of Malta in 1885. Thus, he now belonged to an illustrious Catholic order of chivalry, and had ascended to a lofty position in the social hierarchy, miles away from that of his grandfather who, in spite of relative fame, had 'died in near penury'.[82]

Charles Alban remarked in 1901 that 'towards the end of the year 1900 I signified the desire to terminate my professional employment with the end of the century'.[83] Just as John Ruskin had died so appropriately at the end of the century over which he exercised so profound an influence, it is as though the Bucklers were self-consciously a product of that century. He died without issue in 1905 – and as his three siblings, all Dominican friars known as the 'Buckler Trinity', were unable to carry the mantle on his behalf – the dynasty ended.

UNDERSTANDING THE BUCKLERS

For all the rabid moralism of the Bucklers, they were poorly received in the twentieth century, owing in part to the sustenance of the tradition of moralism in the construction of architectural history itself.[84] According to David Verey, shrewdly paraphrasing Pugin, John Chessell 'dreamed and drew fine things, but realised rather poor ones'.[85] A stronger case in point is Ian Nairn's damning verdict on Charles Alban's Catholic fortress, with its towering lancets, in 1965:

> There is no getting away from the fact that Arundel Castle is a great disappointment. The fault is that of the C19 which would not leave well alone... [namely] an almost complete rebuilding in an unfeeling Windsor Castle style by C. A. Buckler, 1890–1903, which neither amuses nor convinces. That anybody, Duke or Banker, could as late as 1890 have embarked on the pretty complete building of an imitation castle, remains a puzzle anyway, though for the historian of society rather than the architectural observer. After all, during the decade when the Duke had done with it, [Edwin] Lutyens started on Holy Island and Castle Drogo.[86]

While John Chessell had been clinging onto a kind of academic purity that he had helped develop at the start of the nineteenth century, Charles Alban, was an immediate contemporary of George Edmund Street. As Clive Wainwright wrote of him:

> He was an established architect before Pugin died in 1853... and [only] three years older than Burges, Bodley and Seddon... It is essential to see him in this high Victorian context though he lived on until 1905... When he died in the age of Voysey, Lutyens and Mackintosh, *The Builder* gave him a seven line obituary... He had sunk into almost total obscurity.[87]

The cult of so-called 'High Victorianism', that tends to refer to the work of key leading Gothic Revival architects 1850–1870, has in some part affected the legacy of Charles Alban whose work has been seen as derivative, in his own time and subsequently. Yet, as Gavin Stamp, put it, 'the modern critic... looks for originality where it may not be possible, or desirable'.[88] The Bucklers were peripheral from the mainstream and proudly non-innovative – they produced works of architecture safely from a conservative antiquarian perspective that matched the conservative outlook of their clients.[89]

Even in the realm of draughtsmanship, however, the dynasty are often absent from standard surveys, perhaps having fallen victim to the identification of their work as topography, a genre that has long carried the oft-quoted pejorative addendum, 'little more than... [a] kind of map-work'.[90] Topography has recently been re-evaluated as flexible and capacious, rather than as an inferior genre to landscape art.[91] Some neglect of the Bucklers may also be due to their occupancy of the no-man's land between antiquarianism and architectural history. Yet, Simon Bradley has argued that antiquaries and clergy were much in advance of architects in forming and directing neo-medievalism in the years up to 1840 when the Gothic Revival reached its peak.[92] He has argued that antiquarians were responsible for developing the existing climate of opinion, namely 'the widespread appeal which Gothic architecture already enjoyed, not merely as a secular taste, but as what was considered the one supremely Christian style' that enthusiasts like Pugin and the Ecclesiological Society later turned to their advantage.[93]

CONCLUSION

The Bucklers sought to maintain a latent yet stable historicising vision in their art. They found meaning in historical continuity, rather than innovation. As John Chessell put it, not at the height of High Victorian experiment but as early as 1832: 'the love of that fantastic tyrant NOVELTY... so planted in our very nature... the wisdom of former ages contemned [sic] by the vanity of the one in which we live'.[94] Thus, it figures that the Bucklers did not go in for 'ego', or what J.T. Micklethwaite (1843–1906) described as 'the perpetual forcing into notice of the personality of the architect'.[95] With certain exceptions, much of the work of the Bucklers was restrained, almost muting their authorial voice. That is to say, they resisted 'development', which occupied the 1850s and 1860s, a burst of creative fecundity, modernity and self-conscious 'originality'. On the other hand, when given the opportunity, they used their knowledge of Gothic architecture to make a highly conspicuous, often aggrandized display of their patrons' lineages.

By the 1870s, when the Gothic tradition was being challenged by proponents of other idioms, such as Queen Anne, T.G. Jackson (1835–1924), argued anew that contemporary Gothic architecture was mired in antiquarianism and needed developing into a modern style.[96] He might have been referring to architects like the Bucklers, whose antiquarianism – persistent, muted – implied a future that would be built *literally* upon the medieval past. Eastlake, however, while mostly celebrating contemporary vigour and the pursuit of 'development', cast the Bucklers generously in his history of the Gothic Revival. He may well have had them in mind when he said that there were 'but few Medievalists of whom it may be said that they have from first to last pursued one aim unaffected by the strange and conflicting influences which have been brought to bear on the Revival'.[97]

NOTES

1. *The Ecclesiologist* 176 (October, 1866): 295.
2. George Buckler worked under Sir James Pennethrorne at the Office of Works, and also published *Twenty-Two Of The Churches Of Essex: Architecturally Described And Illustrated* (London: Bell and Daldy, 1856). He ensured the safe bequeathal of the family's antiquarian collection in institutions of national standing, principally the family's volumes of drawings at the British Museum (now the British Library).
3. Nd. Oxford, Bodleian Library, MS Eng. lett. a. 1, c. 335, fol. 52.
4. *The Catholic World* 15 (July, 1872): 453.
5. Ed M. Bressani, "Revivalism," in *The Companion to the History of Architecture, Volume III: Nineteenth-Century Architecture*, ed. Martin Bressani and Christina Contandriopoulos (Hoboken: John Wiley & Sons, 2017), 3–18.
6. There are c.130 extant buildings across the UK either designed or conserved by the dynasty between 1805 and 1901. Only a handful are mentioned in this article.
7. Adam Menuge, "Antiquarian romance: John Chessell Buckler at Oxburgh Hall", in *National Trust Historic Houses and Collections Annual,* Supplement, *Apollo Magazine* (London: National Trust, 2007), 4–13.
8. Charles Alban Buckler, *Bucleriana: Notices of the Family History of Buckler* (London: Mitchell and Hughes, 1886).
9. Eric Hobsbawm, *The Age of Capital: 1848–1875* (London: Weidenfeld & Nicolson, 1975) 216.
10. Employed as such in a contemporary novel, A. E. W. Mason, *The Courtship of Morrice Buckler: A Romance* (London: Macmillan & Co, 1896), and implied in the noun 'swashbuckler'.
11. John Mason Neale, *The Rhythm of Bernard Morlaix, Monk of Cluny on the Celestial Country* (London: J. T. Hayes, 1866), 5.
12. The 'trope' of contrasts, notably, can be found in Matthew Arnold, *Culture and Anarchy and Other Selected Prose* (1869; reis., London: Penguin 2015); Thomas Carlyle, *Past and Present* (1843; reis., *Oxford*: Oxford University Press, 1945); Benjamin Disraeli, *Sybil, or the Two Nations* (1845; reis., London: Penguin, 1985); A.W.N. Pugin, *Contrasts* (London: privately published, 1836).

13. M. H. Bloxam, *The Principles of Gothic Architecture: elucidated by question and answer* (London: C. Tilt and J. Weale, London, 1836), iv.
14. See Maurice Wilmore Barley, *A Guide to British Topographical Collections* (London: Council for British Archaeology, 1974). While there are some 89 of their volumes of topographical drawings at the British Library alone, much of their collection is scattered elsewhere including at the William Salt Library, Stafford, the Devizes Museum, Wiltshire, the Bodleian Library, Oxford, and as far as the Lewis Walpole Library in Farmington, Connecticut, USA.
15. William Buckler, *The Larvae of the British Butterflies and Moths*, 9 vols. (London: The Ray Society, 1886–1901).
16. John Chessell Buckler and Charles Buckler, *Remarks upon Wayside Chapels with Observations on the Architecture and Present State of the Chantry on Wakefield Bridge* (Oxford: I. Shrimpton, 1843).
17. Joseph Mordaunt Crook, "The Pre-Victorian Architect: Professionalism and Patronage," *Architectural History* 12 (1969): 62–68.
18. Joseph Mordaunt Crook, "Sydney Smirke: the Architecture of Compromise," in *Seven Victorian Architects*, ed. Jane Fawcett (London: Thames and Hudson, 1976), 50–65.
19. See Norman Shaw and T. G. Jackson, ed. *Architecture: A Profession or an Art* (London: J.Murray, 1892); C. F. A. Voysey, *Individuality* (London: Chapman & Hall, 1915).
20. C. A. Buckler, letter to the Earl of Gainsborough, 17 November 1869, Leicestershire Record Office, DE3214/10037/4, this author's emphasis.
21. C. A. Buckler, letter to the Earl of Gainsborough, 25 February 1871, Leicestershire Record Office, DE3214/10037/6. In lieu of his 10% commission, he paid for the piscina in the sanctuary, 'of which I sh: like the privilege of being regarded the donor' (C. A. Buckler, letter to the Earl of Gainsborough, 28 December 1868, Leicestershire Record Office, DE3214/100376/3).
22. Simon Bradley, pers. comm. 20 June 2024.
23. John Martin Robinson, "How Lady Stafford Revived the Gothic," *Country Life* 197 (April 3, 2003): 82–85.
24. J. Buckler, letter to J. Bloxam, 4 December 1849, Oxford, Magdalen College Archive, Oxford, MS John Buckler, f. 24.
25. Howard Colvin, *A Biographical Dictionary of British Architects, 1600–1840* (London: John Murray, 1954), 105.
26. William Dunn Macray, *Annals of the Bodleian Library,* 2nd edn. (Oxford: The Clarendon Press, 1890), 292.
27. *The Catholic World* 15 (April to September 1872), 454.
28. Many of Buckler's other key patrons for topographical work are listed in Colvin, *British Architects, 1600–1840*.
29. John Harris, *The Artist and the Country House from the Fifteenth Century to the Present Day* (London: Sotheby's, 1995), 347.
30. For instance, the popularity of Revd John Milner's *Antiquities of Winchester* (1798). Buckler was close to Milner, a Catholic bishop, as part of the Gothic-Catholic axis at the Society of Antiquaries.
31. Joshua Mardell, "Blackballing Buckler: the Letters of John Buckler (1770–1851), the Carter School and the Foundations of an Antiquarian Dynasty," *Antiquaries Journal* 102 (2022): 418–446.
32. See also: John Woodcock, "The Buckler Family: A Study in Nineteenth Century Attitudes to Medieval Buildings," *ASCHB – Transactions*, no. 28 (2004–5): 4–22.
33. I am adopting the terminology for Gothic mansions used by Chris Brooks, *The Gothic Revival* (London: Phaidon, 1999).
34. *The Gentleman's Magazine*, January 1852, 103–104.
35. Life expectancy at birth in 1851–1860 was 41 and in 1891–1900 it was 46. Robert Woods, *The Demography of Victorian England and Wales* (Cambridge: Cambridge University Press, 2000), 200.
36. Crook, "The Pre-Victorian Architect," 65; W. J. Reader, *Professional Men: the Rise of the Professional Classes in Nineteenth-Century England* (London, Weidenfeld & Nicholson, 1966), 118–119. See also:

"Appendix C: British architectural pupillage 1740–1840,", in Frank Salmon, *Building on Ruins: The Rediscovery of Rome and English Architecture* (Aldershot: Ashgate, 2000).

37. George Buckler, nd. Oxford, Bodleian Library, MSS Eng. lett. a. 1, ff. 1–220, p. v. It is possible, however, that the respective Bucklers could not afford the premiums to send their sons into an established practice.
38. J. C. Buckler, *Observations on the Original Architecture of Saint Mary Magdalen College, Oxford* (London: John Nichols and Son, 1823), 89 (here, Buckler also argued for Gothic's architectonic superiority).
39. Geoffrey Tyack "Buckler, John (1770–1851), artist and architect," in *Oxford Dictionary of National Biography*: online edition, ed. H.C.G. Matthews and B. Harrison, accessed 27 June 2021, http://www.oxforddnb.com/view/article/3863 (accessed 27 June 2021).
40. The aforementioned *Bucleriana* is mostly made up of genealogical tables, rather than biographical details of the dynasty.
41. For John Chessell Buckler, we find autobiographical passages where we might not expect to, namely in an unpublished manuscript, "Rough Notes Concerning the History of the Hospital of St. John the Baptist" (1856) on the foundational structures (built *c.* 1234) that were granted to William Waynflete for his new college. See: unpublished manuscript "Rough Notes concerning the History of the Hospital of St. John the Baptist" by John Chessell Buckler, 1856, British Library, Add. MS. 27963.
42. *The Gentleman's Magazine*, January 1822, 41–43; Buckler, *Observations*, 89.
43. Julian Munby, "J. C. Buckler, Tackley's Inn and Three Medieval Houses in Oxford," *Oxoniensia* 43 (1978): 123–69.
44. Buckler, *Observations*, 42.
45. John Chessell Buckler, *An Historical and Descriptive Account of the Royal Palace at Eltham* (London: J. B. Nichols and Son, 1828).
46. J. C. Loudon, *Encyclopaedia of Cottage, Farm and Villa Architecture* (London: Longman, 1833), 960.
47. Brooks, *The Gothic Revival*, 77.
48. Joseph Mordaunt Crook, *William Burges and the High Victorian Dream* (London: John Murray, 1981), 22.
49. Nicola J. Watson, "Introduction," in *The Antiquary,* ed. Nicola Watson (1816; reis., Oxford: Oxford University Press, 2002), vii–xxvii.
50. Simon Bradley, Nikolaus Pevsner and Jennifer Sherwood, *Oxfordshire: Oxford and the South-East* [Buildings of England] (London and New Haven: Yale University Press, 1975), 50.
51. J. C. Buckler, *Saint Mary Magdalen College*.
52. *The Gentleman's Magazine*, vol. 78, May 1808, 415. The disclosure of authorship in Associated Architectural Societies' Reports *Anonyms: A Dictionary of Revealed Authorship* (1865) might well have been almost redundant to contemporaries.
53. Buckler, *Observations*, 89. Pugin owned a copy of *Observations*; *The Collected Letters of A. W. N. Pugin: Volume 2 1843–1845*, ed. Margaret Belcher (Oxford: Oxford University Press, 2003), 284.
54. Rosemary Hill, *God's Architect: Pugin and the Building of Romantic Britain*, (London: Penguin, 2008), 546.
55. Except for in an unpublished article, "On Sculpture as Accessory to Architecture", mirroring Puginian dicta on the subservience of structure to ornament, examined in reference to the work of William of Wykeham. Unpublished Manuscript, "Tracts on Architecture" by John Chessell Buckler, British Library, Add. MS. 27773.
56. Another key building they authored together was the Diocesan Training College, Chester (1839).
57. The *Gentleman's Magazine*, July 1840, New Series, vol. 14, 68.
58. Albeit that Perpendicular later came back into fashion. See for instance, J. D. Sedding, "The Architecture of the Perpendicular Period," *Transactions of the St. Paul's Ecclesiological Society*, I (London, 1881), 31–44, reminding readers that 'everybody of consequence, except the great Pugin,

Fergusson, and Freeman, has had an ill word for the Perpendicular' (31). On the return to 'Englishness', see Michael Hall, "The Rise of Refinement G. F. Bodley's All Saints, Cambridge, and the return to English models in Gothic architecture of the 1860s," *Architectural History* 36 (1993): 103–126.

59. The Bucklers' work at Oxford is discussed forensically in Joshua Mardell, "Fidelis ad Mortem: J. C. Buckler, an Oxford College architect." *Oxoniensia* 83 (2018): 73–92. At Cambridge, John Chessell designed the Master's Lodge, Magdalen College Cambridge (1835, demolished 1966) and restored its chapel (1848), removing all the early eighteenth-century fabric to revert back to a fifteenth-century appearance.
60. Edward Cox Alden, *Alden's Oxford Guide* (Oxford: Alden & Co., 1890) 48; John Parker, *A Hand-Book for Visitors to Oxford* (Oxford: J. Parker, 1875), 91.
61. In a number of cases the tops of the gables were deteriorating in advance of their coping or had moved several inches out of their perpendicular orientation resulting in broken joints.
62. Peter Howell, "Oxford Architecture, 1800–1914," in *The History of the University of Oxford*, vol. 7, ed. M. G. Brock and M. C. Curthoys (Oxford: Clarendon Press, 2000), 729–777.
63. Compare the work of H. J. Underwood at Exeter in the 1830s, and Daniel Evans at Pembroke in 1829–30. See Bradley, Pevsner and Sherwood, *Oxfordshire*, 48–52.
64. Hilary Sample, *Maintenance Architecture* (Cambridge, MA: MIT Press, 2006), 7.
65. Qtd. in John Harvey, *The Perpendicular Style: 1330–1485* (London: Batsford, 1978), 20.
66. This appears to be a concession, on the part of the Bucklers, to the thinking of the Ecclesiological Society. The incumbent at Iffley was Thomas Acton Warburton, who was appointed to the living in 1853, and who, as Geoffrey Tyack has learnt, 'followed the lead of the Cambridge Camden Society in condemning "debased" later alterations to medieval churches'. Geoffrey Tyack, "The Restoration of Iffley Parish Church." *Oxoniensia* 68 (2003): 113–130.
67. Joshua Mardell, "Getting into a Scrape: The Buckler Dynasty, Lincoln Cathedral and Mid-Victorian Architectural Politics," *Architectural History* 63 (2020): 191–218.
68. John Chessell Buckler and Charles Alban Buckler, *A History of the Architecture of the Abbey Church of St. Alban*, (London: Longman, Brown, Green, and Longmans, 1847), 1.
69. Archibald H. Kimberlin, *The Return of Catholicism to Leicester, 1746–1946 (*Hinckley: Samuel Walker, 1946) 24. A new Catholic church was built next door (1929–1958) with the present church and Buckler's aisle being incorporated (but surviving) into the Priory.
70. Bryan Little, *Catholic Churches Since 1623: A Study of Roman Catholic Churches in England and Wales from Penal Times to the Present Decade* (London: Robert Hall, 1966), 122.
71. Adrian Forty, "Primitive: the Word and Concept," in *Primitive: Original Matters in Architecture*, ed. J. Odgers, F. Samuel and A. Sharr (Abingdon: Routledge, 2006), 3–14.
72. Qtd. in: Andrew Saint and Colin Thom, *Survey of London: Battersea* (London: Yale University Press, 2014), 159.
73. *The Sacristy* 3 (1881): 165.
74. As did *The Builder*, *The Architect* and *The Tablet*.
75. *The Builder* 40 (May 7 1881): 586.
76. Letter from Fr. R. Buckler to G.G.Scott Jnr. (21 May 1881), London, RIBA, George Gilbert Scott Jnr. Collection, ScGGJ/12 SC/KTSD, emphasis in original.
77. Frank Jenkins, "The Victorian Architectural Profession," in *Victorian Architecture*, ed. P. Ferriday (London: Cape Friar, 1963), 37–50.
78. Letter from Fr. R. Buckler to G. G. Scott Jnr. (4 June 1881), London, RIBA, SC/KTSD/3, emphasis in original.
79. The Howards' was not an uninterrupted Catholic lineage because of the apostate Surrey (the son of the 10th Duke), but Surrey 'continued to maintain Catholic chaplaincies at Arundel Castle', nonetheless. See Mark Bence-Jones, *The Catholic Families* (London: Constable, 1992), 62.
80. The SPAB, founded in 1877, would likely have approved of the retention of fabric, if less so the disguise of Buckler's own interventions.

81. Charles Tracy, "The Real Thing: Choir Stalls of the Fitzalan Chapel," *Country Life* 180 (25 September, 1986): 984–985.
82. Tyack, "Buckler, John (1770–1851)".
83. Charles Alban Buckler (23 November 23) qtd. in Clive Wainwright, "Arundel Castle from 1850," *The Connoisseur* 197 (March 1978): 172–185.
84. E.g. David Watkin, *Morality and Architecture: The Development of a Theme in Architectural History and Theory from the Gothic Revival to the Modern Movement* (Oxford: Clarendon Press, 1977).
85. David Verey, *The Buildings of England: Gloucestershire, the Cotswolds* (Harmondsworth: Penguin, 1970) 442. 'I have passed my life… in thinking fine things, studying fine things, designing fine things and realising very poor ones', qtd. in Benjamin Ferrey. *Recollections of A. N. Welby Pugin, and His Father, Augustus Pugin: With Notices of Their Works* (London: Edward Stanford, 1861), 164.
86. Ian Nairn and Nikolaus Pevsner. *The Buildings of England: Sussex* (Harmondsworth: Penguin, 1965) 91. Nicholas Taylor, writing, as Ian Nairn had done, for the *Architectural Review*, echoed his colleague's damnation of Buckler's masterwork, describing it as 'a clumsy attempt, as late as 1879–1905, at Viollet-le-Duc feudalism'. Nicholas Taylor, "A Duke's Library," *The Architectural Review*, no. 848 (1967): 287.
87. Clive Wainwright, "Arundel Castle", 172–185; *The Builder* described him in unmemorable terms as the 'architect, we understand, of the Dominican Church, near Haverstock Hill, Hampstead' see *The Builder* 89 (July 5, 1905): 46.
88. Gavin Stamp, *An Architect of Promise: George Gilbert Scott Junior (1839–1897) and the Late Gothic Revival* (Donnington: Shaun Tyas, 2002), 134.
89. On writing about non-salient practitioners, see Joshua Mardell, "Book Review of Peter Jefferson Smith, *The I'Ansons: A Dynasty of London Architects & Surveyors*," *Architectural Research Quarterly* 24, no. 3 (2019): 291–294.
90 Henry Fuseli, "Lecture IV – On Invention, part 2," in *The Life and Writings of J. H. Fuseli Esq, MA, RA*, vol. 2, ed. John Knowles (London: H. Colburn and R. Bentley, 1831), 271.
91. A result of this revisionism is The British Library's 'Transforming Topography' initiative from 2019, https://www.bl.uk/projects/transforming-topography.
92. Simon Bradley, "The Roots of Ecclesiology: Late Hanoverian Attitudes to Medieval Churches," in *'A Church As It Should Be': The Cambridge Camden Society and Its Influence*, ed. C. Webster and J. Elliott (Stamford: Shaun Tyas, 2000), 22–44.
93. Bradley, "Roots of Ecclesiology", 22.
94. J. C. Buckler, *Saint Mary Magdalen College*, 132.
95. J. T. Micklethwaite, *Modern Parish Churches: Their Plan, Design and Furniture* (London: Henry S. King & Co, 1874), 265.
96. T. G. Jackson, *Modern Gothic Architecture* (London: Henry S. King & Co. 1873).
97. Charles Lock Eastlake, *A History of the Gothic Revival: An Attempt to Show How the Taste for Medieval Architecture which Lingered in England during the Two Last Centuries Has since Been Encouraged and Developed* (1872; reis., Cambridge: Cambridge University Press, 2012), 360.

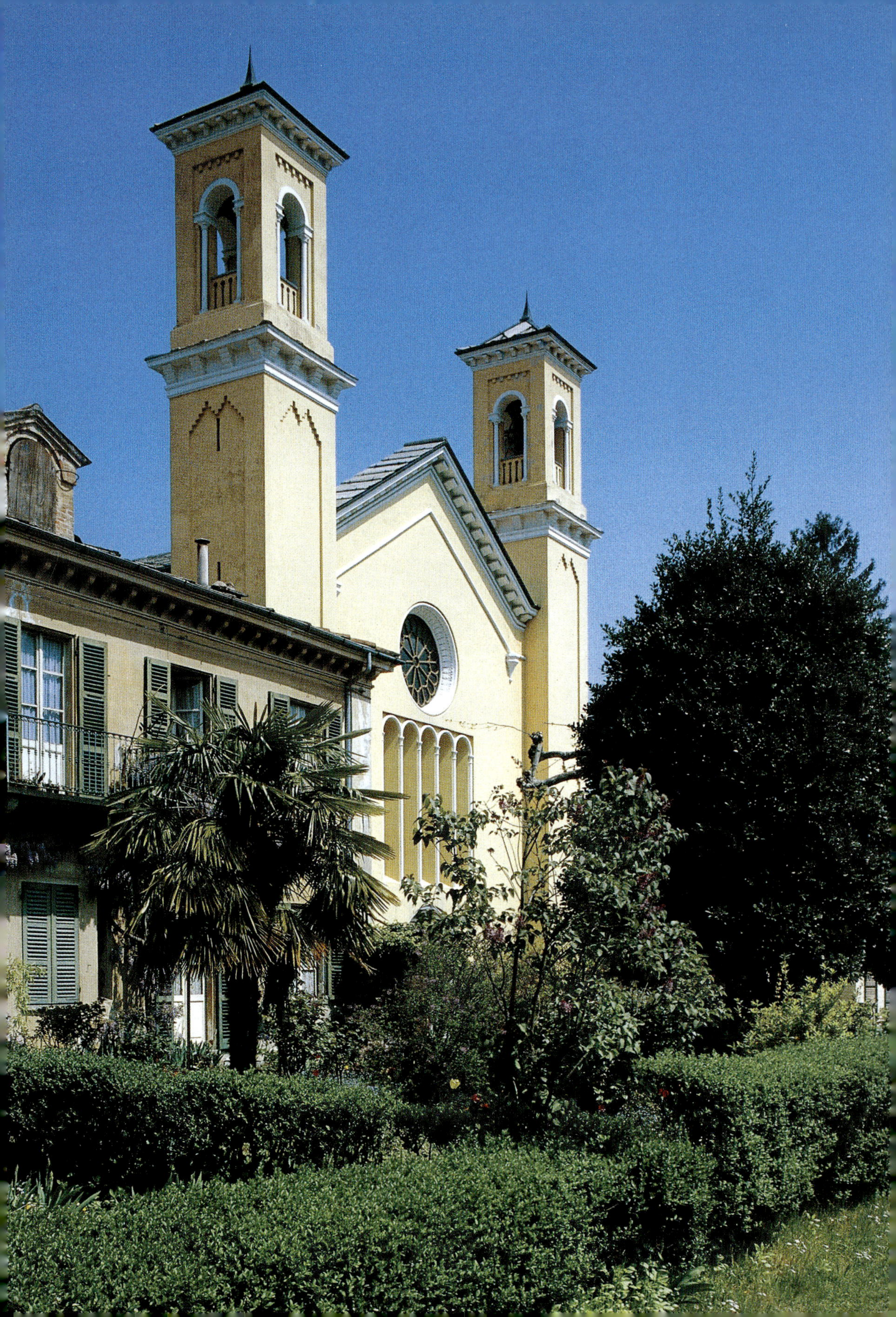

7 · Family and Faith: the Goldie and Bonomi Dynasties of Catholic Architects

PETER HOWELL

Giuseppe Bonomi was born in Rome in 1739; his great-grandson was George Goldie, thus the works of two Catholic dynasties coincided, and are considered together in this article.[1] Giuseppe's family came from Asiago, and his father was agent to members of the Roman nobility. Giuseppe was educated at the Collegio Romano, and studied under Antonio Asprucci and the Marchese Teodoli. Charles Clérisseau probably taught him draughtsmanship.[2] He came to England in 1767 to work for the architects Robert and James Adam, thereafter calling himself Joseph. In 1775 he married Rosa Fiorini, a cousin and close friend of the Swiss painter Angelica Kauffmann. They had four sons. The second, also Joseph (1796–1878), a sculptor, spent many years in Egypt. It was he who designed the Egyptian façade of the flax mill, Temple Mill in Leeds, with the local architect James Combe.[3] He later became Curator of Sir John Soane's Museum. In 1783 the elder Joseph, who had left the office of the Adams in 1781, returned to Italy. He visited Naples in 1784. Failing to find success in Italy, despite becoming a member of the Roman Accademia di San Luca and the Accademia Clementina at Bologna, and establishing a friendship with Canova, he came back to England in that year, possibly at the instance of Lord Aylesford. In 1789 he was elected ARA, on the casting vote of Sir Joshua Reynolds. Reynolds's attempt the next year to get him elected RA failed, since he was a foreigner. He had hoped to become professor of perspective. The offer of appointment as architect to the King of Naples in 1800 came to nothing. Rather surprisingly he was appointed in 1804 Honorary Architect to St Peter's in Rome, for which he had made an unexecuted design for the sacristy in 1776. He died in 1808.

Although strongly opposed to the Gothic style, Giuseppe (since Anglicised as Joseph and described hereafter as Joseph Bonomi the Elder) made an unexecuted design for a Gothic gateway at Merrion Park, Dublin.[4] He built three churches in England. Two were Catholic, the Bavarian Embassy Chapel of the Assumption in

Fig. 7.1 | Ignatius Bonomi, church at Torre Pellice, Piedmont, 1849. Alamy.

Warwick Street (1789–90) London, and the Spanish Chapel in Manchester Square (1793–6), London. For the third, at Great Packington, Warwickshire, see below.

Bonomi was a fine draughtsman, and exhibited at the RA from 1783. He became chiefly known for his country houses, and is mentioned as a fashionable architect in Jane Austen's *Sense and Sensibility.* His houses have interiors which 'are often more robust and architectural and more overtly antique in style' than those of the Adams.[5] They included Longford Hall, Shropshire (1789–92), Barrells House, Warwickshire (1792–4), Ponsbourne Park, Hertfordshire (1792–3), Eastwell Park, Kent (1793–1800), Laverstoke Park, Hants (1796–9), and Rosneath, Dunbartonshire (1803–6, never completed, and demolished in 1961). He had met the Earl of Aylesford in Italy, and decorated the gallery at Packington Hall, Warwickshire, in 1785–8 after the model of 'the Baths of Titus' (really Nero's Domus Aurea). The extraordinary church at Great Packington (1789–92) reflected Aylesford's studies of antiquity. It has Greek Doric columns which support a vault based on the Roman baths. Howard Colvin describes it as 'as radical as anything by Gilly or Ledoux'.[6] Bonomi's mausoleum at Blickling takes the form of a pyramid (1794–6).

Joseph's second surviving son was Ignatius Richard Frederick Nemesius, born in 1787.[7] Trained by his father, he was obliged to start practice on his death in 1808, when he was 21, to support his mother and siblings. He first thought of applying to be a draughtsman for Sir John Soane, but he was wanted in the North to complete Rosneath for the Duke of Argyll, and extend Skelton Castle, Yorkshire (1810–17), for John Wharton. In addition, his father had been employed in remodelling and enlarging Lambton Castle in County Durham.[8] There he built up a substantial practice, including many Anglican and Catholic churches. He was architect to Durham Cathedral. In 1813 he was appointed Surveyor of Bridges for the county. This led to his designing the first railway bridge in the world, Skerne Bridge, in 1825, for the Stockton and Darlington Railway.[9]

In 1837 Ignatius married Charlotte Fielding, a Protestant. John Loughborough Pearson was his pupil, and later assistant, from 1831 until 1841. From 1842 Ignatius was in partnership with John Augustus Cory (1819–87), a pupil of J. J. Scoles. He retired to Wimbledon in 1850, in 1865–6 building a house called The Camels for himself and his brother Joseph, both now widowers. It took its name from a bas-relief depicting camels on the front by Joseph, and was of brick with bay windows and a verandah. It has disappeared.[10] He died in 1870. Cory carried on until 1856, when he formed a partnership in Carlisle with C.J. Ferguson.

Ignatius Bonomi was responsible for 22 churches on his own, and 10 with Cory. Eight of the 26 are Catholic. The most surprising for a Catholic architect, was the Waldensian church at Torre Pellice in Piedmont (1849) (Fig. 7.1). At Brough Hall in Yorkshire the version of the 13th century Archbishop's Chapel at York was designed by Sir William Lawson, owner of the estate, and John Brown, the historian of York

Minster, and only supervised by Bonomi. He also worked on many country house commissions, including three Neoclassical houses in Co. Durham: Eggleston Hall (*c*.1810–15), Windlestone Hall (1821–34), and – the most remarkable – Burn Hall (1821–34) Co. Durham. Colvin comments that the 'channelled masonry and mansard roof suggest the influence of recent French architecture'.[11] His only complete castle was Clervaux Castle, Croft, Co. Durham (1839–44, demolished 1951). As architect to the London Lead Company he designed houses in Co. Durham and Westmorland. He worked on public buildings including bridges, the Durham County Gaol, almshouses, an infirmary, baths, schools, a library, and a poorhouse. Unlike his father, he often built in Gothic, in the rather thin manner of Commissioners' churches, as, for example, St Mary, Sunderland (1830–35). He also used the neoclassical style as at Burn Hall.

George Goldie was born in York in 1828.[12] His grandmother Sophie became a Catholic at Rouen after the death of her husband. Her son George was a doctor, who was active in the Catholic Emancipation movement, and was 'a leading man in all antiquarian matters connected with the city and county'.[13] In 1828 he married Mary Anne Bonomi, daughter of Joseph. They had nine children, of whom three died young. Of the eldest, George Junior's, five siblings, one became a Monsignor, one a Jesuit, and two nuns. He was educated at St Cuthbert's College, Ushaw, at the time when A.W. N. Pugin was working there. He showed so much interest in Pugin's work that they remained friends until Pugin's death. Pugin advised him to study with John Gray Weightman and Matthew Ellison Hadfield in Sheffield.[14] The firm of Weightman and Hadfield had been set up on 1834. They designed many Catholic churches, mostly in a Gothic style derived from Pugin. Goldie trained with them from 1845 until 1851, then becoming a partner. When William Wardell left for Australia they acquired his practice. Weightman left in 1858, and the firm became Hadfield and Goldie until 1860. From 1861 to 1867 Goldie worked on his own in London, at his residence in Kensington Square, until he formed a partnership with Charles Edwin Child (1843–1911).

Goldie had a special talent for the design of ecclesiastical fittings. A magnificent reredos was erected in 1853–5 in St John's Cathedral, Salford, which had been built to the design of Matthew Hadfield in 1844–8. A stained glass window shows Saints Matthew and George, holding the design drawings for church and reredos (Fig. 7.2). The reredos was destroyed by a philistine Bishop in 1990. St Patrick's, Bradford, is a large building in Puginian Gothic (1853). Goldie's earliest works in Ireland were commissioned while he was with Weightman and Hadfield. He was brought in to design the completion of St Nathy's Cathedral, Ballaghaderreen, Co, Roscommon, begun in 1854, but not actually completed to his design.[15] So his first complete Irish church was St Patrick, Bandon, Co. Cork (1855–61). Of his many later works in Ireland the most notable is the Cathedral of the Immaculate

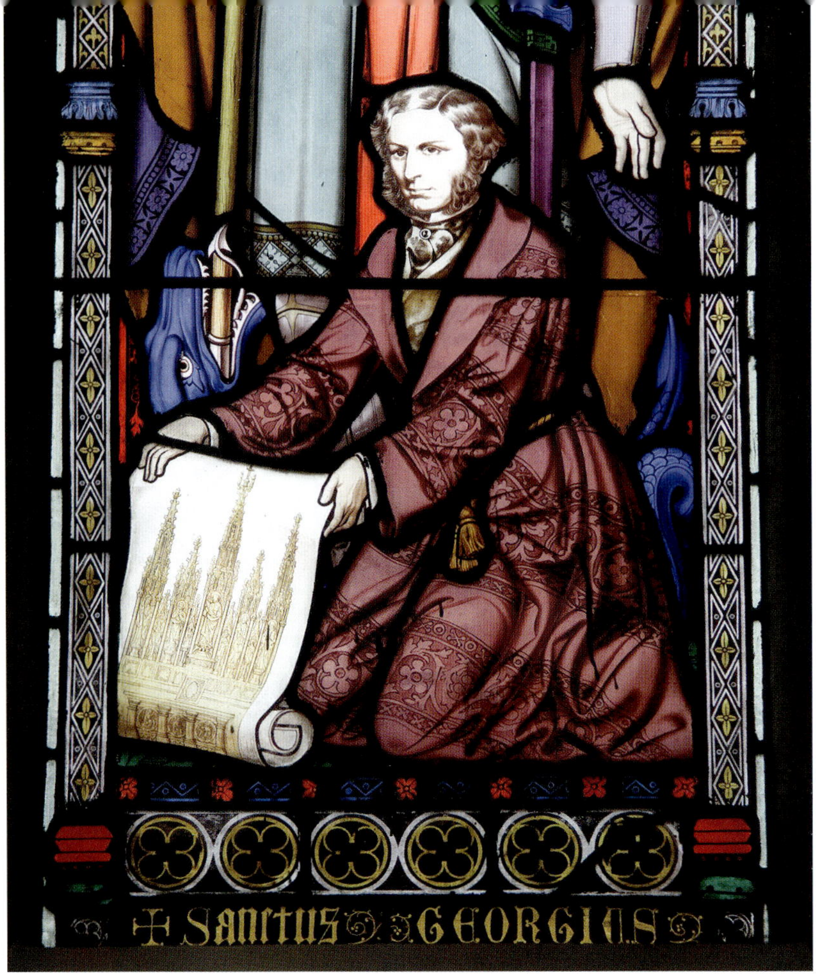

Fig. 7.2 | St John's Cathedral, Salford. Stained glass window showing St. George and George Goldie kneeling holding the design for the reredos. James Crowley.

Conception in Sligo (1867–73), in Romanesque style. At Mount St Alphonsus in Limerick he added the tower (1876–8) and spire, and designed the magnificent altar and reredos.[16]

Goldie later developed his High Victorian French Gothic style, as at Our Lady of Victories, Kensington (1867–9). This grand apsed church was used as the Pro-Cathedral of the Archdiocese of Westminster from 1868 until the new cathedral was ready in 1902. In his *History of the Gothic Revival* (1872) C. L. Eastlake praised the 'fine proportions and rich sculpture' (which was by Thomas Earp) of the western porch.[17] It was destroyed by bombing in 1940. Other works in this style include two large and elaborate institutional buildings, both now closed, St Scholastica's Abbey, Teignmouth (1863), and St John's College, Waterford (1868).

One of Goldie's best, and best known, churches is St Wilfrid's, York (1862–4) (Fig. 7.3), whose elaborate west front and powerful tower dominate the approach to the Minster from the Station.[18] Another important commission was the chapel

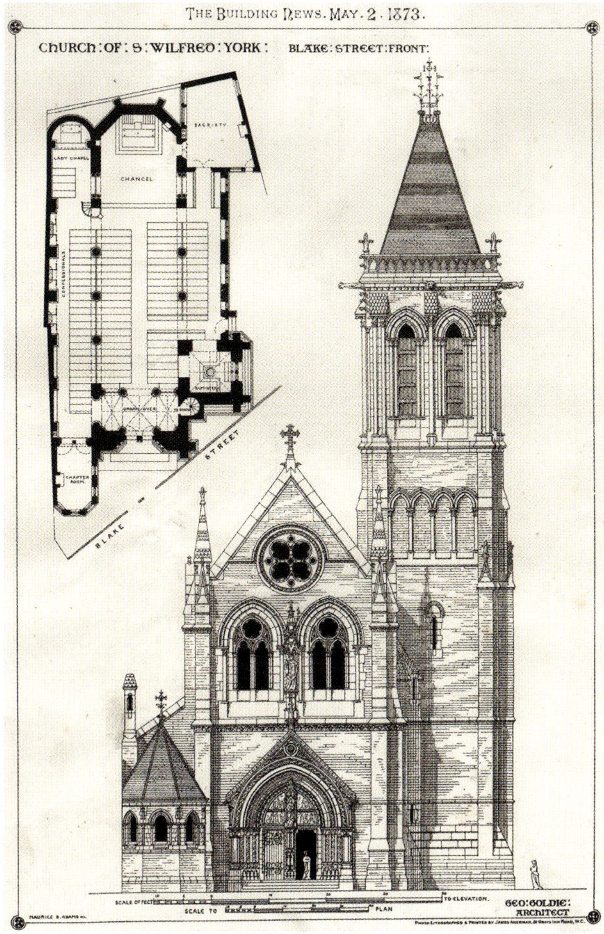

Fig. 7.3 | St. Wilfrid's church, York (1862–4) by George Goldie, plan and elevation drawing as illustrated in *The Building News* (May 2, 1873). Alamy.

of the Convent of the Assumption in Kensington Square, London, of 1870–75. This had an apse, with Aberdeen granite shafts, and was divided into the choir for the nuns, with stalls, at the east end, a central space for the school pupils, and a western part for the public. The carving by Thomas Earp included a lavish reredos, now removed (Fig. 7.4). The metal altar was by F. Russaud of Paris. Goldie also designed the 'large educational building', for the school run by the nuns.[19] St Mary's, Middlesbrough, used as the Pro-Cathedral, was built in 1876–8, enlarged by George's son Edward Goldie (introduced below) in the 1890s, and demolished in 2000.

An unusual country house commission of the 1860s was the enlargement of Pampisford Hall, Cambridgeshire, in a classical style, but Goldie's most notable country house was Upsall Castle, Yorkshire, a great Gothic fantasy, with a tall tower and a huge library (Fig. 7.5).[20] It cost Captain Turton £8,000 before the interiors were begun. It was demolished in 1918 after a fire.

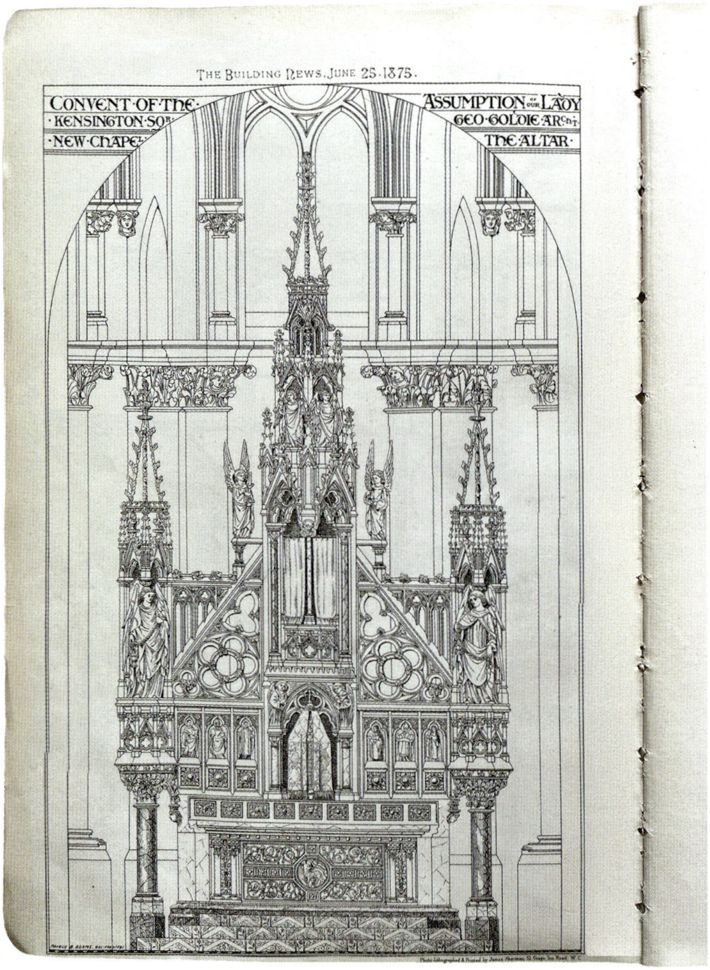

Fig. 7.4 | Thomas Earp, reredos at the Convent of the Assumption in Kensington Square, London (1870-75). *Building News*, June 25, 1875.

Although 'a very enthusiastic admirer' of Gothic, 'he never altogether abandoned the Renaissance style, even for ecclesiastical works', his church in Great Ormond Street 'amply showing his skill and knowledge of that style'.[21] This was the church of the Hospital of Saint John of Jerusalem, and the style was obviously chosen because of the hospital's association with the Knights of Malta. In a letter to Charles Hadfield of 1863, the architect J.F. Bentley wrote 'Goldie is building a Ch in Great Ormond St, in the Italian style, this I think shows but little self abnegation. I thought he was a rampant Gothicist'.[22] In 1898 Edward Goldie moved the chapel to St John's Wood, as part of the Hospital of Saints John and Elizabeth. In 1856 George Goldie gave a lecture in London on 'ecclesiastical architecture, in which he saw the difference between Classical and Gothic as the difference between pagan and Christian.[23]

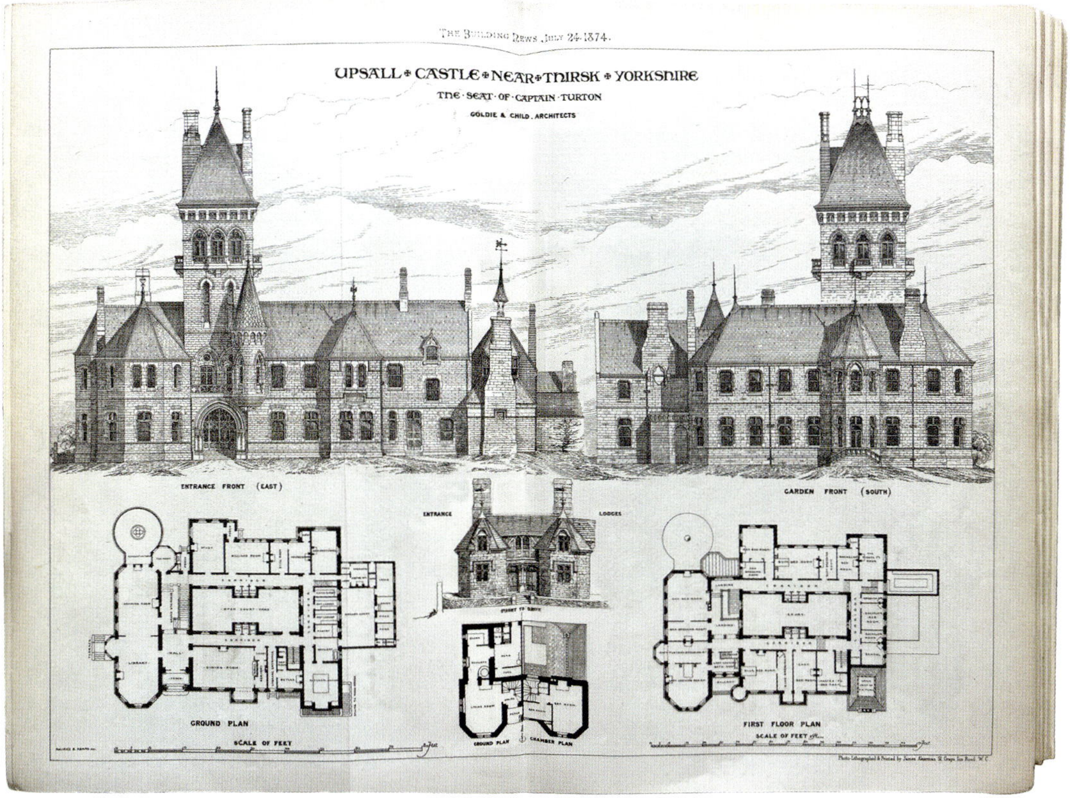

Fig. 7.5 | Goldie and Child, plans and elevations of Upsall Castle, Yorkshire. *Building News*, July 24, 1874.

Goldie entered the competition for the Brompton Oratory church in 1878. The design was required to be in the 'Italian Renaissance' style. His design was not mentioned by the assessor, Alfred Waterhouse, but it was described as 'fine' by *The Builder*.[24] The exterior was to be of Portland stone, but the interior of brick, with marble revetment, columns, and floor. The dome was not included in his entry, to save money. *The Builder*, in its obituary of Goldie, wrote that the design was worthy of being better known, and was published as 'a slight tribute to the memory of Goldie, who has left much excellent work behind him'.[25]

Goldie wrote on archaeological subjects for *The Month* and other Catholic publications. He was a skilled draughtsman, and some of his sketches of ancient buildings were used to illustrate periodicals and architectural books. In 1877 he was awarded the Cross and Order of St Sylvester. He married Marie Madeleine Rose Simeon Stylite Sioc'han de Kersabiec (1830–96), known as Stylite, of a distinguished Breton family, and described as 'propriétaire'. They had several children. Eventually Goldie moved for the sake of his health to his house, the 'malouinière' Le Val Riant, at St Servan in Brittany.[26] When he died there, after a brief illness, he was buried at St Jouan des Guérets.

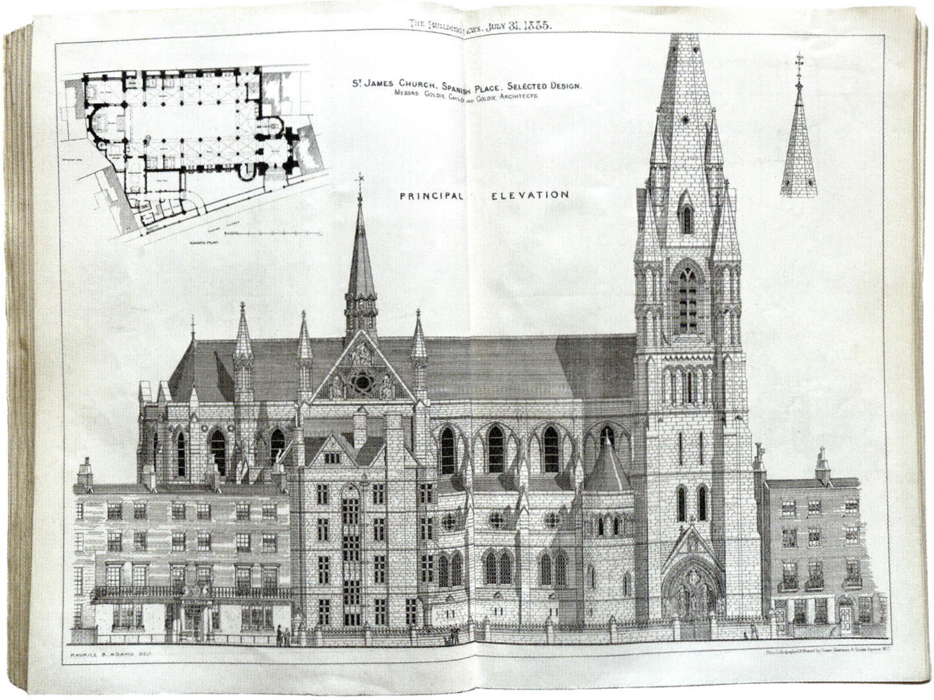

Fig. 7.6 | Goldie and Child, principal Elevation and plan of St James' Church, Spanish Place, London. *Building News*, July 31, 1885.

Goldie had a son who became an architect. Edward Joseph Marie de Kersabiec Goldie (1856–1921) was born in Sheffield and educated at Ushaw.[27] In 1875 he was articled to Goldie and Child, becoming a partner in 1880. From 1893 he practised on his own, until in 1913 he was joined by his son Joseph. The firm was known as Edward Goldie and Son until 1953. His partner Geoffrey Ronald Gilbertson Topham, after training at the Architectural Association and travel in Italy, was articled to Edward Goldie from 1908 to 1911. In 1918 he set up his own firm, dying in 1944. The firm continued as Edward Goldie and Son until 1953.

The Goldie firm won the limited competition for St James's, Spanish Place, Marylebone, in 1885 (Fig. 7.6). Edward's father's failing health prevented him from taking the leading part. In his obituary of George Goldie, T. J. Willson wrote that the design was chiefly due to Edward Goldie, but he subsequently explained that Child was 'equally associated with him in its preparation'.[28] The very large and tall church, in the Early English style required by the competition, is vaulted and has an apse and galleries over the aisles. There is obvious French influence. It was built in 1887–90. The furnishings are mainly by J.F. Bentley. The Parish Priest wanted him to design the church, but Cardinal Manning insisted on a competition, which Bentley refused to enter on principle. The three western bays were added in 1914–8, but the tall spire shown in the engraved designs remained unbuilt.

Edward also designed a large country mansion, Ashorne Hill House, in Warwickshire, in Elizabethan style, for the American Arthur Tree (1895–7). Other works include the former Dominican Priory at Hawkesyard in Staffordshire (1896–1914), with a large and fine late Gothic chapel, and the church of the Most Holy Redeemer and St Thomas More in Chelsea (1895), in Renaissance style.

Joseph Goldie's works include the church of the Assumption, Englefield Green, Surrey (1930–31), a large and powerful Romanesque building.

NOTES

1. Peter Meadows, *Joseph Bonomi Architect 1739–1808* (London: RIBA, 1988).
2. Howard Colvin, *A Biographical Dictionary of British Architects, 4th ed.* (Yale: Yale University Press, 2008), 141.
3. The building is being restored for use by the British Library.
4. Colvin, *British Architects*, 141–43. The drawing for the gateway is in the RIBA Drawings Collection.
5. Colvin, *British Architects*, 141.
6. *Ibid.*, 141.
7. Peter Meadows, "Palatinate Patronage", *Country Life* 183, December 5, 1989, 64–69; see also J. H. Crosby, *Ignatius Bonomi of Durham, Architect* (Durham: City of Durham Trust, 1987).
8. Christopher Hussey, "Lambton Castle, Durham," *Country Life* 139 March 24, 1966, 664–66; Christopher Hussey, "Lambton Castle, Durham," *Country Life* 139, March 31, 1966, 726–729.
9. A.F, Sealey and D. Walters, "The First Railway Architecture," *Architectural Review* 135 (1964): 364–66.
10. Meadows, *Joseph Bonomi Architect,* 22.
11. Colvin, *British Architects*, 137.
12. Anon., "The Late Mr. George Goldie," *The Tablet,* March 19, 1887, 462; *The Builder* 52 (1887): 367; *Building News* 52 (1887): 314; *RIBA Proceedings* 3, NS no. 3 (1887): 357, 387.
13. Anon., "The Late Mr. George Goldie."
14. On this firm see Hadfield Cawkwell Davidson, *150 Years of Architectural Drawings – Hadfield Cawkwell Davidson, Sheffield, 1834–1984* (Sheffield: Mappin Art Gallery 1984).
15. His design was illustrated in *The Civil Engineer and Architect's Journal* 19 (1856): 333; see Caoimhín de Bhailís, "George Goldie, 'a rampant Gothicist' in Ireland", *Ecclesiology Today* 60 (2021): 39–60; for Goldie in Ireland see also Caoimhín de Bhailís, "A Catholic Architect in Post-Famine Ireland" *Studies: an Irish Quarterly Review* 109 (2020): 177–90.
16. *The Builder* 23 (1865): 661.
17. *Ibid.*, 349.
18. *Building News* 26 (1873): 504, 530, 558, 586, 616.
19. *Building News* 20 (1871): 250; *Building News* 28 (1875): 716.
20. *Building News* 27 (1874): 108.
21. Anon., "The Late Mr. George Goldie."
22. J. F. Bentley quoted in Peter Howell, "Letters from J F Bentley to Charles Hadfield", *Architectural History*, vol. 23 (1980): 95–137; *Architectural History* 23 (1980): 100.
23. George Goldie, *A Lecture on Ecclesiastical Architecture* (London: Richardson, 1856).
24. *The Builder* 52 (1887): 367.
25. *Ibid.*, 367, 536.
26. A 'malouiniere' was a 17th or 18th century house in the district of St Malo. The chapel has a stained glass window with his initials and coat of arms.
27. No proper obituary was published, merely notices of his death.
28. *RIBA Proceedings* 3 NS no. 3 (1887): 358, 387.

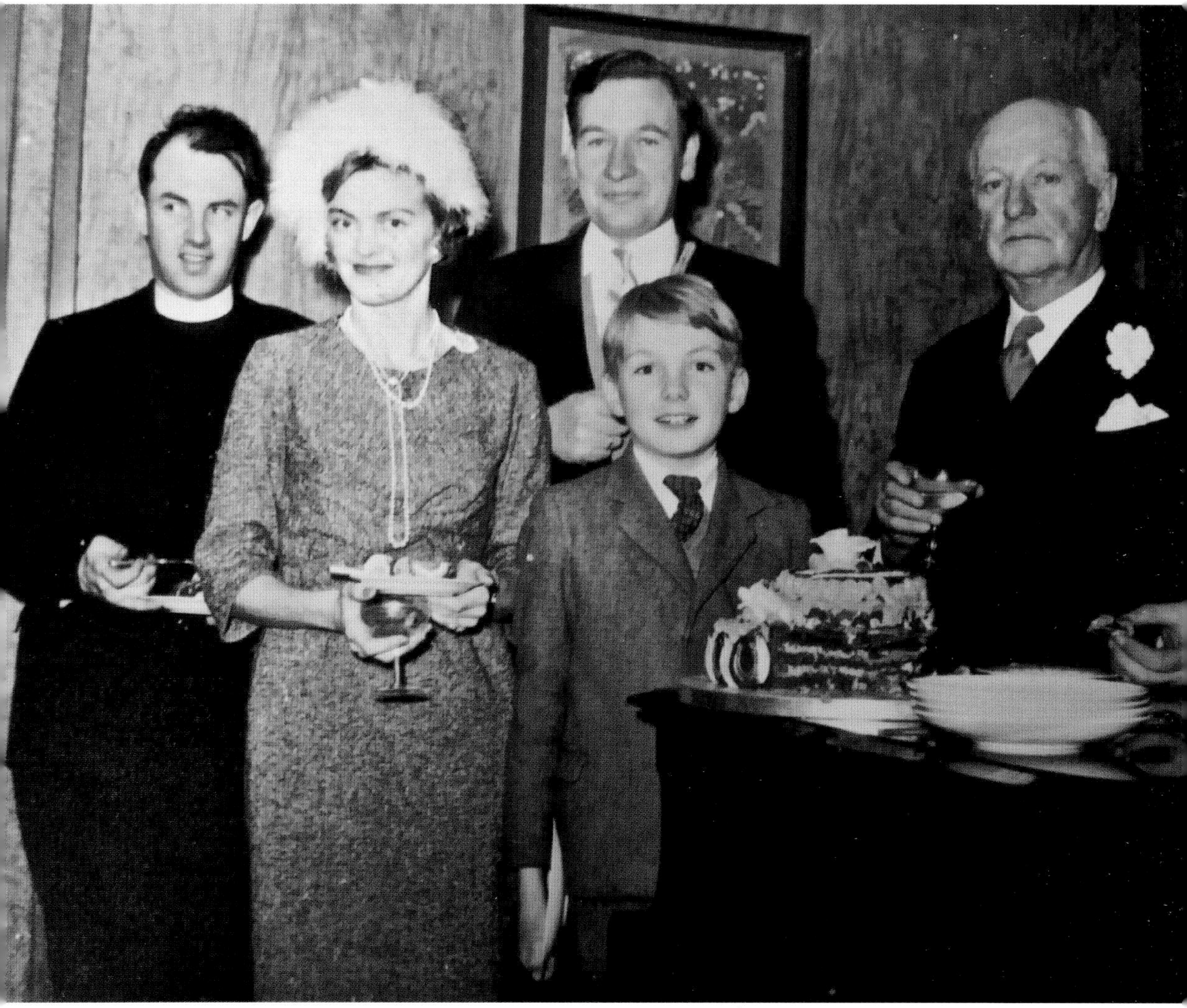

Fig. 8.1 | Three generations of Gilbert Scotts. From left to right after the vicar (name unknown): Eline, Richard, Nick (aged *c.* 10) and Giles. Chester House, London (*c.* 1956–7). Courtesy Nick Gilbert Scott.

8 · Scale, Inhabitation and Detail: In Conversation with a Fifth-Generation Scott

NICK GILBERT SCOTT and JOSHUA MARDELL

Nick Gilbert Scott (b. 1947) (Fig. 8.1), *architect in practice, 1975–2024, is the fifth-generation scion of what Gavin Stamp once called England's 'greatest architectural dynasty'.*[1] *The* paterfamilias *was George Gilbert Scott (1811–1878). The second generation comprised George Gilbert Scott Junior (1839–1897) and John Oldrid Scott (1841–1913). The third comprised Gilbert's sons Giles Gilbert Scott (1880–1960) and Adrian Gilbert Scott (1882–1963), and John Oldrid's son, Charles Marriott Oldrid Scott (1880–1952). Giles' son, Richard Gilbert Scott (1923–2017) formed the fourth generation. Nick's cousins Peter Gilbert-Scott [sic], Robert Gilbert Scott, and John Scott, were also architects.*[2] *While the Scott dynasty of architects ends with Nick, his own offspring continue a professional preoccupation with space.*[3]

Nick set up his own practice in Exeter in 1977. Somewhat contrary to the big practices of his forebears, and, ever conscious of the embodied experience of architectural space – how the environment fits the body and is responsive to it – his focus has been on a local architecture, using local materials and local craftspeople. Yet, as this conversation revealed, his practice is built on the architectural values of 'scale, inhabitation and detail' imbibed by members of the Scott dynasty. He is particularly influenced by proxemics, i.e. 'the ways people interact spatially'.[4] *His interest in the bonds unifying architecture and dance, furthermore, provides a rationale for his own pluralistic practice, while also offering a new lens for examining the oeuvre of the Scott dynasty* per se. *A central part of Nick's practice has been teaching. He has held posts in the School of Architecture at the University of Plymouth (2001–2024), and Trinity Laban Conservatoire of Music and Dance, London (1999–2009).*

Our interview took place on 20 October 2023 at Scott's home in Brampford Speke, Exeter, that he and his wife Sarah built for themselves in 1977. We talked in Scott's office, where a large drawing (1.7 metres high) by Frederick Thomas – of an organ standing on the nave arch of Liverpool Cathedral – leans against one corner of the room.

NGS: This drawing used to be in my father's office in Gray's Inn [Holborn, London] and was handed down to me. It shows the bridge in Liverpool Cathedral with an organ mounted above. This was the intended function of the arch, but the organ was never built due to lack of funds. It was drawn by Frederick Thomas, my grandfather's partner. It is not in great shape – it was in the chicken shed for a while when dad had it.

JM: The drawing must evoke memories of your grandfather?

NGS: As a child I was taken on a tour of the Cathedral. Near the top of the tower, there is a high-colonnaded gallery where I became giddy! At its corners there are little minaret-like structures, suggesting to our imagination distant but accessible places on high. They are like eyries looking out, lifting our spirits as well as our bodies to a higher place.

JM: Since when were you conscious of being part of a 'dynasty'?

NGS: Sir John Betjeman was the first person I ever heard who described my family as a 'dynasty of architects'. He enthusiastically claimed that the Scotts had made a very significant contribution to British architecture. This was news to me!

JM: Did you hear this first-hand, as a child?

NGS: Yes, indirectly. Betjeman became a friend of my parents, Richard Gilbert Scott and Eline Marie Gilbert Scott [née Brodin, 1922–2022], in the 1970s. Betjeman and my father were members of FABS [the Foreign Architectural Book Society]. Dad was very keen on FABS dinners, and both regularly attended them. Betjeman was working hard to save St. Pancras Station from demolition. [...] We lived north of Hyde Park, so it was a child's walk across to the Albert Memorial [in Kensington Gardens] where we were taken up the steps to see the portrait of George Gilbert Scott. We were quietly proud of him.

JM: You lived at Chester House [designed by Giles Gilbert Scott, 1925], in Bayswater, as a child?

NGS: Yes, from 1949, living with my grandfather, my father and mother and two of my younger sisters. The house was designed in a very domestic, simplified classical style. Like my grandfather, it was gentle and relaxed. My own experience of architecture developed during my first twelve years living there, until Giles died in 1960. We have a drawing of it by Raffles Davison. (Fig. 8.2)

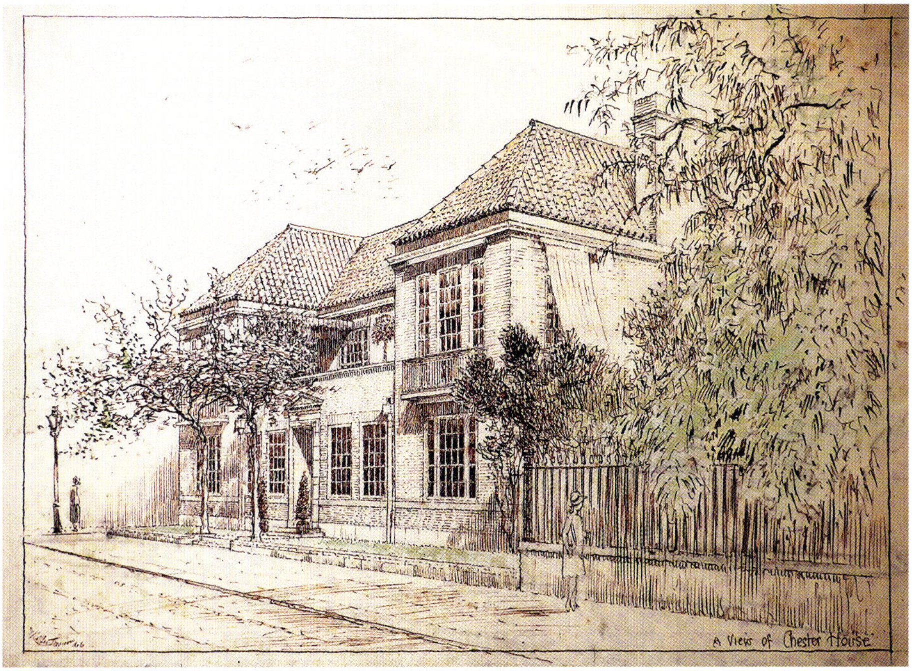

Fig. 8.2 | Raffles Davison, 'A View of Chester House', undated (*c.*1926).

JM: This is something that we might try and unpick across the conversation, but are there 'dynastic' themes across the five generations' work that you recognise, and that resonate with you?

NGS: There is a romantic thread running through the whole thing. For example, the celestial connotations of St. Pancras Station, an earthly heaven. [NGS was referring to John O'Connor's painting of the Midland Grand Hotel, towering over Victorian street life] (Fig. 8.3). Of course, religion is always in the background

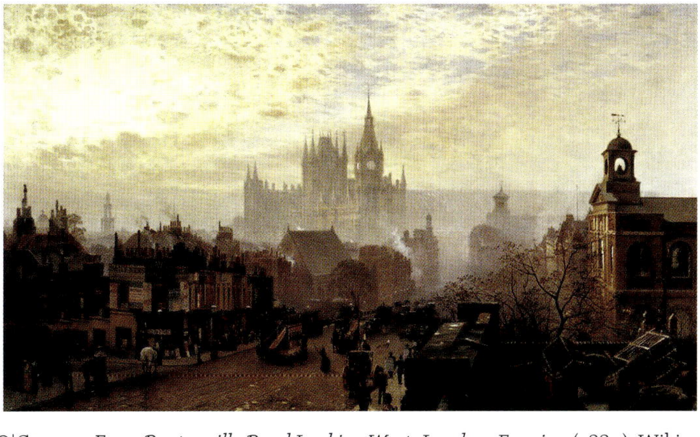

Fig. 8.3 | John O'Connor, *From Pentonville Road Looking West, London, Evening* (1884). Wikicommons.

because Scott Senior's father was a priest. There were a lot of priests in the family. They were either priests or architects! Grandad [Giles] was brought up a Catholic, because of Middle Scott's [Scott Junior's] conversion.

There is a strong spiritual leaning to beauty. I think that aspect runs through the whole thread of Scott work. I get it with my grandpa looking at a chimney at Bankside power station – it gets me. There's something about it that chimes in with a romantic aspiration of celestial beauty of some kind.

JM: Does the romanticism extend to your father's work?

NGS: His favourite building of his own was Portland House at Aldermaston [Berkshire] built as the headquarters of Blue Circle [cement] in the mid 1980s. It was created as part of a lakeside scene. It is a large modern concrete building that meanders sensitively and unobtrusively in a romantic setting, adding to rather than disturbing the peace of the landscape. Dad's first model of the project reminded me of some Eastern temple complex. Now, sadly, the building is unused and being left to deteriorate. What a waste!

JM: And what of the continuation of the Gothic thread in the Scott dynasty?

NGS: Gavin Stamp referred to the new West Wing of the Guildhall building by my father [1970–75] as 'Pop Gothic'. It was very large, ten storeys in all, with three below ground. To keep the scale down, my father reduced the floor heights and subdivided the levels into a hierarchy of plinth, *piano nobile* and roof tier, overcoming the monolithic effect of one mass [...] The mullions, Gothic in their verticality, provide a gentle scale of pattern across the space, forming a background to the Corbusian freestanding porch, with a chamber over it.

I resurrected a Gothic lantern in one of my building projects, a conversion of a Victorian property at Barnhill, Brampford Speke, Exeter (2012–14) (Fig. 8.4). What I brought to it was to make it an escapist, intimate and romantic eyrie. My design involved moving the stair to the central hall and releasing the tower to be used as inhabited space. The lantern itself presented an opportunity to create a secluded lookout – a 'sociofugal' space – reached by a narrow winding stair leading up to the light.[5] It is also a cosy place for family and close friends, so as well as being a hideaway, it can also become a 'sociopetal' space for close encounters. We transformed it from a romantic vision to a romantic experience. It borrows a little bit from Bachelard's *The Poetics of Space* where you go and huddle in a secluded refuge like a nest, and look out across the landscape, the setting sun, the river and dream or drink yourself senseless in a thunderstorm. This is embodied architecture. It's not just the vision, but the *experience* of being there.

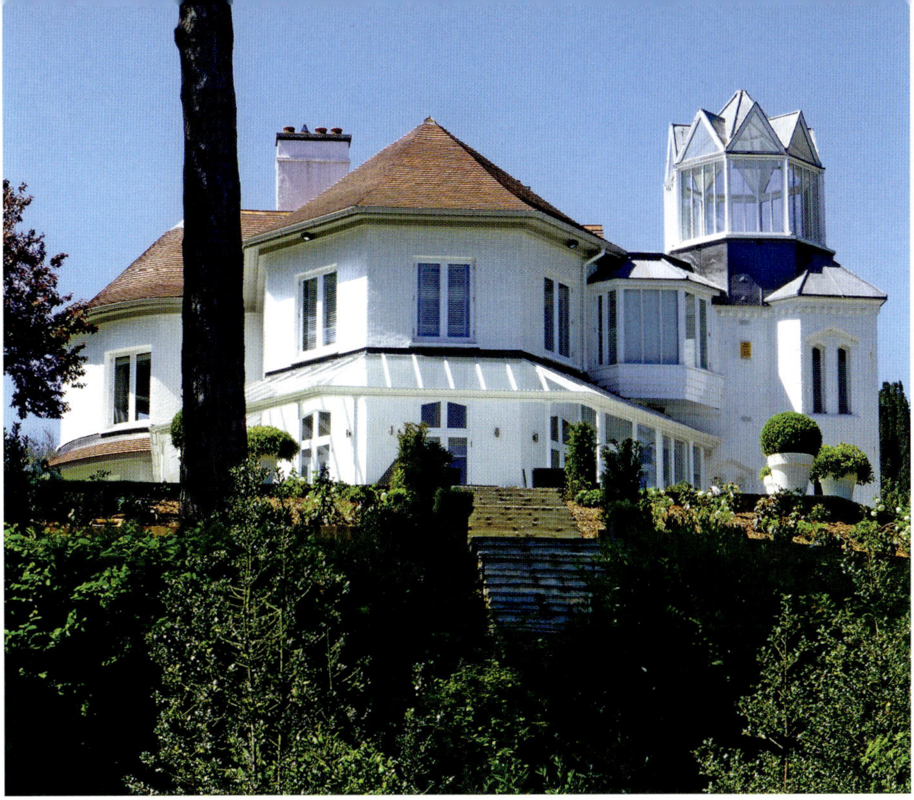

Fig. 8.4 | Nick Gilbert Scott, conversion of Barnhill, Brampford Speke, Exeter (2012–14).

JM: Going back in time again, did you visit your father's and grandfather's office as a child?

NGS: My grandad and dad would drive from Chester House to their office in Gray's Inn, and I visited occasionally as a child.[6] But in Chester House itself there was a study, a lovely first floor room with two drawing boards side by side: my grandfather's to the left and my father's to the right. And there were always drawings out, and models. I remember dad making models there. There was always work in progress and I can remember a Saturday morning going in there with my granddad who was always whistling tunelessly to himself. He was always happy to natter with us kids and we were always stealing pencils and rubbers from his pencil box. We got to know the style of his drawings quite unconsciously. They became part of our life. We could easily recognize his buildings because we knew the drawings.

Dad was a good perspectivist of very contemporary modernist interiors. His board often had perspective drawings of great depth with many straight parallel lines very satisfyingly controlled. He loved his verticals. Lots of verticals. Grandad's board had large, beautiful elevations with ashlar coursing spread out, maybe sketching out detailed pieces of ornamental stone tracery [...]. He would be chain-smoking, with ash everywhere.

JM: Did father and son use the same tools?

NGS: Grandad's pencils were always short with a little rubber on the end – stubby and sat in his hand. Whereas dad had rather formal propelling pencils which were much more suited to his contemporary eye for line. You were looking at a gothic-inspired architect and next to him a young contemporary architect working his way.

JM: Did they discuss each other's work?

NGS: Richard said Giles said little to him about their respective styles and work despite the physical proximity.[7] He [Richard] found it difficult to follow on from such a successful father. Giles' only constant was to say that 'proportion and scale are of paramount importance'. Drawing was *the* medium in which, as a child in the 1950s, I saw my father and grandfather work.

JM: To what extent do you think that the Victorian Scotts were present in the imaginations of your father and grandfather?

NGS: I was under 13 when my grandfather died, so I have a child's perspective. In later life, dad recalled that grandad said that the real artist in the family was Middle Scott. And in my family the highest accolade is to describe an architect as an artist. That's really the highest level of architecture within the family culture.

JM: How did the idea of the architect as artist manifest itself in your predecessors' work?

NGS: I think it refers to the creative sensitivity. My grandfather thought his grandfather's [George Gilbert Scott Senior's] work was over-worked and academic, well informed by his understanding of precedent that he had studied [...] Whereas Middle Scott was seen as a truly creative, imaginative artist. I agree with my grandfather, that Middle Scott expressed feeling, spirit and soul in his work. At Pembroke College, Cambridge, his design for New Court [1883] is classical, with a scale that is both intimate and friendly, while simultaneously being quite formal and dignified. It is a lovely, quirky composition with changes of level and balustrade parapets between the dormers, which are masterfully handled. The whole creates a beautiful space where less is more. In the language of Norberg-Schulz, the space itself becomes the prevailing architectural element.[8] At his tiny church of St Mary Magdalene at East Moors [near Helmsley, Yorkshire, 1882] it is the delicate scale that delights me, with the relationship between the figures and the whole making it so personal.[9]

JM: It seems then, that these delicate inter-relationships between parts and the whole in buildings are another 'thread' within the Scott work?

NGS: I think my grandfather got used to managing great scale, depth and light initially within the discipline of drawing. He explored this in experimental drawings that were called 'Dad's drunks'.[10] They were Piranesi-like, an early exploration of the enormity of scale that he was going to have to handle at Liverpool. He dramatized the height of everything by putting figures in everywhere and by setting the perspective at eye level [...] so the whole thing looked phenomenally enormous.

At Liverpool Cathedral, as built, the enormity of the space is dramatized by galleries, balustrades, doorways, steps, and seats, giving us clues to the size of the human body and the scale of the whole space in relation to it. The building invites and affords movement and exploration. I notice that where places have human scale, that is where they are enriched by stone or wood carving. Giles would often represent natural leaf and floral forms, which would be close enough to touch.

At Biggin Hill Church [St Mark's, Biggin Hill, Kent, by Richard Gilbert Scott, 1957–9], closely spaced, soaring mullions above the entrance to the highest point of the roof all express a Gothic aspiration for height, for the Divine. But also, a modesty of scale with the low eaves, buttressing walls and entrance [that] bring the building right down to the human level. [Nick subsequently sent me a pencil drawing of 1979, of an Edwardian crowd in a futuristic architectural scene, which is another instance of his own exploration of contrasting dramatic scales (and temporalities) (Fig. 8.5)].

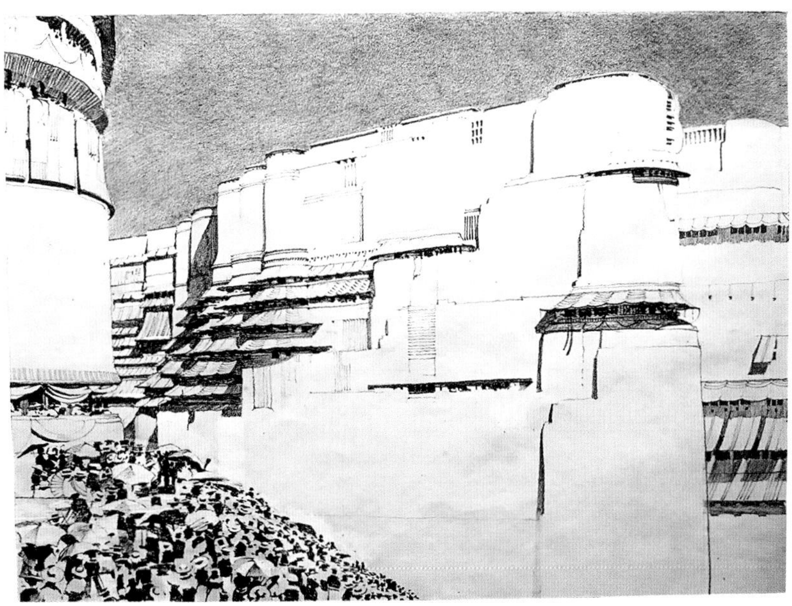

Fig. 8.5 | Nick Gilbert Scott, drawing of an Edwardian crowd in a futuristic architectural scene (1979).

JM: I understand you were born Nicholas Giles *Scott? It is as though your family, saw you quite self-consciously as a dynastic heir?*

NGS: I was born a boy, which in those days mattered a lot. Maybe the next generation of architects was implicit. I was going to be christened Nicholas Gilbert Scott and my grandmother Louise [Gilbert Scott, née Wallbank Hughes [1887–1949]] said, 'go on put Giles in there!' Because Giles was so adored, and adorable. [..] He had nothing of the big ego man that his buildings might suggest. My grandmother chose the name because of the love with which he was held by all of us. [...] Because he was such a gentle, easy-spirited guy who loved drawing, the paradox is that he created these enormous landmark buildings of huge dimensions. But the thing that to me relates me to him in those great buildings is scale because if you look at the detail, it is always to the hand so sweet, so delightfully near. [...] This is where the feeling of the architect as artist comes in because it is a kind of sweet sensitivity to human nature.

JM: Would you say you have inherited some of that intimacy of scale in your own practice?

NGS: I would say so yes, absolutely. There's a kind of tenderness. My father was so besotted with Le Corbusier who rationalised his understanding of scale by working out the Modulor. My father measured us all, how close we were to Le Corbusier's 'ideal'. [...] I was blown away by Marseilles [the Unité d'Habitation]: everything is scaled to the body, even if it's a giant building. And Lutyens' Castle Drogo [Devon]: that porch is grand, yet sweet in scale. I believe in making architecture personal even though it might first appear to be less friendly.

My father regularly said to me 'Always put figures in your drawing as they will give scale to the building.' This had significant consequences to me as this theme developed to become a strong priority in my practice and teaching of architecture.

JM: Were there other formative moments that helped you find your way into architecture?

NGS: One great thing that happened to me as a kid at Chester House was being given some wooden bricks that my grandfather had designed for my father, which got burnt during the war. Giles made another set that he gave to me on two successive Christmases (Fig. 8.6). Some are 2 ft 6 inches long, 3 inches wide, and 1 inch thick. You can really build substantial things with them, and they are beautifully proportioned. Me, dad, and grandad would all try and build towers that would reach the ceiling.

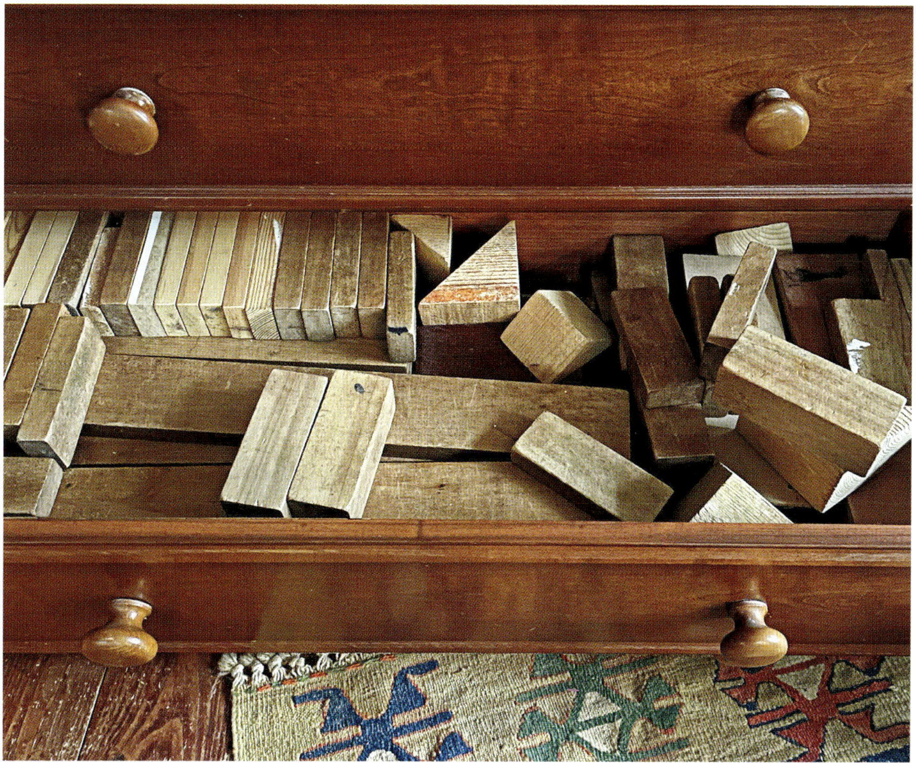

Fig. 8.6 | Wooden building bricks designed by Giles Gilbert Scott for his grandson, Nick, and gifted to him in the early 1950s. Joshua Mardell.

JM: Were they produced just for the family?

NGS: Yes, they weren't produced for a market. Becoming an architect was always on the horizon. By the time I was 16 or 17, I got into painting at the art school at Charterhouse [Godalming, Surrey], and I discovered that I was good at drawing. I shined in the studio under a fantastic art teacher called Ian Fleming Williams [1914–1998]. The studio block [whose building Fleming Williams had supervised, designed by James Dartford] was a refuge for those who didn't fit well into the public-school scene. It was a place of real culture where I thrived.

When I left Charterhouse, I wanted to be an artist. My parents took Fleming Williams to supper one weekend and my dad asked him what I should do. Fleming Williams said I should do architecture and I could be an artist later if I liked. That sealed my fate, to my disappointment. I got into Regent Street Poly[technic], London where my father had studied after WWII.[11] I was antagonised by the functionality of the course, because, after all, I had been taught that good architects were artists. I was less interested in environmental physics. So, I painted as a reaction, before eventually buckling down to architecture.

JM: Charterhouse was a dynastic setting, in a way, noting your grandfather's huge chapel there, and your father's later boarding houses?[12]

NGS: Yes, my father had also been a student there.

JM: Do any of your paintings survive from the 'rebellious' phase?

NGS: I have got one painting from that period on the staircase; it's cathedral-like (Fig. 8.7). I realised while I thought I wanted to be a painter that my paintings were in any case all about architectural space! [*NGS later informed me of a mural he painted on the invitation of his father at the Guildhall, titled* Sails on a Sloping Landscape *(1975) now in the collection of Guildhall Art Gallery. 'It just shows how this kind of yearning for these spatial experiences goes on being expressed in the paintings'*].[13]

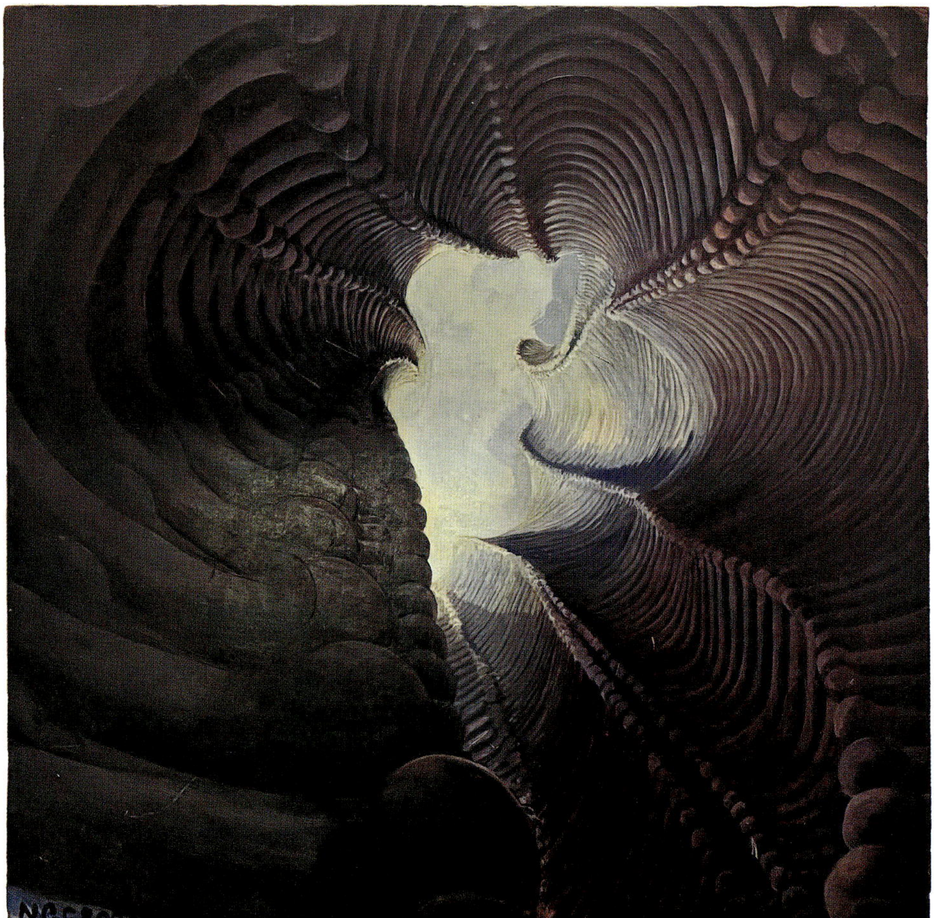

Fig. 8.7 | Nick Gilbert Scott, 'cathedral' painting made during studies at Regent Street Polytechnic (1968).

JM: In a competition entry in the 1980s you called yourself a 'painter-architect'! But let's pick up the competition later. Could you continue describing your early journey into architecture?

NGS: In the autumn of 1966, I helped on a building site at dad's building, Tile Cross [Church of Our Lady Help of Christians, 1964–7] near Birmingham. I was very excited by dad's sketches for it. He had seen Le Corbusier's Chapel at Ronchamp and had come back full of enthusiasm. As built, there was an aspiration to height, with strong structural curving vaults that soar up, Gothic in spirit. In this modern interpretation, the roof hangs and is in tension, using pre-stressed concrete. In Gothic architecture stone arches are in compression. The scale rises from the personal at the entry and grows up to light and lofty grandeur above the altar in the centre – a climax of light (Fig. 8.8).

Both of these commissions for Roman Catholic churches came to my father's office on the death of his uncle, Adrian, the architect of many Catholic churches during the last century.

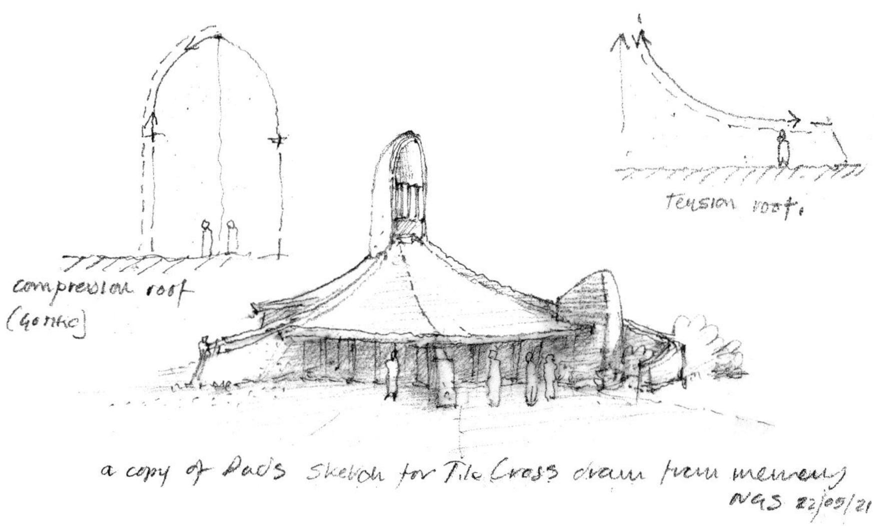

Fig. 8.8 | Roman Catholic Church of Our Lady Help of Christians, Birmingham, drawing by Nick Gilbert Scott, based on his memory of his father's concept drawings, 22 May, 2021.

JM: What are your memories of Adrian?

NGS: He was a great big man, a huge guy, very strong, very present, and quite loud. He liked shooting. When Giles died, he came down to see us at Hollis Street Farm, Ninfield, Sussex, which had become our family home because Giles left it to my mum. We loved to see him because he brought comforting echoes of my grandad back – he chain-smoked too!

JM: What was the nature of your work at Tile Cross, Birmingham?

NGS: I was having a year out [in 1966] and Dad got me onto the site when the job was beginning to go up. Dad wanted a hanging roof, and I was given the job of a steel-fixer's mate putting up the steel reinforcements (Fig. 8.9). I also had a vaguely social mission. I got to learn about the rest of the world outside of my privileged position and education. I'd go back to the YMCA [hostel] in Birmingham and draw built fantasies each evening after working on site. That summer I also went on a Venice course run by John Hall, then newly established, on the recommendation of Ian Fleming Williams.

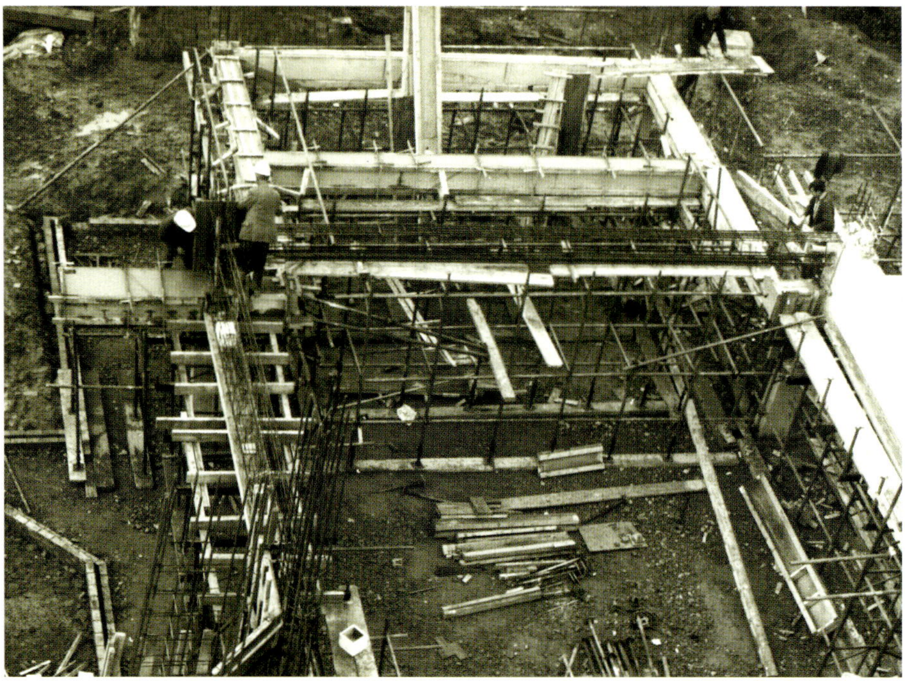

Fig. 8.9 | Roman Catholic Church of Our Lady Help of Christians, Birmingham under construction in winter 1966. Nick can be seen working as a steel fixer's mate on the far left. Nick Gilbert Scott.

JM: Do you remember any influential tutors at the Polytechnic?

NGS: Hans Haenlein [b. 1935] was a wonderful tutor. I slowly began to realise there was a social and personal dimension to architecture, nurtured by Haenlein, that I began to really respond to, especially housing and community needs. I became quite socially- and socialist-orientated. In my third year under Haenlein, I did a housing scheme on the north side of the Thames. I produced these little wooden sheds with gabled roofs, a fishing village, with a little square, like a tiny Venetian piazza, with a stone well in the middle. This was before people were using the word vernacular. And the tutors, who were all trendy modernists, were bemused but found it beautiful. This was our push back on the pressure to follow the modernist line. Robert Adam was in my year, and it turned the switch; it turned *his* switch! Postmodernism was in the air. I got a copy of *Complexity and Contradiction in Architecture* by Robert Venturi.

JM: Did you think of yourself as postmodernist?

NGS: I am a pragmatist. There was a growing anti-modernness [at the Polytechnic]. Our year was probably the first to be explicitly anti-modern. Ernö Goldfinger visited the Poly and was absolutely hammered by the students.[14] We were looking backwards for precedents. And there was excitement about context as a driver of design. We were sensitive to context, both physical and social.

JM: Could you say something about the politics of your family and how this shaped how you thought about architecture? Was there a genealogy there in thinking about architecture as a social good, for instance?

NGS: As a student, I leaned strongly to the left and my father was quite conservative, so at home it was a political battleground. My mother was quite a rebellious woman. She was Norwegian and she had been in the Norwegian resistance as a young woman during the German occupation of Oslo. My dad was a paratrooper and met her in Norway at the end of the war. Mum had been identified by the Germans and had to escape from Norway in disguise in a fishing boat. She got to Sweden and by the time dad got over she had got back. She was a heroine. We all got a rebellious streak from her which genealogically has played into my relationship with architecture and the establishment. She was an independently minded figure, feisty, with her own views.

JM: Were there other women in the family who were influential to you?

NGS: Scott Junior had a difficult relation with his wife, and my great grandmother, Ellen Gilbert Scott [née King Sampson, 1854–1953]. I remember her in her 100th year. She was a scary figure to me, as a toddler at the time. She brought up her four children all on her own, three sons and a daughter: Sebastian (the eldest), then Giles, then Adrian – and finally their daughter, Thea. She encouraged Giles and Adrian to do architecture, so she was the force behind the dynasty. When grandad did the competition drawings at [the age of] 21 for the cathedral, she, along with Adrian, was one of the ones adding texture and colour to the drawings. She was seriously committed to architecture.

In my generation, my sisters got a second-class education in relation to me. I went to a top public school and went to architecture school. But my sisters found their way into being powerfully expressive women as artists, with a spatial bent to their practice. Belinda [Gilbert Scott] is a painter who works mostly in two dimensions but goes into the third dimension with terrific ease. Louise [Gilbert Scott] works mostly in ceramics but creates these great floor-based arrays of tiny pots.

JM: Did you think of the architect Elisabeth Scott as part of the dynasty?[15]

We thought of her as one of us, but distantly. My dad was in touch with her family in Canada. Her Shakespeare [Memorial] Theatre [Stratford-upon-Avon, 1928] is the same period of brickwork that my grandfather was known for. I see a loose genealogy in that.

JM: Was the Scott name noticed at architecture school? To what extent were your famous ancestors in the consciousness of those around you?

NGS: In the 1960s the Scotts were right off the agenda. Giles had got a few commissions late in his life, however. When he died, the office became Giles Gilbert Scott Son and Partner, my dad brought in much more modernist projects. Later when I taught at The School of Architecture in Plymouth in the early 2000s, we were located next to my grandfather's last building [the Roman Catholic Church of Christ the King, 1961–2].[16] Neither he nor his building were ever the subject of conversations in the school – the modernists prevailed!

JM: Was there a resistance, a generational/stylistic tension between your father and grandfather, like there had been between George Gilbert Scott Senior and Junior?

NGS: I think there was between dad and grandad's partner Frederick Thomas who finished off Liverpool Cathedral. But there hadn't been much tension between grandad and dad. Grandad just wanted dad to do his thing – he tried not to influence him by not saying anything. This was painful for dad, but he understood.

JM: When did you first enter a practice?

NGS: In my year out, between Parts I and II at Regent's Street, I worked for Stout & Litchfield who were incredibly formative for me. I worked on 14 new houses at Brookside, Melbourne Port [Sherborne, Somerset] and interacted with ABK [Ahrends Burton Koralek] a bit as some students at the Poly were working with them. We played football with them. They came to our end of year shows. But my last project [for the Part II, in 1973] was a Steiner School. It was in an Edwardian style, combining Steiner with Voysey.

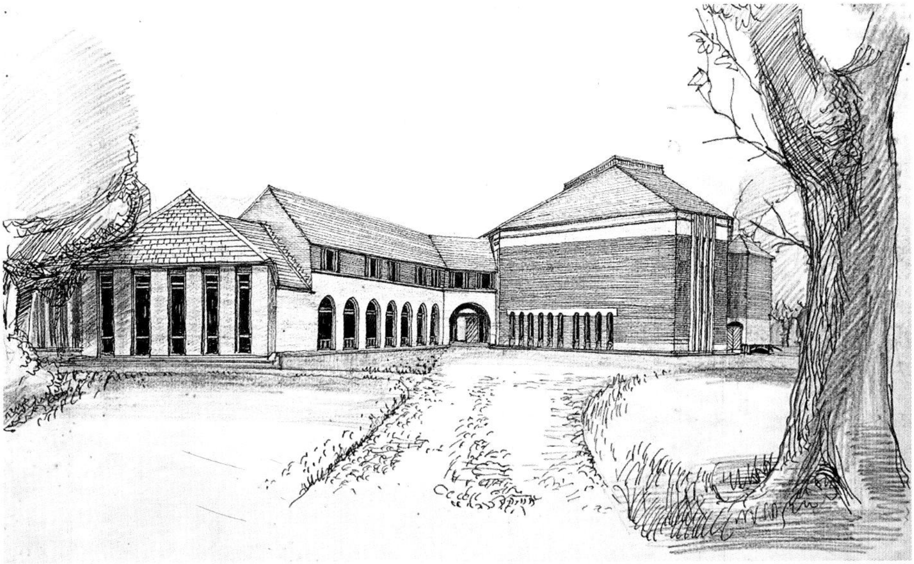

Fig. 8.10 | Nick Gilbert Scott, student project for a Steiner School (1972).

JM: Did it have corners?

NGS: Well, it had arches. The plan was very organic, inspired by Steiner's teaching; drawing on the principles of classroom practice, the views from the classrooms, and the context for learning. The brief came from Haenlein. The Labour government had thought when it was planning to go co-ed nationally that the Steiner school might be the model and produced a brief for a state Steiner school (Fig. 8.10).

JM: Was there a discernible 'Scottness' in it?

NGS: Yes, I'd say so.

JM: Almost Gothic, aren't they? There is Scott-like massing, the gradual building of mass.

NGS: It wanders around the landscape. And little amphitheatres link the spaces. Jim Stirling was my final assessor. He liked the plan, but he couldn't get his head around the retro look for a final year project at the Poly. He was very sweet and generally positive, though.

JM: Did the project help you find your way into practice?

No, I started my own practice completely independently in Devon [in 1973]. Dad was not impressed and thought I should return to doing 'proper' architecture in London. But a bit of nepotism here: dad got me a commission to do a piece of sculpture for Charterhouse School [in 1974] as part of his scheme [for new boarding houses].

I produced a dancing figure, because I had got interested in Contemporary Dance when there were some great American Dance Companies coming to London.

JM: What was the commission for?

NGS: I was asked by the governors to put a sculpture outside the new dining hall at the foot of the tower. My sculpture was made of stainless steel, rather swirling strips of stainless steel, on an eight-sided plinth (Fig. 8.11). The commission inspired me to go to life drawing classes. But it was the dynamic, the living body rather than the statuesque static body that I was interested in, so I went to dance class to see and experience the body in movement.

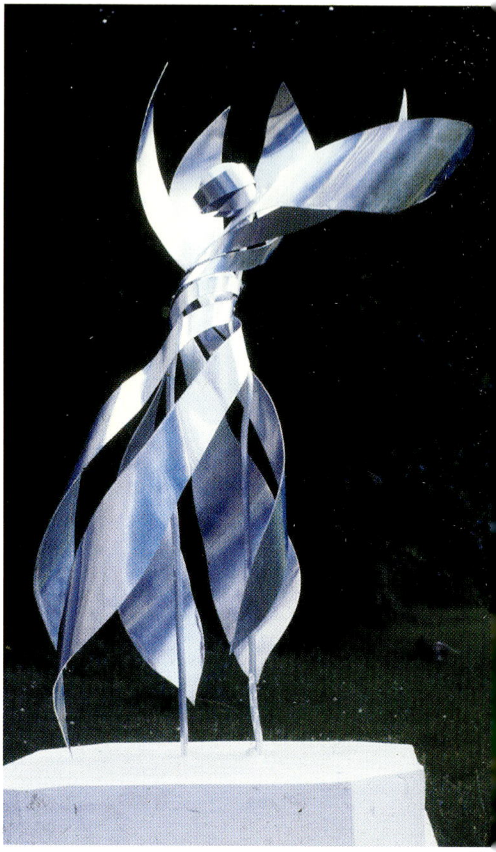

Fig. 8.11 | Nick Gilbert Scott, maquette for a sculpture of a dancing figure at Charterhouse (1975).

JM: Was the sculpture completed?

NGS: No. Michael Woods, the art teacher, thought it was too vulnerable to being vandalised.

JM: But did this bring further opportunities to work with your father, perhaps permanently?

NGS: I said no. Sarah [jokingly] said if you go and work for your father, I wouldn't marry you! [Nick and Sarah married in 1972]. In any case, on qualifying I could not face the prospect of working on my dad's huge projects. He later said it probably wouldn't have worked out anyway because I wanted to go my way and he wouldn't have let me go my way – he was too controlling, dad. Even though I did all this work on the housing at Charterhouse, he wouldn't credit that in any way.[17]

JM: What was your contribution to the boarding house scheme?

NGS: I contributed the idea of the schoolhouses being comprised as a cluster of octagonal plan forms, sitting among mature trees thus breaking down the volumes and reducing the scale (Fig. 8.12).

I worked at Exeter Cathedral with the Gundry Dyer Partnership between 1973–1976. The Scott connection at Exeter Cathedral was huge![18] I was working

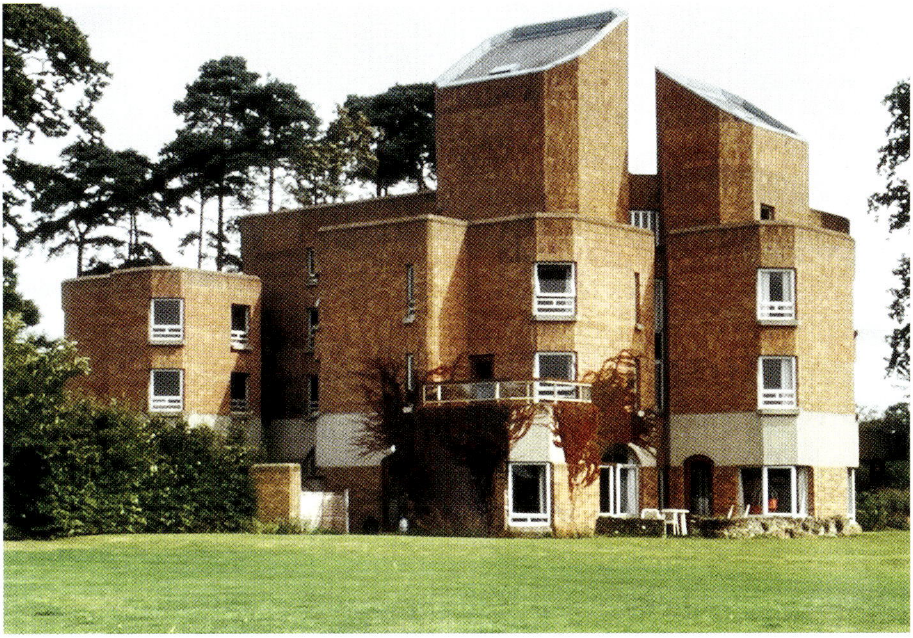

Fig. 8.12 | Nick Gilbert Scott, New Boarding Houses for Charterhouse (*c.* 1974).

with Peter Gundry, Surveyor to the Dean and Chapter and doing quinquennials [...] The main work I did [for Gundry Dyer] was to design a massive housing scheme for a building developer on the hills outside Exeter based on some Swedish models.

JM: What was the name of the scheme?

NGS: Luggs Farm housing estate. [*We went looking for a picture of these houses in Nick's file system, expecting to find it under the practice name*] Oh, it looks like I filed it under my own name. That's courageous!

Only a fragment of my challenging design was built. The developer wanted to put a standard housing layout plan on a 1 in 3.5 slope, very steep. You quickly realised that the houses on one side were way above the access road, and the others were way below it. So, a garage would have to be on the top storey of a three-storey house on one side, and in the basement on the other! It was patently not sensible. It was nonsense to suggest lofts with garages in them and the developer could not think in three dimensions! It was an education in the world of spec developing. Cheap houses were miles away from world I was brought up in.

I am still concerned about the need for new affordable houses. Recently, I have been involved with conceiving of an initiative to bring social housing back into our village, on a rural exception site. Being housing in a rural context, the scheme takes inspiration from local barns, and agricultural groupings.

JM: Was there much in the way of cheap, or speculative housing in the broader Scott oeuvre?

NGS: I found a drawing in the attic the other day by my grandfather, of proposed social housing in front of Liverpool Cathedral (Fig. 8.13). It's post-war housing [1949] but with a touch of grandfather's ornament, drawn by the illustrator A. C. Webb. It shows an interesting mix of modernist cantilever balconies and deco/gothic fenestration and decoration. My grandfather also designed a house that was going to be prefabricated. A post-war brick-clad system build. [The Boxgrove House, near St. George's, Surrey, *c.*1950s]. Only one was ever built. My dad's brother Maurice and his family lived in it. It is one of three prototype designs.

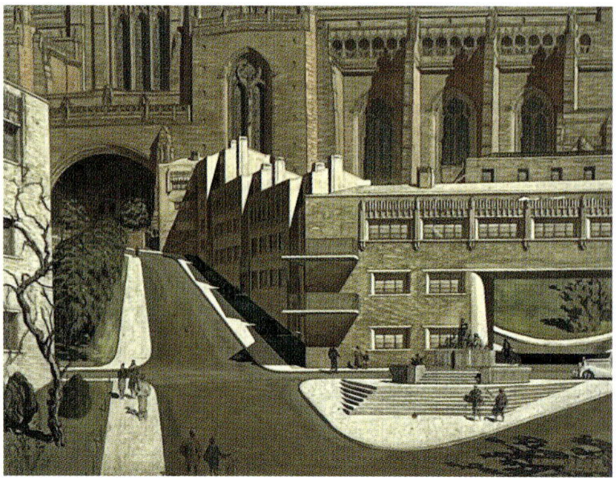

Fig. 8.13 | A. C. Webb drawing of proposed housing in front of Liverpool Cathedral designed by Giles Gilbert Scott (1949). Nick Gilbert Scott.

JM: Returning to your *trajectory, was it the Gundry Dyer work that brought you to Devon?*

NGS: I moved to Lympstone with a friend from the Poly just for a summer shortly before the miners' strike [1972]. Then, there was a recession in the building industry, and I found it hard to get back to London. Then Sarah inherited a modest amount of money in about 1976 which was enough to purchase a building plot and to design and build a house with our own labour.

JM. Tell me more about the house, does it have a name?

NGS: It is called New House. It was named by the Post Office as we couldn't think of a name. It was finished in 1977. It is rendered to fit in with the village, all historically cob buildings. I always call it a segmented pyramid. The roof structure ascends into one point, a central chimney. If you cut segments out of a pyramid, the roof sloops on four sides (Fig. 8.14). I think it's a de-segmented pyramid rather than a segmented one. I wanted to start a self-build housing co-op but was scared off by the local Housing Corporation who advised that it would be hard to ensure that people did their share of the work.

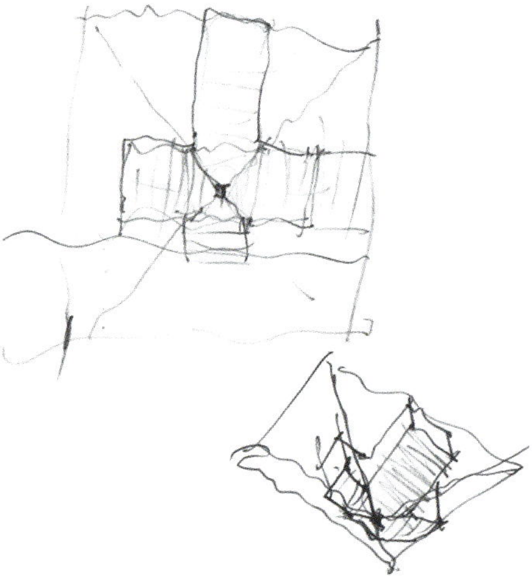

Fig. 8.14 | Nick Gilbert Scott, sketch of the de-segmented pyramid concept of his and Sarah's house in Exeter, for Joshua Mardell (2024).

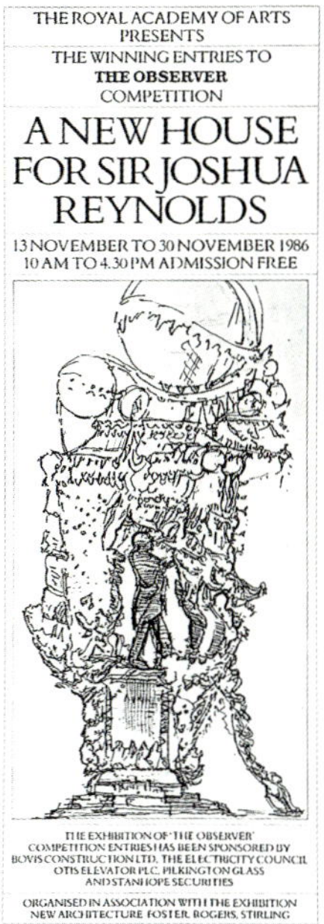

Fig. 8.15 | Poster advertising an exhibition at the Royal Academy of winning designs for 'A New House for Sir Joshua Reynolds' competition. It illustrates the winning design by Nick Gilbert Scott and Willy Grylls (1986).

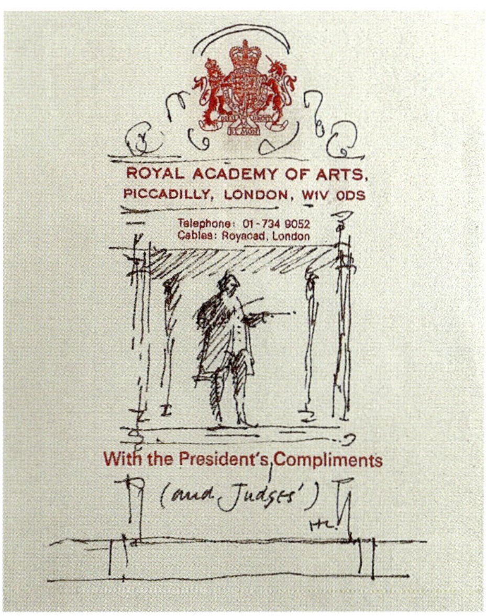

Fig. 8.16 | Memo from Hugh Casson, President, and one of the competition's judges, to Nick Gilbert Scott (*c.* 1986).

JM: You mentioned nepotism a moment ago, but competitions were one way of helping to alleviate nepotism historically. Did you enter many?

NGS: You're right. With my friend the engineer Willy Grylls, I entered a competition at the Royal Academy in 1986, to design around the statue of Joshua Reynolds [in the forecourt]. It was organised by the *Observer* newspaper [in conjunction with the *New Architecture* exhibition]. Ours was a very playful collaboration and we won (Fig. 8.15), much to our surprise![19]

In the event, though, the scheme was not executed.[20] The RA said they would build it, but they funked it in the end because it was too difficult and expensive. But they commissioned me to make a 1.5m-high plaster on fabric maquette with the help of Roger Dean and the sculpture department at the Exeter School of Art. Hugh Casson sent me a little drawing, converting his letterhead to our scheme (Fig. 8.16).

JM: In the Observer *write-up of the competition, they captioned a drawing of your winning scheme 'High Baroque and surely by a stage designer. What do you think of that characterisation in relation to your work?*

NGS: This Baroque style of architecture had come from my organic painting style, slightly mystical in intention, but not serious architecture for my future practice. For many years, I was involved in building large-scale public spaces, outdoor, and yes, primarily for theatre productions,

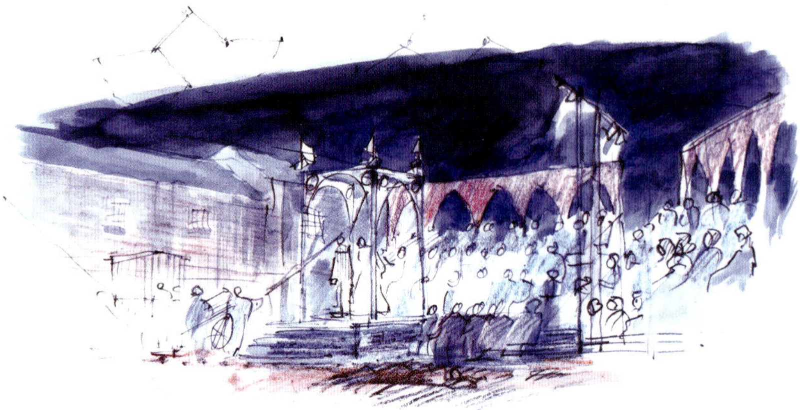

Fig. 8.17 | Nick Gilbert Scott, drawing of the Night-time Auditorium of Scott's structure for 'Measure for Measure', Crediton Town Square, Devon (2007).

which I also designed. One was designed for the play 'Measure for Measure' [in Crediton Town Square, Devon, 2007] (Fig. 8.17). The spatial relationship between actors and audience drove the design. The plan is like a circus, a 'theatre in the round' arena with the 400-seat audience looking in towards the centre ('sociopetal'). They are in the same space as the actors, very close to the reality of their bodies and voices. The perspective sketch visualizes the arrangement.

Also, Spacex Art Gallery, Exeter [*c.*1994–96] (Fig. 8.18) was a National Lottery-funded project for an Arts Council supported gallery. I created an internal meeting space out of an outside sunken yard and so the focus was also very much an inward ('sociopetal') focus on a raised floor and reaching for light. A Richard Long sculpture on the floor echoes the circular rim of the glazed roof. Spacex was potentially a springboard for cultural projects, which I was offered, but I went instead to do a Dance MA because of my reactive nature to architecture.

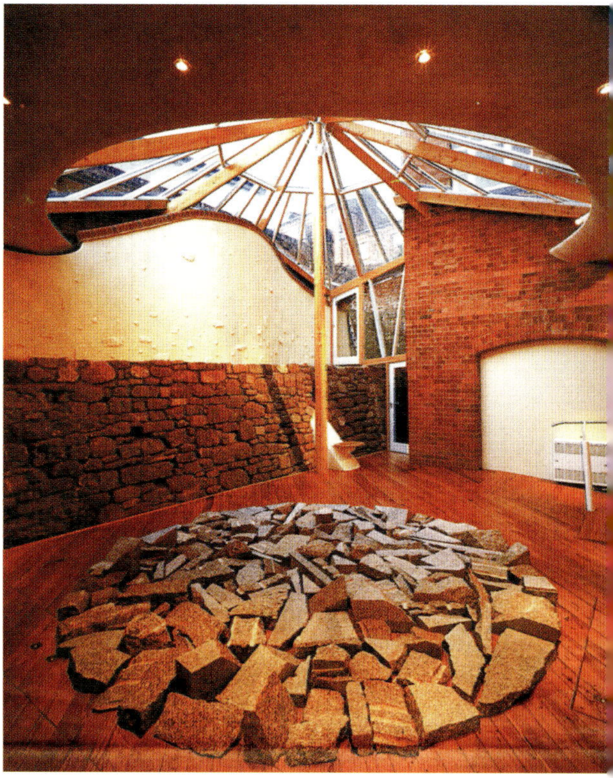

Fig. 8.18 | Nick Gilbert Scott's Spacex Gallery, Exeter as illustrated in *The Times* (April 28, 1998), 35. Warwick Sweeney.

JM: I think you said you started dance classes in 1978?

NGS: 1977. This developed over some years in a series of dance projects where I was able to design sets. By the late 1980s, I was able to combine working as a designer, dancer and chorcographer, to create dance pieces where the drawings, the painted design and the spatial setting were the generator for movement ideas. Finally, to resolve my yearning, I applied to The Laban Centre (now Trinity Laban Conservatoire of Music and Dance), London, in 1996 to study a part-time MA in Dance Studies. To my terror, and delight, I was accepted. I was 49 years old.

Laban was transformative. I learnt so much theory and practice about the body – my body – and space. For example, I discovered 'Relative Movement', namely, how we perceive all movement relative to its context and how this varies depending on the spatial context.

JM: And how did this change the trajectory of your work?

NGS: Following my MA, I began teaching at Laban and at the University of Plymouth School of Architecture on the same subjects but seen from differing points of view. For dancers, it is about the need to learn ways of seeing and experiencing space as intrinsic to dance practice [...] Rudolf (von) Laban [1879–1958, founder of Laban Conservatoire] had had an architectural training and he understood this. For architects, it is about the need to learn about the human experience in relation to architectural space, the life of buildings, as well as the form of buildings.

JM: Laban had studied architecture at the École des Beaux-Arts in Paris. Was his connection to architecture articulated or made visible to you during your training?

NGS: Yes, because Laban stressed that an intrinsic feature of dance was space. This was intrinsic to a dancer's perception of their own movement. During teaching sessions for students and practitioners, I developed the use of 1:10 scale models as a way of demonstrating ideas of spatial behaviour derived from the study of proxemic theory in relation to architectural space types. This is about how we behave spatially in relation to each other; how trust affects the distance we keep from each other; what makes for friendly or anti-social spaces; and, how we can create our own places for coming together or for seeking separation and seclusion. Students could easily project their own spatial sensibilities on to the models and the spaces around them.

JM: Can you see a dynastic link, thinking 'proxemically', across the broader Scott oeuvre?

NGS: I have said that my grandad had a great sensitivity to the scale of the human body in all his projects. Even in the grandest projects if you investigate them, the scale of the body is very implicit and quite tender, in contrast with the great areas of surface which he created. But he had a feeling for the nearness of detail and the scale of use […] Even Battersea, although it looks unbelievably big was never quite as big as people imagined, because he played with the scale in that rather unfathomable way. My father was fascinated by scale, to focus in on the body itself and how architectural form should relate to it.

When I went into dance and learnt about non-verbal communication, the way dancers and people relate in a non-verbal way and how we use space in relation to each other, I realised there was a connection between the kind of intimacy of what I had been talking about in architectural scale and personal space in dance and movement – the space around the body. If you look at Liverpool Cathedral there are all these cues of places for people to go: stairs, steps, the little minarets on high. They are all frames for human behaviour and human movement and are all very intimate in scale and help us 'read' the building as an experience of moving through it.

JM: One of the themes loosely explored in this volume is that old idea, debated by the late Victorians and others, of whether architecture is an art or a profession. Sometimes, to dynasties, it is seemingly a vocation, even a calling. Is this your experience? Architecture as a calling?

NGS: I take comfort in any connection with my grandfather and his spatial sensibility which I had dreams about as a kid. You talk about a calling. Certainly, there is a mysticism in all this that is not to do with a monetised career, but a deep belief or revelation of some kind about being moved in some ways. I think in my case, there's been a real conflict in terms of professionalism. I have always rebelled to an extent, against my architectural journey by trying to escape it routinely, for instance, into the theatre, into choreography, into painting […] but I keep bouncing back because architecture seems to win out.

What you say tempts me to say that I've tried to escape the dynastic – that continuity. How about if you come from this dynastic background and put yourself in the position of someone else, outside of the Gilbert Scott [phenomenon], and just say I'm a local architect? […] It was a challenge to dynastic thinking. I've not traded on dynasty, but tried to build on it in an organic way locally for local builders for whom the name means very little.

If you take the Gilbert Scott out of it, it's just me doing my thing down here.

NOTES

1. Gavin Stamp, "Richard Gilbert Scott obituary," *Guardian* (12 July 2017), https://www.theguardian.com/artanddesign/2017/jul/12/richard-gilbert-scott-obituary
2. Peter Gilbert-Scott trained at the Architectural Association and became a church architect. He also restored Daphne du Maurier's house, Menabilly, Cornwall. His first job, aged 19, was drawing (to Richard Gilbert Scott's design), a new organ case for Christchurch Cathedral, New Zealand. Robert Gilbert Scott worked in practice with Ian Simpson, as the Simpson Scott Partnership from 1988–1998, before moving to Brooker Flynn Architects until 2012. John Scott chairs the Victorian Society's Southern Casework Committee.
3. Nick's children comprise a 3D designer, a film cameraman and Director of Photographer, and a user experience designer.
4. Oxford English Dictionary.
5 In proxemic parlance, discussed below, "sociopetal" means coming together and "sociofugal" is separating from each other.
6. Adrian Gilbert Scott worked there too.
7. See Richard Gilbert Scott's talk at the Art Workers' Guild on 14 December 1962, published as *Giles Gilbert Scott: His Son's View*, edited by Penny Granger and John Martin, London: Lyndhurst Road, 2011.
8. Christian Norberg-Schulz, *Intentions in Architecture*, London: Allen & Unwin, 1963.
9. It was completed by Temple Moore after Scott Junior's death.
10. Some of these are published in Granger and Martin, *Giles Gilbert Scott*, *op. cit*. "Dad's drunks" refers to Giles' drawings, not Richard's.
11. Richard Gilbert Scott had initially studied architecture at the Bartlett School of London University which was evacuated to Cambridge during WWII. He completed studies at the Regent Street Polytechnic.
12. The school chapel by Giles Gilbert Scott was designed in 1927. The boarding houses were designed by Richard Gilbert Scott, 1971–74.
13. *Pers. comm*. 18 December 2024.
14. Nick was there between 1966 and 1973 for parts I and II, with a year out 1970–71.
15. Outside of the immediate genealogical line, the architect Elisabeth Scott (1898–1972) was a great-niece of George Gilbert Scott and the second cousin of Giles Gilbert Scott.
16. The church was finished posthumously by his office after Giles Gilbert Scott's death.
17. On the Charterhouse Boarding Houses, see: Anon., "Architecture of the Old School", *Building* 229, (18 July 1975): 55–62; and Anon. "Charterhouse Revisited: A Study in the Craft of Brickwork," *Redland Record* 41 (1975): 12–16.
18. Principally, the restoration by George Gilbert Scott Senior, 1870–77.
19. Out of 198 entries. The judges were Hugh Casson, Katherine Hamnett and Stephen Gardiner.
20. This is explained in the minutes of the Academy's Council meeting (15 July 1986): "Serious misgivings had been expressed already in the General Purposes Committee about the ideas behind this competition, but it had been allowed to proceed, without any commitment to build the winning design, in the hope that it would stimulate public interest in architecture and the exhibition." Royal Academy Archives (no ref.). The Georgian Group, furthermore, feared it would become a permanent fixture. Amanda Baillieu, "Georgians Hit Out at Academy Competition," *Building Design* 793 (27 June 1986): 40.

Contributors

MIKOŁAJ GETKA-KENIG, PhD, DSc (habil.), is an associate professor at the Institute for the History of Science, Polish Academy of Sciences, Warsaw.

PETER HOWELL taught Classics in the University of London. He is a former Chairman of the Victorian Society.

JOSHUA MARDELL F.S.A. is an architectural historian, a Tutor at the School of Architecture, Royal College of Art and co-editor of the *Journal of Architecture*.

JULIAN POOLEY F.S.A. is Public Services and Engagement Manager at Surrey History Centre and Honorary Visiting Fellow of the School of History, Politics and International Relations, University of Leicester.

NICK GILBERT SCOTT, Architect in practice, 1975 to 2024, lectured at the University of Plymouth School of Architecture and at Trinity Laban.

MATTHEW WELLS is a lecturer in architectural history at the University of Manchester and the author of *Modelling the Metropolis: The Architectural Model in Victorian London* (2023).

HELEN WILSON is an independent scholar and award-winning author of *The Remarkable Pinwill Sisters* (2021).